DAZZLING IMAGES

DAZZLING IMAGES
The Masks of Sir Philip Sidney

Alan Hager

Newark: University of Delaware Press
London and Toronto: Associated University Presses

© 1991 by Associated University Presses, Inc.

All rights reserved. Authorization to photocopy items for internal or personal use, or the internal or personal use of specific clients, is granted by the copyright owner, provided that a base fee of $10.00, plus eight cents per page, per copy is paid directly to the Copyright Clearance Center, 27 Congress Street, Salem, Massachusetts 01970. [0-87413-390-4/91 $10.00 + 8¢ pp, pc.]

Associated University Presses
440 Forsgate Drive
Cranbury, NJ 08512

Associated University Presses
25 Sicilian Avenue
London WC1A 2QH, England

Associated University Presses
P.O. Box 39, Clarkson Pstl. Stn.
Mississauga, Ontario,
L5J 3X9 Canada

The paper used in this publication meets the requirements
of the American National Standard for Permanence of Paper
for Printed Library Materials Z39.48-1984.

Library of Congress Cataloging-in-Publication Data

Hager, Alan.
  Dazzling images : the masks of Sir Philip Sidney / Alan Hager.
    p.   cm.
  Includes bibliographical references and index.
  ISBN 0-87413-390-4 (alk. paper)
  1. Sidney, Philip, Sir, 1554–1586—Criticism and interpretation.
2. Role playing in literature.   3. Disguise in literature.
4. Persona (Literature)   I. Title.
PR2343.H27   1991
821'.3—dc20   89-40767
                                                              CIP

PRINTED IN THE UNITED STATES OF AMERICA

Contents

Introduction	7
1. A Dazzling Mirage	19
2. Charted Problems	33
3. Sidney's Official Indirection	41
Rhomboid Logic (1578) 42	
Advice to the Queen (1579) 52	
Naming and the Blatant Beast (1584) 56	
4. Astrophil's "Tragicomedy of Love . . . Performed by Starlight"	63
The Prologue 67	
The Catastrophe 69	
The Recognition Scene 73	
The Epilogue 78	
5. "Darknesse Cleare": Seven Levels of Starlover's Ambiguity	82
Names 83	
Complex Words 87	
Oxymorons 90	
Ambiguous Metaphors 93	
Allusion to Myth 95	
Descriptio 97	
Narratio 100	
6. The Sonneteer's Mock Encomium of Self	103
7. The Anti-Platonic Platonic Monologue	115
Popular Philosophy 117	
Restrained Lust 118	
Prophetic Craft 121	
8. Retroactive Reading	130
9. The "Unflattering Glass": Sir Fulke Greville's Theory of Reader Identification and Sidney's *Arcadia*	145
Musidorus's Eyes 150	
The Icon of Cupid 157	
10. The Irony of the *Eiron* and *Alazon*	167
Parodic Design 167	

      Narrative *Eironeia*   171
      Dramatic *Alazoneia*   173
11. Sidney's Self-Effacement   176

Notes   188
Bibliography   207
Index   215

Introduction

This book maps the fictive impersonation of a Renaissance artist who made only brief forays into the world of dramatic writing, as we shall see in chapters 3 and 11, but whose major theme in essay, poem, and romance was that of roles and how we play them, from transvestite to savage. Thus he helped usher in one of the supreme eras of the stage and of fictional characterization in general. In the second eclogues of the *Old Arcadia,* one of Sidney's many personae, Duke Musidorus ("gift of the muse")—like his author,[1] in some sense, an aristocrat gone proletarian[2] for love—disguised as the novice goatherd, Dorus, in order to approach his mistress in pastoral seclusion, sings a eulogy of the green world and its simplicity.

Musidorus fails to share such simplicity not only because of his disguise, but for two other forms of deception: covert self-praise and devious creation of a rival for his affections. Musidorus has wooed Pamela ("all honey" or "sweetness") by delivering heroic tales about himself in the third person, and by affecting love for her maid and keeper, Mopsa. The use of these erotic weapons of deceit is far from innocent, yet, in a rhetorical question, he sings sweetly of the custom of cutting names in trees: "What man grafts in a tree dissimulation?" (69).[3] Musidorus, the poetic lover, can no longer tell his disguise. By means of his purposely confused persona, here, I argue, Sidney causes us to share Musidorus's indirection and its consequences at first hand.

Society has always condemned disguise—except on holidays when rules are meant to be broken—because masking one's identity connotes subterfuge, even loss of identity or transformation into one's new persona. In Elizabethan England, the London parliament—of which Sidney was a sometime member—even attempted, on occasion, without notable success, to color-code its citizenry in order to facilitate identification of rank of individuals by sight,[4] and sumptuary laws specified a wide variety of dress codes to designate identity at least in terms of the social order. Although laws could not touch the extremes of society in the largely fictive parody of majesty, the fool, and the monarch, custom prescribed the outfit of the court's official pauper,[5] in his or her hand-me-down patchwork and other trappings, as well as the ruler's corporate finery and accouterment. Deviations were generally considered dangerous.

When Sidney's narrator remarks, at the close of "The First Book or Act": "and as for Dorus, a shepherd's apparel upon a Duke Of Thessalia will answer for him" (55),[6] he suggests that his disease lies not only in his deception but in the internal metamorphosis brought on by his new outfit. Human identity and sense of position are so tenuous for Sidney that new clothing can alter them. That a duke, Musidorus, dresses up as an apprentice goatherd and cannot tell its dissimulation, suggests for that first audience a special kind of "rank disorder": a case of clothing not only nullifying position in society but character as well. The duke, in fact, becomes the rude goatherd of his own making in a central moment of *Old Arcadia,* when he contemplates rape as a solution to his longing for his sleeping princess, and Sidney makes us know his exposure because Musidorus is another conscious authorial persona.

Musidorus's narrative, a boast from the defilade of a distant point of view, that goes out of control, recalls Sidney's own characteristic fictive maneuver of masking autobiography in the crises of his heroes and heroines, and this consciousness gives us overview of his authorial manipulation of the whole narrative of the *Old Arcadia.* When, for example, Musidorus allows his erotic contemplation of Pamela's sleeping form to overwhelm all aristocratic restraint, he is interrupted by a mob of shepherds, seeming "savages" (202), who parody his descent into sexual assault. Thus, Sidney, by the very structure of his narrative, asks the reader, in this jarring and comic moment, to compare Musidorus's "low" desires to members of a mob in action who mirror the levelling in Musidorus's own soul. Indeed, the duke has already announced his disease of undifferentiation in a song that proposes he abandon his own identity in favor of that of his disguise:

> Come shepheard's weedes, become your master's minde:
> Yeld outward shew, what inward change he tryes:
>
> (13)

The clothes have become the man. Masking and disguise are that dangerous to one's own being as well as to the state and due process.

Such contrived enigma on Sidney's part invites misinterpretation. Warring factions of historical interpretation, old and new—each with considerable acuity—have alternately suggested that Sidney is either a case of perfect self-creation (with Musidorus) in the tradition of idealist and sometimes jingoist Renaissance English interpretation, or

Introduction 9

that he is a self-fashioned rebel (with Musidorus), albeit unsuccessful, to such an enormous and corporate concept. I place him and his various personae, however, in a third and very special Renaissance tradition of self-design: purveyors of a rainbow of identities, from self-denigrator to self-promoter, for a higher ironic and curative purpose—sometimes propagandistic—following the humanist praisers of folly. No wonder his subtleties sometimes escape polemicists who look for leads to expropriate Sidney as icon for old or new historicist cults. Sidney is, as Arthur Kinney and others have shown,[7] a crucial figure in danger of falling into a critical gap of the sort Milton fell into at the beginning of this century, in part, because of a critical debate that fails to come to terms with his conscious role-playing.

The two kinds of irony, constructive and self-serving, look alike, and Sidney complicates our response to his works by portraying egoistic dissimulation in characters who are veiled versions of himself. In order to stir "the affects of admiration and commiseration" (96)[8] in his audience, Sidney—as confirmed by writers who followed him, such as Thomas Nashe, Fulke Greville, and John Hoskins—presents us throughout with characters who lose a sense of their own identity under the strain of desire. Some of Sidney's best readers take his maneuvers to be the product of political and poetic anxiety. My book argues, however, for another Sidney who dissembles for the purpose of what Barbara Bowen calls, in a discussion of the masks of Rabelais and Montaigne, "bluff." Serious jesting makes "us stop and think, either about the subject under discussion or about the literary techniques being used."[9] "Bluff" is a form of impersonation designed to trap a reader in a truth of the human nature we all share. It is dissembling for the purpose of showing how we can lose ourselves in self-fashioning.

In his critical theory, Sidney returns again and again to the image of a conscious deceiver who treats human ills by catching his auditors up in their own foolery. A court jester, an orator, or, indeed, a senator in Menenius Agrippa or a prophet in Nathan, this dissembler traps an audience by adopting a mask below the level of his or her understanding, then exposing its artifice. Aristotle in the *Rhetoric* that Sidney translated makes a distinction between the joking lie (βωμολοχίον) that points outward, and irony (εἰρονεία) that points back at oneself.[10] The two masks appear at first identical, but the latter has the curative function I discover in Sidney; the former is dominated by too much self-interest to enjoy negative capability.

I find ironic purpose in Sidney's personae even, as in the case of *Arcadia's* Amphialus ("between two seas"), when Sidney pictures tragic dissolution. This mother-dominated hero of his romance remains an image of comic self-destruction, whether he is lending his murky personal desires political validation, or stealing a beloved's glove, thus ensuring her hate. Amphialus, living with dreams of political and sexual conquest, remains a candidate for the amorous conversion Sidney's incomplete narrative seems to guarantee.

Of course, Philip Sidney's role in the consolidation of power in Elizabeth's England hardly constituted that of court jester to the queen in London palaces. The historical Sidney designed for himself an image of courtier, author, and protagonist of symbolic entertainments, patron of the arts, adventurer, ambassador, and general. When he traveled as Queen Elizabeth I's representative, Collins reports he hung a tablet below his coat of arms that referred to himself as "most illustrious," "most generous," finally as "English." Wallace notes that such posturing promoted the greater glory of the queen of England;[11] but we cannot disregard Sidney's manipulation of his own image. Here I suspect another version of a minor diplomat's self-irony. Unlike some Elizabethan image-making noted by Stephen Greenblatt and others,[12] this author, I argue, remains shielded from view by his masks through conscious dissimulation.

John Nichols's *Progresses of Elizabeth I,* which provides invaluable chronological descriptions of entertainments, pageants, and other displays that fulfilled the aims of Elizabethan propaganda (with special attention to Sidney's activities, as we will see in chapter 3), also records Christmastide gifts received by Elizabeth, roughly listed according to the rank of the donor, for each new year in Sidney's era. All gifts have iconic significance as well as monetary and functional value. Bejewelled scorpions, serpents (basilisks?), hawks, dolphins, icons of Jupiter and Pallas, and miniature military hardware, such as helmets, daggers, and lances abound to remind the world of Elizabeth's power. Phoenixes, butterflies, icons of Diana, swans, lambs, white hinds, a great mass of white objects of clothing, and furs tell of the queen's mystical position of unattainable virgin. No gift, however, reveals more than Sidney's offering for the new year of 1580–81 in the wake of circulation of his *Letter to the Queen Concerning Monsieur:* "Item, a juell of goulde, being a whippe, garnished with small diamonds in four rowes and cordes of small seede pearle."[13] Sidney's standard biographer, Malcolm William Wallace, claims the gift is "in token of his submission to the will of Her Majesty,"[14] but beyond its significance as an icon of rule, I glimpse another self-ironic reference on the part of the queen's cup-bearer in the role of a rebellious boy, one of his recurring self-images, the failed "amatorious" double of Cupid submitting himself to his idol. This bestowal of the bejewelled whip was a semipublic act that seems to belie the image of the naive rebel that informs the work of writers as diverse as E. M. W. Tillyard and Michael Walzer.[15] Sidney's public impersonation of an adolescent adventurer providing the means of deserved flagellation connotes to this reader not masked highwayman, radical aristocrat, or resentful courtier, but master of indirection in support of the queen and her purported white Machiavellian policies of rule.

Sidney's masked assault on his reader in palaces and armchairs apparently involves two steps, as demonstrated earlier in his century by Desiderius Erasmus's female embodiment of serious jesting, Stultitia. You make your audience laugh at symptoms of folly in others by pretending to catch the fever yourself. Since, however, your spectators clearly share those affects, they must then, with the fool's guidance, proceed to laugh at themselves.

In the audience we identify with the smiling persona; we join in on the hilarity only to discover that this jester was only pretending levity. Stultitia points out to her spectators that when she makes her appearance to deliver her speech, everyone's face shines "forth with unaccustomed mirth,"[16] but her overview makes it impossible to know where she really stands, or rather her exterior encodes a deeper message. Her outfit of all the colors of the rainbow symbolizes shape-shifting—as well as such poverty as she would have no cause to hedge—a warning to beware the truth knitted up in her dazzling variety.[17] Following our cure, only that immediate puzzling mask remains visible, but with the purpose of having us taste our own folly.

Greenblatt has shown that many Tudor courtiers and poets—notably those on the rise in Elizabethan England's society—developed self-images that expose their maneuvering when the posing goes beyond their conscious control. The stresses and strains of their self-fashioning reveal internal and external imperatives of power in Tudor England. What was conscious becomes unconscious in their conflict with authority. But his studies, even in the case of such public figures as More and Ralegh, overestimate, I argue, the unconscious in such posturing, and ignore, on the whole, one of the most significant Renaissance intellectual traditions: the serious jest.

Although Elizabethan authorities stressed, as I have noted, the dangers of impersonation of any sort, Sidney is not alone in licensing a conscious form of benevolent deception or *serio ludere*. Invoking Erasmus, More, and Agrippa, Sidney remarks that the voice of serious jesting "sportingly never leaveth till he make a man laugh at folly, and at length ashamed, to laugh at himself, which he cannot avoid without avoiding the folly" (95). His "critic" describes an audience's process of self-discovery, brought about by a ruse, a trick of impersonation that requires our identification with his persona.

For the great ironists of the court of Henry VIII and their followers, such as Rabelais, Montaigne, and Sidney, violent opposition over theological, historical, and philosophical issues bred a reaction against open debate that took the form of its ironic containment in works whose significance has a way of slipping through the grasp of contemporary readers. Is it surprising that modern polemicists such as Greenblatt, Helgerson, McCoy, Ferguson, and Montrose, albeit subtle in their rhetorical applications, sometimes miss the effect of the distortions of the conscious antipolemicist?

In a review article summarizing the aftermath of deconstruction and Marxian readings of Renaissance and nineteenth-century texts, Joseph Litvak points out that new historicists represent "an approach that looks both politically savvy and historically responsible precisely *because* it can (appear to) accommodate such traditionally 'literary' values as instability, irony, ambiguity, and paradox."[18] Studies of Sidney may provide the supreme test of such apparent accommodation, because the very fabric of his works is unstable, ironic, ambiguous, and paradoxical for a purpose his first readers would have best known. Only seeming adaptation to his self-contradiction is, in fact, misreading. It reduces his controlled irony to accident and unconscious manifestation of resentment.

Although Sidney had great impact on the age that followed him, recent critical and literary circles represent him as an exemplar of defensive hurt and huff partly because, as we have seen, he demands initial misinterpretation of his intentions. His personae all clearly suffer from self-inflation. Surveying the ground of *Arcadia*'s ironic design, for example, McCoy remarks that the characterization of Amphialus in Sidney's final narrative efforts, shows "blurring of purpose . . . typical in Sidney's fiction, as the conflict between sovereign and subject frequently descends to a more covert psychological level."[19]

McCoy legitimately locates an autobiographical element in Amphialus; a fictional descent into internal disorder; and a "covert" element in Sidney's creation of protagonists. "Covert" and its synonyms often appear in McCoy's analysis, in part, because the word implies the subterfuge of all deception. Although McCoy allows Sidney great intelligence in his subversion, "blurring" also suggests a lack of control he connects to Sidney's supposed aristocratic resentment of "diminishing feudal power," of "courtly dependence and intrigue,"[20] or of the power of his uncle, Robert Dudley, the Earl of Leicester, or of the queen. Thus he denies the possibility of a conscious presentation of Amphialus's own blurred motivation. Borrowing a phrase from William Blake, Margaret Ferguson notes that Sidney the critic is "a master of 'deep dissimulation,'" but, like McCoy, she sees his deception in his *Defence of Poetry* largely as negative—if intelligent—masking of "political and autobiographical issues."[21]

In *Dazzing Images*, I argue that Sidney, as an Elizabethan political poet, supported Leicester and the regime of Elizabeth I, as required by the censors and his own inclination, but saved a special kind of Renaissance self-irony for his reader. As designer of his fiction, as dissembling narrator, and as persona within the narrative, Sidney ultimately asks us to share overview of the disease of the dissembling soul, but only when we experience it ourselves. I argue that Sidney, in all his works, public and private, adopts a set of roles for a peculiar purpose, like the praisers of folly he admired from the early part of his century.

This study shows that Sidney develops personae to include precisely those comic manifestations his rhetor identifies by type in his discussion of comic masks in his *Defence of Poetry*—"a busy loving courtier and a heartless threatening Thraso; a self-wise-seeming schoolmaster; an awry-transformed traveller" (116)—in order to fill his readers with mirth and to cure the disease of undifferentiation in them. In the Renaissance tradition of praisers of folly, including Agrippa, Erasmus, More, Rabelais, Montaigne, and others, Sidney designs his masks in order to help his readers diagnose themselves.

As a creator of fictions, a critic, a poet, even at times as a citizen, as we will see in chapter 1, Sidney leads his readers into discovering how they could fool themselves both in the context of the psychic inner world and in that of the outer realm of social position. Like the Socratic ironist, he "nothing affirms, and therefore never lieth" (102). Because his personae are fictional constructs, he "never maketh any circles about your imagination, to conjure you to believe for true what he writes" (102).

As a "self-wise-seeming schoolmaster," Rombus, in *The Lady of May*, he warns the world of the dangers of erotic and political idealism and provides an ironic cure for recusancy. As a less pedantic courtier in a letter to his sovereign, he speaks smoothly of the queen's hopes for a marriage and of the problem of the good and bad subject. As the boasting and "heartless threatening" young man of the *Defence of Leicester* he defends his uncle—impossibly—against slander and libel. As the first lover and "busy loving courtier," Astrophil, in his sonnet cycle, he spins a tragicomedy of lost love. As sonneteering poet and rhetor of his *Defence of Poetry*, he leads his reader into discovering paradoxes of poetic production and fiction's appeal. As narrator and character—often dis-eased female—he leads the audience of the *Old* and *New Arcadia* into a variety of discoveries about passion, in both senses of the word, and human motivation. As teller of the tale, he develops a thoroughly puzzled and reductionist Chaucerian persona. As Philisides, he complains of career, love, political, and cosmic melancholy. As a host of characters in the fiction—notably his central "awry transformed travellers," Pyrocles in a dress and Musidorus in an apprentice goatherd's outfit—he puzzles his reader about paradoxes of sexual and social identity and leads his audience into contemplation of the paradoxical mysteries of love and politics. Sidney's critical voices, I argue, reflect rather than mask Elizebethan doctrine on monarchic rule, but they also dazzle us, in the great Renaissance tradition, with dialectical complication of moral and philosophical issues.

My notion of Sidney leading and drawing his reader into self-scrutiny by assuming voices helps resolve recent critical debate about his "vanishing distinctions"[22]: his tendency to sport with the outcome of dialectical oppositions, yet his ethical bias and critique of idealism. Sidney's voices draw us into a maze of experience with no exit to educate us "on the job" without injury. His impersonation lures his readers "ere themselves be aware, as if they took a medicine of cherries" (93). Controlling reader response through surprise is Sidney's announced goal. He requires what I call "retroactive reading." In their examination of other major Renaissance works of the English tradition, such as *Paradise Lost, The Faerie Queene,* and Shakespeare's sonnets, Stanley Fish, Paul Alpers, and Stephen Booth,[23] have all discovered strategies of dissembling and "medicinal" effects that this Renaissance poet and critic takes care to describe in theory and use in practice.

Sidney, the aristocrat and artist, I argue, like Aristotle's and Theophrastus's *eiron,* when he dissembles, steps down, not up. In adopting personae, even the boaster, or *alazon,* Sidney ensures that the mask will conceal him. Greenblatt, in his most eloquent presentation of the theory of self-exposure in Elizabethan role-playing, quotes Spenser's Calidore, a figure at least partially based on Sidney, as evidence of the concept of total self-creation; but he fails to note that, in this context, self-creation is internal and hidden to the world. Midway through book 6 of *The Faerie Queene,* the Knight of Courtesy, about to ask for exile in Melibee's lowly cottage, admits finally that one cannot blame Lady Fortune for one's real or supposed reversals in the world, "Since then in each mans self / It is, to fashion his owne lyfes estate" (6.9.31.1–2).[24] Development of one's image, in this special case of stepping down, unlike Musidorus, into a shepherd's world, exposes the disguise but not the individual and his ambitions in the discourse of power. It is the unseeable ordering of the estate of one's soul, an internal preservation of one's superiority to mutability. As image-maker, like the consummate serious jester, Sidney, by his "unflattering mirror" and the dazzle of disguise, continues to frustrate our vision, but to help cure us of our folly, to help us glimpse paradoxes that live beyond the threshold of controversy, personality and difference. Beyond the largely unquestioned authorities of Elizabeth and Leicester, his masks trick us into consciousness of what he presents as twofold truth.

In my first chapter, I show how Sidney's self-irony shines through a magnified public image. In chapter 2, I show how redaction and criticism, sometimes baffled by his supposed egoism, lead to discovery of his true nature. In chapter 3, I look at the masks he adopts in his public writings and their purpose. Chapters 4 and 5 show how Sidney uses an image of *adolescens,* from *commedia dell'arte*, Greek romance, Roman comedy, Greek new comedy, and before, in his sonnet cycle, in order to "psychoanalyze" a case of love melancholy. Chapters 6, 7, and 8 show how the persona of love poet exposes the operation of poetry and its ontology. Chapters 9 and 10 show how the narrator of the *Arcadia* controls reader response by overview, as explained by two men who knew Sidney and his works, Greville and Hoskins. My final chapter demonstrates how Sidney could cause his persona to shrink to self-effacement or magnify into the *alazon* for self-ironic purposes. In this book, I hope to show that Sidney is England's Renaissance man, if you will, not because he combines courtliness and heroism, or because he purveys outsider resentment, but because he manages ironic impersonation, when called upon, even in those two realms.

DAZZLING IMAGES

1
A Dazzling Mirage

The limitations of Sir Philip Sidney's biographical image may well have proceeded to limit our critical appreciation of him. His own concept of the fallacious process of making history in his *Defence of Poetry* would serve a prophetic function in relationship to his reputation as an author. When Sidney complains of the "historian . . . authorizing himself (for the most part) upon other histories,"(83), we may be reminded that the image of Sidney as "Calvinist," "idealistic," "heroic" and "serious," that found a recent form in a BBC comedy series, in which he plays a feisty censor of pornographic literature,[1] is, on the whole, a file copy that has been dusted off periodically since his death.

Attitudes towards Sidney change as many times as attitudes towards serious, heroic, idealistic Calvinists change. However, his posture as the "ornament of his age," in and out of favor, seems constant in a way that fulfills Sidney's own worst apprehensions about historical inquiry. When, with sarcasm, he goes on to complain that historical authority is based on the "notable foundation of hearsay" and rues the necessity of picking "truth out of their partiality" (83), he could just as well have been referring to some of the origins of his historical image in legendary anecdote and biased treatise. Since the mirage of Sidney has sometimes cluttered our reading of his works, an elementary goal of criticism of his poetry and fiction, which seem on the whole ironic, comic and "amatorious," must be a reconstruction of an accurate historical reading of those works. In some criticism, this activity need not be as conscious as it is in the case of this Elizabethan courtier, who was made to play a popular "role" central to our understanding of Elizabethan culture.

I argue not only that Sidney's exemplary image is the product of Elizabethan propagandistic design, but that Sidney is aware and attempts in his own life—and works—to make us aware of the ironies of being identified with such a role. Indeed he sets out to expose the dangers of the very idealism with which he has been traditionally identified. Our final image of Sidney is that of a critic of human aspiration, a ventriloquist didactic poet working by indirection and irony even in his own behavior, a master of the overview that his exemplary image would deny him. In his poetry, criticism, and fiction, Sidney presents us with a sequence of over-reachers who are undercut or trapped by rhetorical and narrative irony, but these glorious over-reachers are all self-images. For example, his *Defence of Poetry* opens with the self-glorious haranguing of Sidney and Wotton by the esquire of the stables of the court of Maximilian II in Vienna, John Pietro Pugliano, an example of how "self-love is better than any gilding to make that seem gorgeous wherein ourselves be parties"(73).

Here we might take the Italian instructor of horsemanship to be our only butt, but Sidney's persona immediately goes on to describe himself, the defender of his own poetic craft, as the "scholar . . . to be pardoned that followeth the steps of his master" (73), Pugliano. As elsewhere, Sidney demonstrates an overiew of his own "gilding," that glittering image of the "Renaissance man" that was becoming an official Elizabethan external standard. This ideal Sidneian image exaggerated his historical importance, as it sometimes confounded efforts to get a handle on the variety of his literary works. Of course, a few friends—a significant group, as we shall see—knew this self-ironic Sidney in real life, and they provide a key to understanding those works.

Although Sidney's ideal in his *Defence of Poetry* was the popular poet—and his works are ultimately exoteric—his real audience was limited. We may recall that he, in the only wholly unfacetious moment of the close of his *Defence of Poetry,* warns us "to believe, with me, that there are many mysteries contained in poetry, which of purpose were written darkly, lest by profane wits it should be abused" (121). Sidney is suggesting, with strenuous self-avowal, that even a contemporary, if he fall into the category of "profane wit," will suffer the puzzlement of a benighted reader with some particular poetic work.

No matter how many editions the *Arcadia* went through, beginning three years after his death, he indicates a select audience for his work, a coterie under a metaphoric bower: his sister, the Countess of Pembroke, and certain "friends"(3),[2] Greville, Dyer, Ralegh, Fraunce, Nashe, Hoskins, Bacon, Penelope Rich, Frances Walsingham, even Queen Elizabeth herself, that was likely to know his personality, life, and some of his ideas intimately. The first step in approaching an accurate historical reading of his works, then, is to apply our best analyic tools to what we know of Sidney's life, in order to reconstruct an understanding of what his friends—his first readers—already knew, to wipe clear a historical lens that has become dusty over the ages.

It is impossible to ignore the numerous facts about Sidney. Not only do we have contemporary sketches of his life, but also a mass of letters and official documents that were either written by him, to him, or about him. His portraiture alone has been the subject of a delightful but incomplete book—the Paul Veronese portrait remaining lost.[3] What we still need is a consistently plausible interpretation of the hard facts of his life, and we must overcome, in the process, a rather imposing deductive construct. Frances A. Yates, John Buxton, and Jan Van Dorsten, in taking a close look at the thought of Sidney's English and continental acquaintances, and Richard Lanham, Richard McCoy, and Richard Helgerson, in testing historically a notion of Sidney as antihero or conscious failure,[4] have already raised enough questions about traditional concepts of Sidney's idealism to make critics wary of the assumptions that lie behind Tillyard's early comment that "platonizing created an enthusiastic idealism . . . that impelled Sidney to seek education through his love for Stella and honour in sordid battles in the Low Countries."[5] Such assumptions about Sidney the man, rarely stated in such bold terms, but often implied by Sidney critics, would make the skeptical thinker and comic poet of *The Lady of May, Astrophil and Stella*, his *Defence of Poetry* and the *Old* and *New Arcadia* an impossibility.

The biographical concept of Sidney as the epitome of Tudor leadership is first the product of the enshrinement of Sidney as the "hero of Zutphen" following his early death at the age of thirty-one. As Richard Lanham writes of Sidney's standard biographer, "here Wallace, and indeed all of Sidney's biographers, have been the heirs of a legend which was created not by Sidney's life so much as by his heroic death."[6] Elizabethan and Jacobean memorial literature is unequivocal praise, but the genres themselves are panegyrical. Of the more famous examples, Edmund Spenser, in *Astrophel*, characteristically mixes genres in order to create a pastoral elegy for a hero of action. Thomas Moffet's *Nobilis, or a View of the Life and Death of Sidney*,[7] is largely a treatise on university learning, where the dead Sidney serves, as best he can, the function of exemplum for his own apparently rakish nephew, William Herbert.

Fulke Greville's later-named *Life of Sidney* is a version of a genre conventionalized by Foxe's *Acts and Monuments*, the Protestant saint's life. Sir Walter Ralegh's epitaph builds to a stanza of self-denigration and hyperbolic comparison of Sidney with Scipio, Cicero, and Petrarch. It would require a largish monument to reflect this range, though no monument to Sidney exists.[8] In accepting the body of Sidneian memorial literature as sincerely biographical, historians overlook factual distortion caused not only by conventions of genre but also by specific rhetorical purposes.

The abundant memorial literature of the period on Sidney is compromised by two propagandistic motives. For one, the Leicester faction and Greville in particular used the occasion to promote their "hawkish" position, that of hoping for a combined Protestant military offensive against Spain on the European continent, waving, so to speak, the bloody shirt of their lieutenant. Lanham writes, I think fairly, of Greville's treatise: "It is an elaborate justification of the bellicose foreign policy which Walsingham and his party were trying to persuade the queen to pursue on the continent."[9] Here, Sidney becomes a martyr to the cause of the Protestant League. Perhaps it is in this capacity that John Philip has Sidney return from the grave, in a dream vision, to warn the "noble Brutes"[10] to beware Popish espionage in their midst. Yet Wallace has carefully documented Sidney's comparatively lenient attitude towards Catholics and towards the Jesuit Edmund Campion in particular.[11]

The second transformation of Sidney is the product of Elizabeth's own aims in upholding the notion of her court as the late flowering of chivalry in fealty to the virgin queen. Here, Sidney is metamorphosed from a complicated, often-neglected courtier into the ideal of chivalric heroism and courtesy, an ideal that would serve to control the impetuosity of some of her courtiers. In her articles for the *Journal of the Warburg and Courtauld Institutes*, "Queen Elizabeth as Astraea," and "Elizabethan Chivalry: The Romance of the Accession Day Tilts,"[12] now collected in *Astraea*, Frances Yates implies that Elizabeth's tilts were a means of building up a body of quasi-religious imagery around her person in a festive chivalric setting. Her goal was political consolidation on the largest possible plane. The images connected with Elizabeth on these occasions, such as Astraea, Cynthia, Diana, vestal virgin, and even, apparently, the Immaculate Mary herself, had profound affect not only on poets, but also on the aristocrats and the populace.

In part, the outdoor masques and tilts, such as Woodstock 1573, were designed to replace former saint's day celebrations. Sir Henry Lee is seen as the mastermind of what Yates calls "an imaginative feudalization of culture"[13] in the English court. But she also hints at an imperial propagandistic intention behind these tilts when she points out that "for the expense of a few pence . . . the rude country people may now instead behold the worship of Elizabeth by her knights."[14] Clearly adulation of the commoners would follow hard upon apparent adulation by the leading figures in the realm. To effect this, she would have to reduce her leading courtiers, at least symbolically, into worshippers of a queen with the rank of idol.[15]

Contemporary accounts of Elizabeth in court emphasize her very special regard for rank. In the *Apophthegmns*,[16] Francis Bacon recounts the anecdote of Elizabeth intentionally bypassing Burleigh's row of men to be knighted more or less in order of importance of service, and knighting them in reverse order, more or less by rank. If the tale were not true, it would certainly be symbolic truth. When the Queen found herself in the central role of Sidney's quasi-masque, *The Lady of May*, she seems at first to have made a simple error in choosing the rich but ineffectual shepherd, Espilus, over the poor but spirited forester, Therion, to wed the lady in question. As Stephen Orgel has shown,[17] the drama was designed to favor Therion in the debates and resolve his victory in the final songs, which open with the lines

> Silvanus long in love, and long in vaine,
> At length obtain the point of his desire.[18]

On the other hand, we should consider the possibility that Elizabeth intentionally chose the rich, unerratic shepherd to remind Sidney and the public of the importance of economic and social hierarchical relationships. If she did so, as with Burleigh's prepared ceremony, she must have intentionally left Sidney's "entertainment" in a state of considerable disarray, with a victorious shepherd singing a song in praise of the god of the woods, Silvanus, and a forester ruing the defeat in love of Pan, the god of shepherds. We should remember that Elizabeth's main cause for anger with Sidney in the tennis court incident with Oxford was not its near violence, but Sidney's insufficient regard for his inferiority of rank.[19] Recognition of social hierarchy was, naturally, of special importance to Elizabeth. Her own claims to the highest rank in the kingdom were questioned on several scores and periodically challenged by plot and rebellion. And she was a woman, surrounded by impulsive gallants of the new and old aristocracy, Drake and Leicester, Ralegh and Essex. These men were not easy to rule.

Bacon, in his Plutarchan version of her life, *In Happy Memory of Elizabeth, Queen of England* (1608), hints at her solution to the problem of imposing obedience on major peers and favorites alike. Having mentioned that Elizabeth surrounded herself with would-be lovers "beyond the lot of that time of life," he adds that these activities "certainly were in no way detrimental to her majesty."[20] Is not Bacon suggesting that these activities were designed specifically to increase her majesty? And if obedience to the virgin queen was absolute for the courtier-lover, the commoners would follow suit. Joseph Levine has made the following comment about the queen's problem and solution: "If Elizabeth could become their lady and they the love-sick knights of chivalric tradition, awkwardness could be made to disappear and the problem of obedience might be resolved. What a grand performance this required!"[21] Largely in death, it seems, Sidney became part of this performance and gained the rank in overplus that he never had as Leicester's heir.

Alive, Sidney was rarely an apparent favorite, though he had a nickname, "Phip," and made an appearance in several tilts. He himself complains, I think undramatically, in a letter to Walsingham, the year of his death, "how apt the Queen is to interpret everything to my disadvantage."[22] But if his youthful death were to be seen as the sudden and irreparable loss of perfection, Elizabeth could set up a competition in her court to try to fill the ensuing vacuum. At least on one occasion, four years after Sidney's death, the 1590 Accession Day Tilt, the earl of Essex took Sidney's part. George Peele, in the most extensive description in his commemoration of the event, *Polyhymnia* (1590), calls our attention to Essex, with company, lancers, horses, armor, and staves,

> in funerall blacke,
> As if he mourn'd to thinke of him he mist,
> Sweet Sydney, fairest shepherd of our greene.[23]

Because of rather unusual circumstances, Essex had, by a special clause in Sidney's will, inherited his "best sword."[24] But he had also married Sidney's widow, Frances Walsingham, the year of this tilt. Peele refers to this twofold identification with Sidney in the lines that follow the above:

> Well lettered Warriour [Sidney], whose successor he [Essex]
> In love and Armes had ever vowed to be.

This extraordinary reference to the sword as well as to the widow of Sidney, as somehow honors to be reaped, could not have been lost on the courtiers if on the populace. The presence of staves clearly connected him, however, with all as the inheritor of the mantle of "fairest shepherd of our greene." The quasi-mystical *concordia discors* implied by the appearance of a herder of sheep at a tilt was clearly the self-image of the ever ironic Sidney.

Essex, having replaced Leicester as master of the horse, was already the queen's favorite, and destined to be, away from court, her most unruly courtier-lover. The kind of restraints she imposed on him as the inheritor of the mantle of the perfect shepherd-knight, Sidney, served the specific political purpose of keeping him in check. As Bacon later advised the queen when she was angry with the proceedings of Essex in Ireland:

> If you had my Lord of Essex here with a white staff in his hand, as my Lord of Leicester had, and continued him still about you for society to yourself, and for an honour and ornament to your attendance and Court in the eyes of your people, and in the eyes of foreign Embassadors, then were he in his right element.[25]

Here we have an extroardinary glimpse of the immediate purpose of the cult of Elizabeth. When Bacon mentions the ornamental badge of office, the "white staff" of Essex, we may be immediately reminded of the artificiality of the ruffles and other trappings of the portraits of the courtiers, that, in Sidney's case, caused an emergency borrowing of money to pay his tailor. The extreme amount of ceremony and ornament in Elizabeth's court, from the nicknaming, sonnet production, and oral euphuism, to the masques, tilts, and processions, served not only to impress the public and, through report, foreign rulers of a "woman's rule," but also tied the hands of an aristocracy now used to thinking of the royal succession, perhaps, as the prize of military conquest, a very male activity. Bacon blames this attitude, in part, on Henry VII who decided after his military victory over Richard III to claim the English throne on the basis of the house of Lancaster's "ancient and long disputed title (both by plea and arms)"[26] rather than the house of York's more sound hereditary claim. Ironically, Elizabeth had to suffer for her grandfather's refusal to allow her grandmother, Lady Elizabeth—for whom she was named—a share in the royal title.

Bacon seems to have had the fullest understanding of the Machiavellianism that lay behind the artifice of Elizabeth's court, and it is clear, here, that he could discuss it openly with the queen. Danger was created by the fact that Essex had gone out of his "role," a role that was deliberately tied to that of the Shepherd Knight, Sidney. That the master of the horse should hold a shepherd's staff was part of her design, a design that in Essex's case failed. It seems probable, then, that the queen, through her chief propagandist, Sir Henry Lee, created the cult of Sidney to which modern biographers, as well as critics, have responded. The cult of a shepherd-knight, Sidney, who is metamorphosed so often in literature of the period into Calidore, Philisides, Astrophil, etc., served as a damper on the impetuous knights Elizabeth had some difficulty controlling. That her personal feelings about Sidney were more complex can be shown by her reaction to his death. She was moved for a period of time apparently, and then seems to have bitterly complained to Sir Charles Blount that he had thrown away a noble life with an ordinary soldier's death, as if he had never fully understood rank.

In his own fictional constructs, however, Sidney seems determined to bring us to a realization of the importance of fulfilling the requirements of social position. For example, he shows in *Arcadia* the chaos that follows a king adopting a shepherd's life by monarchic fiat, or one prince disguising himself as a shepherd in a courtly environment and another eschewing his true identity in donning Amazon's garb and renaming himself for a thwarted lover, Zelmane. The very relationship between sexual passion and disregard of social identity—or identification with the beloved—is a theme from his first works to his last. Nor does he overlook the limitations of rank and the psychic strain created by the transaction of moving from one role to another. To carry off serious jests in his life and works Sidney adopted a series of personae from court jester to grandiloquent courtier, but he seems to have done so in order to show us the dangers of social masking and force us by irony to gain overview about the moral imperatives that go with degree. Such shape-shifting, however, invites misinterpretation, and the difficulties of interpreting disguise appear in criticism of his works as well as in interpretation of aspects of his life to include his soldierly demise.

Sidney's death may have contained deeper irony than the distortion, post mortem, of a complex career into one of simple heroism and virtue. A chronology of the period brings into focus what is, at least initially, a coincidental juxtaposition between the arrangements surrounding Sidney's death and the trial and beheading of Mary, Queen of Scots. Sidney died, after nearly a month of medical care on 18 October 1586, two days after the recess of the original tribunal assembled for the trial of the eloquent Mary on attempted regicide and treason. The trial was then taken up by the Star Chamber, a week later, on 25 October. Sidney's body arrived at port in England on 2 November, when mourning began. Until Sidney's funeral, for instance, courtiers wore only black. But when Mary was finally beheaded, three months later, on 8 February 1587, Sidney's funeral was still a week and a day off. The initial delay of the interment was caused by Secretary of State Walsingham's slow liquidation of his son-in-law's debts. Perhaps by a legal oversight, Sidney had attempted through his will to pay off debts by the sale of mortgaged lands. At any rate, the law stated that only fee-simple land could be sold, post mortem, to pay off creditors, and Walsingham had to find other means to raise approximately six thousand pounds.

It seems reasonable, on the other hand, to assume that Elizabeth was party to the decision for the exact date of Sidney's extravagant funeral at St. Paul's in London, the last on its scale before Admiral Nelson's.[27] The ceremonial parade through the capital, lavish and well-attended, would have helped turn the minds of the populace from the beheading of Mary. Two continental biographers have noted this possibility. Berta Siebeck merely notes the proximity of the two dates and suggests that Elizabeth may have had such a propagandistic scheme: "Perhaps Elizabeth was not sorry to see the people's attention diverted from the painful memory and the execution by a harmless spectacle."[28] Michel Poirier, however, considers the possibility of a Machiavellian subterfuge on the state's part a strong theory for explaining the date and extravagance of the funeral parade: "It was perhaps in order to distract the attention of the people from a regicide that risked shaking its own loyalty that the English government decided to surround the burial with such glamorous occasion."[29] Like so many modern historians, Poirier prefers assigning subtle policy decisions to a vague political force, "the government," rather than to Elizabeth herself. Bacon was always less reticent. If the irony of the "smokescreen" funeral exists, Walsingham must have been deeply exasperated, since he went into debt for the lavish funeral parade when Elizabeth and Leicester refused to defray the costs.

No contemporary commentary on the juxtaposition of events at this time survives, nor are we likely to discover any, since such maneuvering would most likely remain a state secret. But however we interpret the timing and extravagance of Sidney's funeral, we are left with a widespread, intentional use of Sidney's death for propagandistic purposes. Sidney's role, for instance, as the "hero of Zutphen" is largely the product of Greville's second-hand account of his part in the battle and the decay and collapse of his medical condition.[30] That is to say, the heroic image we have of him now is not a product of his own "self-fashioning," but of the image-making of a second party, unlike, for example, what Greenblatt has shown[31] in the case of Ralegh at the time of his execution. Self-fashioning or assumption of roles for the purposes of advancement or self-justification, or, on a higher level, for the sheer artistry of it all, was a conscious activity perhaps of a whole generation of Elizabeth's younger courtiers. But the circumstances of Sidney's death, if we can be certain of them, seem too severe to allow for the artifice that such self-dramatization would rquire.

One of Greville's "facts" about Sidney before the battle, that he threw away his cuisses, his thigh guards, because the marshall of the camp was lightly armed, furthermore, was contradicted by Moffet, who may have been present at the battle and who claimed Sidney was not fully armed because he was in haste. And whatever we do with the image of Sidney offering water to a dying soldier, furthermore, when he is in great thirst from loss of blood, saying, "thy necessity is yet greater than mine," we know that Sidney could not have designed the act for effect, whereas Ralegh, when he imitated Sidney's supposed action offering his hat to a bald fellow in his way to the scaffold, was probably exclusively concerned with effect.[32] We cannot hold Sidney responsible for the perpetuation of his heroic image, and his friends would have known this.

Evidence that Sidney took a modest view of his own achievements as a diplomat, courtier, and author appears so often that we are forced to accept, I believe, the image of a man who saw his own life as a kind of irony. It would be too easy to see his deprecatory references to his own writings, for example, calling his *Defence of Poetry* an "ink-wasting toy" (121) or the *Arcadia* "a trifle, and that triflingly handled,"[33] as manifestations of rhetorical humility, of *sprezzatura*,[34] if he did not treat things supposed more important for a gentleman with similar, often self-disparaging, humor. In regard to his religion, he let it be known that when he was three years old, during Mary's reign, when, incidentally, the Sidneys were all ostensibly Roman Catholic, "with clean hands and head covered" he prayed to the moon.[35] Here he forces his friends to take the reign of Mary with a kind of humor. To joke about religion at all, of course, is a surprise, and we are forced to interpret in our own way what praying to the moon signifies. Perhaps he feigns anticipation of the moon-goddess, Cynthia-Belphoebe-Luna-Elizabeth I.

As for his career, he appeared in the tilt following the news that Leicester had produced another heir with *impresa* altered from "SPERO" ("I hope") to "SPERAVI dashed through" ("I hoped" with a bar)[36] to indicate that his hope was past and to draw a laugh on that score. Here the solemn allegorical circumstances of the tilt are surprised by a personal joke on what was in the context of Sidney's life an important reversal. Finally on his deathbed, his shoulder blades having already broken through his skin,[37] he insisted that a poem of his own making, "La cuisse rompue" ("the broken thigh")[38] be put to music of his own choice and sung to him.

Greville, somewhat puzzled, attributes this act "partly" to show "that the glory of mortal flesh was shaken in him,"[39] but it seems to this reader to be another manifestation of a special kind of humor, a kind of constructive irony, a dissembling, a pretending that he is less than he is, or that circumstances are less grave than they are, something far more "humorous" in all senses of the word than *sprezzatura*, which is a more voluntary posture than Sidney's reflexive irony. What Sidney has performed in these cases is a corrective irony. He creates the special effect of surprising us into going back and reevaluating aspects of what are conventionally understood to be solemn affairs. His characteristic mode of thought in his own life as well as in his art seems to be a criticism of weaknesses in our conventional understandings or constructions of experience. Of course, I have given here only a few examples of a kind of humor that found its most permanent form not in "hearsay" but in those other "facts," his literary works.

An ominous mark or blemish in a personal *impresa* and emblem suggests a paramount self-irony that Sidney developed in both his life and works. At one moment in book two of the revised *Arcadia*, a shepherd knight, Philisides ("star-lover," "Phil-Sid"),[40] makes a brief appearance (in Pyrocles's account to Philoclea of the annual Iberial tilt) looking up at a lady in a window, "the 'star,' wherby his course was only directed."[41] "His impresa was a sheep marked with pitch, with this word: "Spotted to be known." As D. Coulman and Katherine Duncan-Jones have pointed out, the motto is identical with one of Sidney's own Latin "words" in an emblem described by Abraham Fraunce in a manuscript at Penshurst:[42] "A sheep marked with the planet Saturn, with the motto *macular modo noscar.*" ["to be stained merely to be known."] Like Moffet, Fraunce—among other interpretations—insists that "spotted" actually means "spotless": "No blemish is found on the peerless body."[43] But he also notes that Saturn is a symbol of melancholy—in his explanation, irreconcilable sadness over mutability. Philisides's obsession with his star, however, leads this reader to connect both spots with Sidney's love for Stella ("star")—the Earl of Essex's married younger sister, Penelope Devereux Rich—and the blame that went with it. He called this passion in Gifford's account of his death, "a vanity wherein I had taken delight, whereof I had not rid myself."[44] It is suggested by all his references to loving stars in the devices and pseudonyms and sonnets. Note, for example, that the first appearance of a melancholic Sidney persona in *Arcadia* is "upon the ground at the foot of a cypress tree,"[45] a traditional symbol of death and melancholy. Pitch suggests shame and its blackness the color of the bile or humor. Gloomy Saturn is the god of melancholy. In each case, Sidney is providing us with an ironic self-portrait of the sad, young lover; he is gently mocking his blameful passion as he mocks his own choleric tendency to sudden rage at supposed slights—at Oxford, to whom he gives the lie for being called a "puppy," in the tennis court incident perhaps—in the Philisides passage mentioned above.[46] There an older friend's, Lelius's special treatment of him in the Iberian joust causes Philisides to be "much moved with it, while he thought Lelius would show a contempt of his youth." Here Sidney is employing *esoterica* for the purpose of self-irony, in exposing his own would-be adulterous love. In general a spot may suggest all the aspects of mutability such as "infected will," desire and egotistic passion, but this spot specifically symbolized the love melancholy brought on by his longing for his star. In adopting this heraldry, Sidney is going one step further than the woeful Elizabethan courtier in conventional black attire, arms folded, seeking shade, tongue-tied yet vigorously producing sonnets to the virgin queen and to his mistress. When C. S. Lewis suggests that Sidney's complaints about melancholy were a product of "yielding somewhat to the fashion,"[47] he is, I believe, interpreting Sidney's tone according to that bright image of a serious young man who lacks the overview to be self-critical.

Based perhaps on his self-image as "marked" love melancholic and emphasis on love-crises in his works, there have been traces of an antitradition of Sidney throughout the centuries. A "spot" always existed in the development of the heroic image of Sidney, and it is perhaps the exception to his systematic idealization that proves the rule. It concerns those sexual maneuvers with Penelope, which apparently continued after she became Lady Rich and perhaps even after he was married to Frances Walsingham. Observing little of the secrecy recommended in the manuals of courtly love,[48] he unfolded aspects of the quasi-affair in his sonnet sequence, which travelled around enough in manuscript so that many at least knew it existed if they had not read it. Protective poetic reaction to contemporary blame of Sidney seems to appear in Spenser, Greville, Ralegh, and Jonson. In fact, Gifford's prose account of Sidney's death, as Duncan-Jones suggests, seems to have been doctored to remove Sidney's last words on the subject, although "Lady Rich" is at least mentioned by name. And Moffet is probably referring to this matter when he spices his otherwise unrelieved praise in *Nobilis* and *Lessus Lugubris*[49] with disparaging references to Sidney's youthful exuberance, especially in matters of love.[50]

While Moffet and others seem to be directly contradicting the idea of the "spotted" knight by referring to Sidney as "spotless," there has been maintained in Sidneiana an undertone of disapproval and uneasiness with the difficulty of holding Sidney up as a perfect exemplar of social virtue when he was apparently a man of considerable sexual appetite. It will be noted that for all his supposed political acumen, his sonnet sequence and the *Arcadia* unfold a series of sexual intrigues only occasionally relieved by "heroic" or "political" matter. Undertone of disapproval may take the form of somewhat veiled remarks from Dobell and Wallace[51] that Sidney was too preoccupied with sex.

The most intriguing example of the preservation of the image of Sidney's sexual "spot" is contained in Aubrey's *Brief Lives,* where Sidney's death is not laid at the door of his wound but of his refusal, over the best medical advice, "to forbeare his carnall knowledge of" his wife, Frances, when his wound needed healing "upon which occasion there were some roguish verses made."[52] Whether the story is true, it is an interesting tale because it is another manifestation of the image of Sidney's flaw or "spot" that has lived a subterranean life, even in ballads, alongside the exemplary image of Sidney through the centuries. It is hardly a surprise to find that a modern edition of Aubrey's Brief Lives, which in general shows little sign of bowdlerization, substitutes "(acted)" for "would not . . . forbeare his carnall knowledge of her,"[53] obfuscating Aubrey's sense. If the positive tradition were not so strong, it could not have contained the antitradition so easily.

The permanence of the cult of Sidney results, I think, from the fact that its image of Sidney is so appealing. If no "ideal courtier," if no "Renaissance man" ever existed, we would have had to invent one. Even if one had been developed for specific political purpose, we would still want to preserve him. But somewhere buried in eulogy and panegyric and negative reactions to that rhetoric exists the other Sidney semi-defined by his known literary works. Often, however, the works themselves, that best evidence of the "other Sidney," are read allegorically to suit that all too attractive image of what C. S. Lewis called "that rare thing, the aristocrat in whom the aristocratic ideal is really embodied."[54] In fact, that the bright light of that image might distort our reading of his works is suggested metaphorically by many of his most sensitive readers. William Hazlitt, for example, compares its splendor to something

> Like a gate of steel,
> Fronting the sun that renders back
> His figure and his heat.[55]

And Lewis says that "even at this distance, Sidney is dazzling."[56] The image is blinding, in part, because it is a fictive achievement of the Renaissance mode, yoking the opposites of shepherd and knight, contemplative and active, love and friendship, nature and art, nature and grace, fulfilling a synthetic ideal of varied accomplishment. This is an ideal we would or should not part with easily, even in search of the truth through "partiality," but in discovering it in Sidney's works we may be practicing circular logic; we may be proving our assumptions about history.

The development we are led to expect of criticism of Sidney's work has not been fully realized. Since an unsound legendary image is often both our critical point of departure and our point of return, theses and antitheses about Sidney's works have accumulated somewhat unprogressively. Something of worth has accumulated, of course. The many analyzers of moments in certain traditionally chosen passages of his works have located problems in the text the way, perhaps, the Babylonian priests charted problems in the location of heavenly bodies, if only on the assumption that the gods were exerting their immortal free will to move around. My proposed Ptolemaic or Copernican demythologized reading of Sidney's works would owe a great debt to those charts, but it would begin, I hope, with an approach to a more accurate "contemporary reading" of those works.

What I here propose is a first step in search for that experience: The deconstruction of a biographical image that Sidney's friends could not have shared, even if some of them helped develop that precious Elizabethan propagandistic ideal. Sidney's friends and contemporary admirers, such as Thomas Nashe, John Hoskins, Sir Fulke Greville, Ben Jonson, and Edmund Spenser, point, in general concert, to a reading of Sidney as a serious jester, a master of disguise, setting out to entrap his readers in the ironies of existence, for their own benefit. Those friends lend Sidney, the creator of personae, a complex didactic goal and method later ages would deny him.

2
Charted Problems

Traditional "charts" of Sidney's poetry and fiction have failed to provide us with a coherent reading of his works because criticism of Sidney's style and content—generally taken separately[1] was determined by a largely posthumous notion of Sidney as courtly hero. The Arthurian ideal that Elizabeth and her propagandists promoted is uneasy in actual life, intentionally so. The courtier works by indirection, the hero not. In the romances, the heroic reputation of a knight of the round table was largely the product of quests that took him far from Arthur and his influence. But in actual life, Elizabeth, never in greater danger than when her impetuous courtiers were seeking *aventur* in Guiana, Cadiz, or Ireland, vigorously promoted the ideal of a heroic courtier stationed at home, a contradictory concept connected with Sidney and promoted by him and Sir Henry Lee as two of Elizabeth's leading apologists and writers.

Sidney's posthumous reputation as a hero of the Protestant faith and the British aristocracy, yet a poetic technician of cavalier ostentation, however, creates nagging problems for his critics, because it so easily replaces the "unified" concept of the master of voices that Sidney's contemporaries apparently shared. Instead of "hearing" ironic personae, in other words, romantic readers, made out two separate voices of courtliness and heroism that contradicted each other. Sensibly, they asked: "Why would simple virtue express itself in such a devious and figurative manner?" But if courtly style could be divorced from heroic content, the problem of reconciling Sidney's reputation as complex stylist and yet developer of a simplistic moral could easily be solved. Understandably critics overlooked those self-ironic personae designed to trick us into contemplation of a complex dialectic on life's difficulties. Complex words from heroes always look like fanfare.

In his own literary argument about elaboration and indirection, however, Sidney concentrates so much on the purpose of poetry, as well as on the necessity of hiding art, that the distinction between style and content vanishes. Meaning and form jointly comprise a "voice," a persona. Matter and words must be apposite for effective discourse, and elaboration, because it is ostentation, simply becomes a new argument, argument for self. Such elaboration substitutes self-glorying for "earlier" thesis, a statement in itself. Desire for ornamentation produces our new appearance, symbolically speaking: "Like those Indians, not content to wear earrings at the fit and natural place of the ears, but they will thrust jewels through their nose and lips, because they will be sure to be fine" (117). If your words become ornate you alter content. And by such mutilation or adornment of your argument you are now boasting or being fine.

Although Sidney often employs the metaphor of eloquence as apparel, he never implies that style should be considered the "clothing" of content. Altering diction and syntax causes intrinsic change in discourse: "So is that honey-flowing matron Eloquence apparelled, or rather disguised, in a courtesan-like painted affectation" (117). You are "dis-guised"—"unfaced"—by "painted affectation" if your manner becomes periferal to your intent. Notably in criticism of *Arcadia*, and *Astrophil and Stella* critics have made a distinction that would have made Sidney uncomfortable. They have divided and conquered his impersonation by means of a doubtful distinction. And Sidney's own words about style come to haunt him, because his manner is taken to be affected, but only for the purpose of self-aggrandisement, clearly a necessity in maintaining a self-image of that impossibility, the courtly hero.

William Hazlitt's pejorative analysis of *Arcadia* and Charles Lamb's answer to his "accidental prejudice,"[2] for example, at the dawning of modern criticism in England shared and bred assumptions about the meaning and style of Sidney's romance without coming to terms with the work as a whole. They also indulged in biographical heresy. Both writers compared Sidney with Milton in the opposite "roles" of supposed reactionary courtier for Elizabeth and supposed radical administrator for Cromwell, and they fought over a limited plot of Sidney's output. Had they chosen to base their analysis on two court entertainments, *The Lady of May* and *Comus*, or even on two sets of sonnets—as Lamb does briefly—they would never have been able to make the distinctions they discovered in restricting themselves to comparison of *Arcadia* and *Paradise Lost*.

The Lady of May and *Comus* are two versions of the masque, mocking the conventions, so to speak, of their own formal requirements; and the two sets of sonnets are moments in a relatively unified tradition of English introspective and critical poetry. Even though both creators of narrative remind us that their competent audience is "few,"[3] *Arcadia* and *Paradise Lost* are designed, at least ostensibly, for two different kinds of readers, one alert to wit and entertainment values, and the other diverse, even missionary. Hazlitt and Lamb both consider *Paradise Lost* a "coherent" work. *Arcadia* is seen as a parcel of style and content, although they do not at first appear to find common ground for its discussion at all. Hazlitt's essay analyzes Sidney's rhetoric, while Lamb intends to fix his place in the history of ideas. Yet both draw the same conclusions about both aspects of Sidney's art of romance.

Hazlitt complains about Sidney's style and restricts himself to three examples that show how the power of human love can "move" inanimates to action:

> the wind, which seemed to have a sport to play with it [Pyrocles's hair], as the sea had to kiss his feet;
>
> (8)[4]

> her breath is more sweet than a gentle south-west wind which comes creeping over flowery fields and shadowed waters in the extreme heat of summer.
>
> (5)

> Most blessed paper, which shalt kiss that hand, whereto all blessedness is in nature a servant.
>
> (155)

All sense of purposeful "pathetic fallacy" set aside, Hazlitt decries Sidney's susceptibility to the "original sin of alliteration, antithesis, and metaphysical conceit,"[5] conceding, however, that without such rhetorical excess in, for example, Pyrocles's description, "there is hardly a more heroic one to be found in prose or poetry." Lamb "answers" his friend by justifying Sidney's content. He points out that "the noble images, passions, sentiments, and poetical delicacies of character scattered all over the *Arcadia* (spite of some stiffness and encumberment) justify to me the character which his contemporaries have left us of the writer."[6] In his parenthetic reservation about the style—"stiffness," "encumberment"—however, Lamb is in agreement with Hazlitt. But he is really referring to the noble content, something on which Hazlitt, merely in passing, is in total accord. The strained idealism implicit in the comparisons Sidney develops in the above examples is reduced to ostentation—"painted affectation"—the veneer of an idealized content.

The fact that the disagreement between Hazlitt and Lamb had political overtones often made it appear that they were disagreeing about *Arcadia*, when they were actually at odds about the function of the state. Lamb insisted that Hazlitt's negative feeling about *Arcadia* was predicated on the fact that in choosing Milton over Sidney, Hazlitt was arguing with "wantonness" at the expense of a court poet for a "king-hater"[7] like himself. What kind of courtier Sidney was never entered the question. Hazlitt's sole remark about *Arcadia*'s potential for instruction lies in his sarcasm that "it no longer adorns the toilette or lies upn the pillow of Maids of honour and Peeresses in their own right (the Pamelas and Philocleas of a later age)."[8] He sees *Arcadia* as a handbook for a complacent upper crust—notably female—which he fears and loathes politically.

On the other hand, Lamb, who neither questions the value of handbooks of court etiquette, nor challenges the belief that *Arcadia* is such a work, proceeds to construe even the most ambiguous plot motifs as bright examples for an institution he respects. Thus when Pyrocles adopts a transvestite disguise in order to invade a pastoral court with a seducer's intent, in fact when he begins to use his "female" charm in a similar way to the lovestruck Zelmane, for whom he has renamed himself, Lamb insists:

> Sir Philip has preserved so matchless a decorum, that neither does Pryocles' [sic] manhood suffer any strain for the effeminacy of Zelmane, nor is the respect due to the princesses at all diminished when the deception becomes known. In the sweetly constituted mind of Sir Philip Sidney it seems as if no ugly thought or unhandsome meditation could find a harbour.[9]

The emphasis on "Sir," furthermore, conveys a sense of respect for the kind of spotless mind that could never have produced the set of personae that convey the dissimulations and larger paradoxes of *Arcadia*, much less those of *Astrophil and Stella*, the *Defence of Poetry*, and his public works. Sidney's courtly indirection must be sacrificed to the deity of the heroic image propagated by received biographical interpretation. This unanimity posing as debate has recurred periodically up to the present moment of consensus on Sidney among old historians and new historicists.

In the last thirty-five years, no important critical analysis or evaluation of Sidney's works has failed to emphasize the necessity of accommodating concepts of *Arcadia*'s style to its meaning. Since the encyclopedic reevaluations of *Arcadia* and other works by E. M. W. Tillyard and C. S. Lewis appeared in 1954,[10] critics have generally related stylistic antithesis to larger antithetical designs found in the work, but they have also noted that the dichotomies that lie behind such contrasts are rarely, if ever, resolved.[11] Taking this apparent equivocation as a sign of weakness, two of Sidney's most articulate critics, Helgerson[12] and McCoy[13] conclude that Sidney's works, though vastly popular and consistently echoed in their own age, were interesting failures—the product of a curious linking of artistic to historical and biographical collapse mapped out in Lawrence Stone's *Crisis of the Aristocracy: 1558-1641*.[14] While Helgerson suggests that Sidney's *concordia discors* "managed to still the clash" of the conflict of "love and honor, wit and judgment, pleasure and profit,"[15] his *Defence of Poetry* fails[16] as the prodigal fails in relation to paternal authority. And because Sidney lacks "negative capability," because his works are "dominated by the 'egotistical sublime,'"[17] the failure of the works reflects the failure of the man. In McCoy's subtly psychologistic theory, by an urge to rebellion Sidney fails to finish. The unresolved conflict between youthful error and parental severity causes the ending of *Old Arcadia* to slip into obscurity. The confusion is necessary because Sidney did not want to pursue these conflicts to a developed conclusion.

Nancy Lindheim, in her recent analysis of Sidney's antithetical structures, seems to be puzzling over this failure to resolve—though she is ostensibly very positive about Sidney's achievement—when she writes: "While it is easy to demonstrate that Sidney had frequent recourse to a three part tonal structure comprising positive, negative, and humorous perspectives in writing the *Arcadia*, it is difficult to say whether the structure in itself has meaning."[18] Elsewhere she speaks of the "defeat"[19] of distinction between the male figures of *Arcadia*, and also of "Sidney's sleight of hand, the vanishing distinction."[20] That Sidney may be creating such distinctions—and undercutting them—for purposes of "game" has been suggested by several recent critics.[21] Here Sidney's work becomes a courtly entertainment, and an intellectual exercise in Renaissance ambiguity for its own sake—an assault on the reader's expectations that is unresolved and unrelieved. Sidney, thus, becomes the Cusanus of the English court. On the other hand, David Norbrook[22] and Annabel Patterson[23] would usher us out of the maze by testing Edwin Greenlaw's reading of Sidney's works as political allegory. Certainly valid, such procedure could facilitate, however, no more than a critical escape from all those collapsing dichotomies.

Perhaps Margaret Ferguson comes closest to my interpretation of Sidney's irony when, in speaking of Sidney's apparent dissimulation in his *Defence of Poetry*, she says the examples "frequently serve to complicate or undermine the points they are supposed to prove."[24] Sidney's ethical bias, emphasized by William Craft and others,[25] suggests that we see his "vanishing distinctions" as strategically undermining conventional dichotomies that serve to explain experience, because they are mere tools for interpretation not answers, and the author must "surprise"[26] us into that discovery. When Lindheim suggests that for Sidney "parody" or "humor" follows his positive then negative antithesis, she insists that the negative and parodic merely reinforce the positive.

In part, she may be holding out for the Sidney of Lamb whose princes she claims are perfect heroes, not, as I argue, comic protagonists. Her narrator's wit sometimes become the brilliant ostentation of a self-aggrandizing Sidney, Hazlitt's rhetorician, capable of sacrificing, as she says, "content to virtuosity."[27] But, if she acquiesces in the courtly hero opposition, I am certain she is on the right track. I argue that the parodic or humorous version is undercutting the initial distinction, and the reader must understand the irony of its collapse, and then move beyond the rubble to the paradox underneath. Why does Sidney create such oppositions, including style and content, only to collapse them? Because, like his great philosopher friends, Peter Ramus, Giordano Bruno, and other congenial Renaissance thinkers, Sidney has a profoundly paradoxical view of experience. True experience is a paradox. Comically collapsing distinctions not only clears the air in order to venture on higher levels of thought, but it also yokes those original distinctions in a harmony of opposites. In a mystical as well as a linguistic sense, all distinctions should generate clarity, but none is final or infallible.

Sidney anticipates the quandary that dichotomizing interpreters have with his fiction when his rhetor pictures, in his *Defence of Poetry,* "the moral philosophers, whom, me thinketh, I see coming towards me with a sullen gravity, as though they could not abide vice by daylight" (83), rigidly fixing the poles of moral distinction, "casting largess as they go, of definitions, divisions, and distinctions." Their dark vice is their substitution of dichotomy for analysis of persona and intention not their lack of a sense of humor. In Sidney's example, such readers of experience display affected knowledge: "rudely clothed for to witness outwardly their contempt of outward things, with books in their hands against glory, whereto they set their names, sophistically speaking against subtlety" (83). Such moralists are engaged in the art of defining virtue but also "making known his enemy, vice, which must be destroyed, and his cumbersome servant, passion, which must be mastered; by showing the generalities that containeth it, and the specialties that are derived from it" (83). Sidney's personae always gently criticize the use of such generalities in fiction or poetry.

Sidney's rhetor, in this passage, parodies the workings of the polemicist's kind of fiction. He reveals a morality play where the master, "Virtue" painted on his forehead, perhaps, destroys "Vice" on stage, and overthrows a rebellious majordomo named "Passion" on the boards. This fiction provides an experience of binary abstraction, an apologue that affirms its own anterior assumption that distinctions between virtue and vice and reason and passion are infallible aids to interpretation of experience. Sidney's persona undermines such oppositions, and criticizes our dependence on categorization of the raw material of experience because it welcomes, as in the case of his moral philosophers—"angry with any man in whom they see the foul fault of anger" (83)—simplism and hypocrisy. Behind that satiric mask, however, lies a truth that informs all Sidney's works. In *The Lady of May* and the *Arcadia,* for example, Sidney's dialectic asks us to consider whether the court offers an active life and the country a contemplative one, but then he merges the worlds. We experience active contemplation in such a way that reminds us that activity and thought always fuse in the human political animal. Sidney's persona in the *Defence of Poetry,* taunts the philosophers' "wrangling . . . whether the contemplative or the active life do excel" (93) not only because they cannot move men by their exercises but because such abstraction from experience is only a method for explaining life not a truth. Sidney and his contemporaries, like Spenser and Shakespeare, never shy away from asserting the lifelike content of high art as well as its necessary paradoxes.

When the rhetor of his *Defence of Poetry* comes to define the nature of fiction, he surprises us with new meanings for the same words, forcing us to go back and recollect what happened. He says, "the poet only, only bringeth his own stuff, and doth not learn a conceit out of a matter, but maketh matter for a conceit" (99).[28] In each case the repetition[29] modifies the meaning of the word in question. The meaning of "only" shifts from "merely" and "strictly" to something closer to "solely" and "alone." "Conceit" travels semantically from "assumption" to "idea"; "matter" from "fictional matter" to "suggestive substance." To paraphrase: "The writer of fiction strictly and alone brings in his own content, and does not extract an assumption from fictional matter, but creates suggestive substance for an idea." In other words, fiction, like life, does not serve our concepts; rather it provides, like experience or nature at large, food for interpretation. Allegory is not poetry. Poetry is not allegory.

Sidney's persona implies in this oblique manner that poetry abhors abstraction, as nature does a vacuum. Fiction cannot beg the questions so many critics discover in Sidney's discourse because there are no categorical moral assertions there. To answer critics who say poets do not tell the truth, Sidney's voice must answer "paradoxically" (102). The poet "nothing affirms, and therefore never lieth" (102). He "never affirmeth" (102). He never conjures "you to believe for true what he writes" (102) by schematization. He depends on "knowledge of mankind" (102) to suggest a profounder truth beyond all ready distinctions. I argue in this book that Sidney's dissimulating attitude towards the univeral reader produces the variations of tone in the narration, description, and speeches of the 1590 *Arcadia* and his other works, even the official ones. He adopts the voice of the serious jester bent on leading the reader into entertaining likelike contradictions. If Sidney's personae of the moment can reduce the distance between reader and text, he can correct in gentle ways his reader's passionate, rationalizing, dichotomy-loving nature, and force him or her to experience at one remove the paradoxical nature of experience. In so arguing, I hope to demonstrate the validity of Sidney's text, not allowing it to be reduced to a pawn in a skirmish between old and new historical consciousness.

3
Sidney's Official Indirection

To show how Sidney's strategy of involvement functions, I would like to briefly examine three of the official works he produced. These, I assume, were commissioned by his uncle, of whom he was the sometime heir, Robert Dudley, earl of Leicester. The first is a court entertainment similar to a masque; the second is a letter of protest or advice to a sovereign; and the third is a formal defense of the earl himself. With the now fragmentary *Discourse on Irish Affairs*, and the symbolic pageant, *The Four Foster Children of Desire*, these works represent the extent of Sidney's intended "publications" in his own lifetime, although the *Defence of the Earl of Leicester* apparently saw precious little circulation in manuscript.

Like much of the "golden" poetry and prose of the age of Elizabeth I, these works promoted political positions of the Leicester faction, but more significantly, as demonstrated by Frances Yates, Dorothy Connell and others,[1] of the cult of Eliza. Elizabeth's surrounding herself with relatively satisfied—that is, relatively free and uncensored—writers, mostly under Leicester's aegis, became a weapon of rule and order in a traditionally fragile and heterogeneous union. Maintaining identity in the social order was so often their theme, that reading such poets, one would never suspect that hereditary rank would virtually be done away with in the years following 1642. Sidney is not, however, merely a propagandist of monarchy and traditional aristocracy in these works, although these aspects are at times dominant. He seems a serious jester from the first, seeking ways to force us to entertain the paradoxes he sees in human existence and what he apparently takes for its universal conditions. In fact, his humor appears full-blown to this reader in his first "publication," his comic court entertainment, designed for Elizabeth's visit to Robert Dudley at Wanstead Garden, recently acquired from Lord Rich, in 1578,[2] now known as *The Lady of May*.

Rhomboid Logic (1578)

On Wanstead estate in Essex, now in the northeast of greater London, Queen Elizabeth was spontaneously entreated to choose between two suitors for the May Lady's hand, either a shepherd who the May Lady says has "very small deserts and no faults" (25.12)[3] or a forester who has, also according to her, "many deserts and many faults" (25.11).[3] Rightly or wrongly, the queen chooses the shepherd and establishes her political and religious authority, in this green world in some comic disarray, with an assist from a schoolmaster, Rombus. Probably, along with his dramatized tournament of Witsun 1581, this quasi-masque is Sidney's only dramatic work. It borrows its form in part from George Gascoigne's *Princely Pleasures,* produced by Leicester at Kenilworth in July 1575 during one of Elizabeth's progresses, in part from innovative Italian and French pastoral drama. Like the masque to which it is akin, it revolves around the physical presence of the flattered monarch, airing topical and philosophical issues that go well beyond allusion to present parties.

Traditional readers delivered the verdict that Sidney's court entertainment was a mere bagatelle. Given the peculiar light and comic veneer of his quasi-masque at Leicester's newly acquired Wanstead Garden, old historians condemned it as lacking merit, unworthy of the exemplar of serious Anglo-Saxon empire-building. As entertaining and nicely structured as it is, it must be the accidental product of a Calvinist dispositon, a diversion both in the sense of merely diverting for audience and reader, and as departure from an activist career. Perhaps Roger Howell says it best in *The Shepherd Knight,* when, baffled by growing interest in what he insists is a "trifling work," "a slight royal entertainment," he asserts, "there is little to be gained from detailed analysis."[4] But new historicists and recent allegorical interpreters, who take it far more seriously, have had trouble with Sidney's drama as well, because they are also influenced—often negatively—by a received notion of Sidney as heroically minded, secretly or not. Both the paradoxical image of "courtly hero" and the notion of a self-conscious or egoistic rebel that it helped spawn, I maintain, have impeded our appreciation of Sidney's text.

Above all, discovery and publication[5] of the Helmingham Hall manuscript of this described quasi-masque have generated responses that emphasize its author's purported naive idealism. These studies interpret the work as political argument on the question of the queen's marriage or her foreign policy, or as Platonic allegory or stoical apologue. They take Sidney's "*idea* or foreconceit"[6] of the drama to be manifestation of his "active" (to comprehend love and war, that is, high politics) or "contemplative" (philosophical) idealism. William Ringler, Jr., who first reported in print Jean Robertson's discovery of the manuscript papers,[7] notes an internal argument in favor of aggressive foreign policy symbolized by Therion, whose name suggests "wild beast,"[8] the erratic forester suitor of the May Lady. Robert Kimbrough and Philip Murphy, who produced its transcription, see an idealized Leicester in the same figure, symbolizing all that Leicester represents.[9] Louis Montrose[10] proposes that Sidney's representation of his own idealistic rebellion against the queen as monarch, mother, and love object, is sublimated in Therion and more especially in a senior forester, Rixus. And Christopher Martin[11] takes the mini-drama to be a piece of exasperated—and therefore dangerous—satire of prolixity and indecision in the queen's chambers.

In these cases, Sidney is seen espousing, in the realm of action, Leicester's supposed love-suit to the queen, or the Leicester-Walsingham faction's proposed system of alliances designed to oppose Papism in the late seventies on the mainland—the Continental League: in other words, immediate and decisive causes in love and war. Thus we hear scholars on the time-honored and perfectly valid notion of the masque as a high symbolic airing of topical issues. On this side, McCoy, Montrose, Helgerson,[12] and others present a "serious" and single-minded Sidney producing ready answers to the issues behind current events.

On the other hand, Penny Pickett,[13] Robert Stillman,[14] and others present Sidney encoding his work with his Platonic and stoical idealism. In the realm of contemplation, Pickett see Therion and Espilus representing the wild and tame horses of Socrates's triadic view of ideal government or control in the *Phaedrus*. Sidney's "full-fledged Platonic poem"[15] thus benignly represents a metaphor for the unresolved yoking of contraries in the operation of power. Stillman argues that Sidney leads his audience into an understanding of an ideal Stoical and Horatian bonding of words and things in the healthy rhetoric of Rixus the forester. High Neoplatonism and its traditional stoical ally are at center stage in both critical analyses.

Stephen Orgel, however, who, in good part, opened the debate about Sidney's complex purposes in *The Lady of May*[16] by observing Sidney's opposition of active and contemplative life in the work—as well as the queen's apparent misinterpretation of its tendency to favor the forester—early cautions us that "here, as everywhere in his writings, Sidney is above all a criic."[17] Orgel implies that Sidney in this drama critiques the very binary oppositions—such as active and contemplative or pastoral and courtly—that help design his work. In support of Orgel and others, I further propose that Sidney's larger criticism in *The Lady of May* extends to the idealism implied by the characters, action, and structure of the work itself.

In respect to the active life, Sidney examines, with a simultaneously admiring and skeptical eye, the urge to true love implied by Petrarchanism as well as the impetus to create a collective paradise implied by his pastoral modes of shepherds and foresters. Annabel Patterson points out that Sidney espouses what she calls the "standard Renaissance reading of Virgilian pastoral"[18] as not only a criticism of established hierarchy, but also as a "revolutionary" proposal to consider the possibility of a society without hierarchy. But Sidney, I argue, remains skeptical of that pastoral mode and its implied political ideal. In respect to philosophical contemplation, furthermore, I argue that Sidney remains a Platonic anti-Platonist, a wry analyst of the political thought of that philosopher of whom the rhetor says in his *Defence of Poetry*, in a rare moment of relatively direct speaking, "the wiser a man is, the more just cause he shall find to have him in admiration" (109).

Use of the Helmingham Hall manuscript restores to the established text of Sidney's drama the peculiar macaronic epilogue delivered by the schoolmaster Rombus—whom I assume Sidney played—that completes the work's anti-idealistic argument in respect to action or contemplation.[19] This speech also produces a self-ironic cure for recusancy in its promotion of "Roman Catholic" worship of Elizabeth.

Through Rombus, Sidney implies that monarchic political control certainly contains a paradox. This paradox is a Platonic yoking of the "horses" of laxity and rigor—but a pragmatic one that informs Elizabeth's propagandistic image as unattainable virgin and forceful queen, as replacement for the Petrarchan idol as well as the Virgin Mary, and as creator and curer of disease—most notably recusancy—in the body politic. The very absense of this closing oration in the otherwise excellent 1598 printed version of the text, in fact, may serve to warn us of controversy surrounding Rombus's argument that Elizabeth substitute for the Immaculate Mary. Finally, Sidney tempers all rhetoric in the drama by exposing the gap that always exists between language and actuality—*verbum* and *res*—by means of self-irony in his dramatic characterization of Rombus. Gentle irony, in fact, as always in Sidney's work, gives this mini-drama its low-key, congenial quality.

In other words, although he is capable, as C. S. Lewis has shown,[20] of perhaps the first and certainly some of the most spectacular flights of golden poetry in England with all its violent hyperbole, Sidney remains at heart—paradoxically—a deflator of the strained ideals such poetry expresses, or, shall we say, a critic of the dangers to identity and rank that inevitable yearning for those ideals entails. In fact, if Marlowe's hyperbole explodes, Sidney's has a peculiar way of imploding with considerable violence. His crash anticipates Marlowe's blaze. In our introduction to *The Lady of May's* Edenic green world of true love and cooperation, for example, we discover paralyzing indifference on the part of the beloved and envious faction on behalf of the lovers. What the terrestrial paradise could be, it is not. Far more than in mutations of idyllic worlds from Theocritus to Sannazaro and Tasso, pastoral conventions are here reversed.

We hear Queen Elizabeth interrupted by a mother's suit to decide a match between a shepherd and a forester for the hand of a daughter, the May Lady, who later admits: "I like them both, and love neither" (25.2). Then in dumb show we see a would-be policeman, the town Latin instructor, Master Rombus, beaten by a mob made up of elements of warring factions of shepherds and foresters who champion one or the other lover. In other words, a landscape that should provide a life exempt from the sexual politics and envy of the court, yields us very un-pastoral humans, whose great erotic and political ideals lead them into rivalry, then factionalism—the enemies to pastoral selflessness and Melibean peace.

Topically the specific location in Wanstead Garden in a period of heavy recusancy begs for a picture of disorder and strife—specifically suggested in the drama—but the problem of a pastoral paradise gone awry applies to all England as well, and to what Sidney and the censors apparently took for the constants of the human condition that tend to disorder and, *in extremis,* demand the imposition of monarchic order. Ultimately all difficulties of this real and ideal garden are resolved by the queen's assumption of the role of arbitrator, although she may have intentionally mischosen the rich shepherd Espilus over the erratic forester Therion, as I have suggested in chapter one, thereby putting the entertainment in mild disarray.[21] The irony of an entrepreneurial shepherd who counts his sheep with an auditor's zeal might well have appealed to the economically conservative queen.

Sidney's self-ironic mask in this skit belongs, as we have seen, to the would-be peacemaker and "self-wise-seeming schoolmaster" (116), Rombus, the object of both factions' abuse in the second scene of the anti-masque. Rarely in this era is a "literary" professor sympathetic. Yet, as Duncan-Jones points out,[22] our empathy extends to all the local and rustic characters in this garden, who remain nearly on a par with the courtly elements caught up in the action. Rombus is also the victim of love—or at least sexual desire—and, in ludicrously garbled fashion, he creates the serious jests of the wise fool. Delivering in the manuscript version the greatest number of speeches as well as lines, Rombus provides an epilogue that acts as an ironic solution to amatory and political disease.

This Latin instructor thus becomes our focus of attention, and sympathy, partly because "poor" Rombus (24.13) is not only the butt of the disorderly shepherds and foresters but of the May Lady herself. The queen, however, tolerates his pedantry, and at the entertainment's close, accepts his gift of a rosary "stolen" from Robert Dudley. With the queen, we in the audience listen carefully to his instruction, although we cannot always be sure we understand what we hear. Stillman, in his dense and provocative discussion of Sidney's picture of rhetorical corruption in *The Lady of May*, justly asserts that "as a rhomboid lacks right angles Rombus lacks rightness in his reasoning."[23] But if he remains off-center in redundancy and obscurity—if his *verbum* strays far from his *res*—Rombus alone suggests the possibility of geometric order in the political worlds of Wanstead Garden and its environs.

When the Renaissance resurrected the stock comic figure of the doctor or savant from Greek New Comedy,[24] by way of Plautus and Terence, it not surprisingly transformed this more worldly pedant into a professor. This figure could be used to sustain the attack on logic-chopping scholiasts whether in the form of *commedia dell'arte's dottore* from the University of Bologna or that of Schoolmaster Rombus and his progeny in Shakespeare's Holofernes and others. Like the moral philosophers of Sidney's *Defence of Poetry*, Rombus casts many "definitions, divisions, and distinctions" (83), in macaronic and obscure Latin.[25] As one shepherd later says to himself: "O poor Dorcas, poor Dorcas, that I was not set in my young days to school, that I might have purchased the understanding of Master Rombus' mysterious speeches" (28.4). "Mysterious" remains Rombus's definition of the May Lady: "*O Tempori, O Moribus!* In profession a child, in dignity a woman, *in ceteris* a maid" (24.6). And he "divides" and "distinguishes" the merits of the rival claims of forester Therion and shepherd Espilus with more energy than depth, albeit in Latin: "For thus I must uniform my speech to your obtuse conceptions; for *prius dividendum oratio antequam definiendum, exemplum gratia* [First a speech must be divided, before it is defined, for instance]: *either Therion must conquer this, Dame Maia's nymph, or Espilus must overthrow her*" (27.27). Giving a false impression of making distinctions, Rombus merely wallows in the obvious, his leading characteristic suggested by his looking at marriage strictly from the point of view of its consummation, or first "overthrowing."

This self-styled *corpusculum* [little body] (27.23) shows sparks of a fine appreciation of female charms. Thus the May Lady who sends him off with "tedious fool" and "good Latin fool" for his pains, in his macaronic remains "a certain *pulchra puella profectò*" ["a pretty girl indeed"] (23.25), and Queen Elizabeth becomes "your excellent formosity," or "Juno, Venus, Pallas *et profecto plus*" [and, indeed, more] (31.21), the apotheosis of female form in this odd version of the judgment of Paris.[26] If we go no deeper in the quasi-masque, Rombus has made us laugh and has, no doubt, pleased the queen.

Rombus's definition of love, however, exposes one of Sidney's dearest paradoxes. As Stillman says, "Rombus elevates the dispute, predictably and pedantically, into a comic mythological love story."[27] But we hear something more: "The sovereign lady of this, Dame Maia's month, hath been *quodammodo* hunted, as you would say, pursued, by two, a brace, a couple, a cast of young men, to whom the crafty coward Cupid had *inquam* delivered his dire doleful digging dignifying dart" (23.27). Redundant overemphasis on the rivalry between the two young men leads to his applying contradictory, albeit alliterative, affective adjectives to Cupid's arrow. As Stillman has it, "he is hunting the letter," but I challenge the assertion that "only by accident do the words makes sense," since these adjectives share a degree of truth intrinsic to our wise fool's analysis. Love is "dire," sudden and destructive, "doleful," creating pain and sorrow in the lover, "digging," spurring.[28] But love's dart is also man's urgent internal motivator to self-improvement. According to the rules of courtly love, one is "dignified" by the desire to be worthy of the beloved.

Yearning for true love, however, as Sidney often shows, can create dangerous desires, even self-destructive ones. Such passion creates an internal usurpation of reason that may cause suicidal melancholy or violent rivalry. It fosters egotism in the lover as well as in the beloved. For example, when Rombus accuses the May Lady of a tendency to "turpify the reputation of my doctrine with the superscription of a fool" (24.7), of not having respected his rank or position as schoolmaster, he could have predicted the May Lady's own self-inflation in the presence of the queen. She will deign to accept queen's decision, "nor yet because of your great estate, since no estate can be compared to be the Lady of the whole month of May, as I am" (24.20). Love can both dignify and degrade. Its flattery might lead to self-importance. The very enchantment of unrequited love of the May Lady or of the queen also establishes identity. Rombus then moves on from the paradox of love to deliver his blundering wise picture of that of man's politics and society.

Master Rombus remains the Cassandra-like prophet of proper rule and peace in Wanstead Garden. That no one except the queen listens, indeed that the parties to the quarrel—"nothing duteous to his clerkship" (23.4)—answer him with "many unlearned blows" (22.22), does not detract from his presentation of what I call the rhomboid logic of rule. Naturally the classroom represents our schoolmaster's model of ideal monarchy.[29] There, Rombus declares, he is "one not a little versed in the disciplinating of the juvental fry, wherein (to my laud I say it) I use such geometrical proportion, as neither wanteth manseutude nor correction, for so it is described: *Parcare subjectos et debellire superbos*" (23.13). Self-glorifying and misquoting *Aeneid* 6.853, even hinting at the unsquare figure of his own name,[30] he calls for a balance of graciousness and punishment to spare the humble (*subjectos*) and war on the proud (*superbos*) as the elementary principle of monarchic rule.

Here Rombus espouses a Heraclitan or Platonic (and, of course, Virgilian) opposition of *parcere* (Rombus's *parcare;* to abstain, desist) and *debellare* (Rombus's *debellire;* to conquer completely, vanquish) to suggest the slow hastening of monarchic justice. At the moment, in Wanstead and the country at large, the queen's classroom, *parcere* has ruled, even to breeding in counties nearby to Wanstead Garden a community of lapsed Anglicans. Dorothy Connell in fact demonstrates Elizabeth's difficulties with recusants in her progresses through Suffolk and Norfolk late in the summer of 1578, noting where, in specific cases, she must "overturn" her "double" in the image of the Virgin Mary.[31] In Sidney's drama, pastoral order in the country—which, ideally, might provide a picture of cooperation used rhetorically to criticize the corrupt hierarchy of the court—has been disturbed by a lapse in control, and perhaps in religion, tempting forester and shepherd to battle in desire for the May Lady.

The factions of proud foresters and shepherds have even come to rule bystanders like Rombus, releasing energy by beating on him. Rombus implies that by pride of possession and rivalry, *superbia*, elements of the green world have, in fact, become bestial. When he refers to the foresters and shepherds as rude subhumans, as "rural animals" (23.12), "brute nebulons" (27.22) (from the Latin *nebulo*, worthless fellow), "plumbeous cerebrosities" [leaden minds] (27.25), "inscitium vulgorum et populorum" [of the ignorant multitudes and peoples] (27.21), he is not just condemning their education, their "disciplination," but their contagious unruliness in a crowd, their animal-like collectively violent selves, who have just joined in showering him with blows.

Inevitably Rombus associates himself with the central hero of the

Roman literature he teaches, the demigod who suffered so much in his efforts to love and rule fairly in the voyage of life. In high elegiac mode, he again misquotes the Aeneas of Virgil (1.203) "when he sojourned in the surging sulks of the sandiferous seas: *Haec olim memonasse iuvebit*" [one day it will be a joy to remember these things] (23.23). In his self-glorifying way, Rombus has raised the painful question of rebellion, war, turmoil, and religious conflict crucial to Elizabeth's rule and to Tudor England, and parallel to the struggles of pre–Augustan Rome.

For an audience that had suffered a rhythm of attempted revolutions and rebellions, Sidney's theme could not be lost. English authorities, since the days of Edward VI, regularly compared themselves directly to heroes of the Augustan Romans, also survivors of a century of civil strife. The English in general may have even exaggerated Virgilian horror of civil disturbance on this score.[32] Insurrection in *The Lady of May* is thus both interior, caused by what the elderly shepherd Lalus calls a "certain fransical malady they called 'love'" (22.34) or "flat folly" (23.1), and exterior caused by undisciplined *superbia*, the hubristic desire to impose the peace of marriage and unity that, given human perversity, always creates strife, here in the escalating vendetta of shepherds and foresters.

If forester and shepherd only join to victimize our policeman, however, each agrees that their natural world teaches cooperation. Thus for the shepherds the sheep act as models "among whom there is no envy, but all obedience" (28.11). For the foresters, the "hurtless trees" exemplify the social ideal, who "though never so high, they hinder not their fellows; they only enviously trouble, which are crookedly bent" (29.19). Yet every regular inhabitant of this springtime green world has become twisted, even devious though monarchic license and internal disorder.

A failure in rule and a raging desire for the love object have locked them in reciprocal strife, only relieved when they irrationally focus their energy on "the poor schoolmaster" (24.13), or, finally, when they most carefully and most rationally respond to Queen Elizabeth, ironically, not only as "the law" but also as the ideal love object. The dynamics of the queen's rule depend on her collapsing distinctions that cause strife, here, by becoming in an improbable combination both nonpareil Petrarchan love object and the Roman Catholic queen of Heaven.[33]

In the quasi-masque, Rombus, of course, cannot achieve the "square" geometrical peace he hopes for. The queen must be imported into its true center. Rombus having failed "to have parted their sanguinolent fray" (23.19), Elizabeth must separate those who would be "at this present, without your presence redress it, in some bloody controversy" (21.23). Of course, such a masque inevitably propagandizes the importance of the queen for peace in the commonwealth. But in this dramatic work Sidney chooses to convey Elizabethan doctrine, in part, by means of suggestive metaphor, with Petrarchan forebears—that of catching disease from the queen's eyes. The queen is pictured as fighting disease in the populus by creating it. The first speech of the play, that of the May Lady's mother, ends with the odd declaration: "I dare stay here no longer, for our men say here in the country, the sight of you in infectious" (21.25). The reference is topical to the extent that Elizabeth's courtiers literally carried contagion into the country.[34] On the metaphoric level, however, Rombus glosses one aspect of this universal disease as the symptom of a hit by Cupid's arrow of love. Such an arrow feels like the symptoms of oppressive disease, and sudden blinding: "where ears be burnt, eyes dazzled, hearts oppressed" (22.8), here in erotic response to the May Lady. Furthermore, on the high political level, the eye of the queen's authority works like the basilisk, killing with the ruthless evil eye. Rixus the forester later says that Elizabeth "even with her eye can give the cruel punishment" (27.15). Now eyes can quell civil strife only by meeting violence with the violence of law. Thus Dorcas responds: "Hold thy peace, I will neither meddle with her nor her eyes. They say in our town, they are dangerous both" (27.17). Both love and punishment can be caught from her gaze.

In this odd compliment to the queen—an echo of the pleading mother's version of what "men say here in the country," lies a concept of the two "disciplinators," the bewitching eyes of love and the basilisk-like eyes of the law.[35] Thus, the queen's face hurts oft, but still it doth delight" (22.10). Both "visual" assaults are dangerous as well as generative, and both are paradoxically connected with the image of the queen as unattainable love interest and as ruler. Sidney will say of the paradoxical nature of medicine in the *Defence of Poetry:* "Do we not see the skill of physic, the best rampire to our often-assaulted bodies, being abused, teach poison, the most violent destroyer?" (104). And of legal science: "Doth not knowledge of law, whose end is to even and right all things, being abused, grow the crooked fosterer of horrible injuries?" Medicine, love, and law ideally would cure, according to Sidney, but they might well destroy. In the case at hand, the law had been lax. Rombus will be safe from what he calls "the contaminating hands of these plebeians" (23.18) only when the factions resubmit to the sceptre of England's true policeman, Elizabeth. Thus, although Rombus's macaronic formulae remain barely understood, he suggests a powerful idea of internal and external disorder that provides that "matter for a conceit" (99) Sidney saw peculiar to fiction's power. Sidney's own version of the "self-wise-seeming schoolmaster" shares more of his maker than a susceptibility to female charms. He is exposing Sidney's favorite paradoxes of love and rule.

In his final disquisition on the idolatry of Elizabeth, Rombus proposes an ironic cure for the fallen paradise of Wanstead Garden that collapses the distinction between the icon of Elizabeth and that icon of Mary, blessed among virgins, which threatens to break up the kingdom. As if Sidney's uncle, Robert Dudley, had not suffered enough slander from English Roman Catholic militants on the continent, Rombus, in the concluding speech, accuses the earl of being, in fact, a Roman Catholic fanatic, another violent religious deviant. Levels of irony exist in the accusation of Dudley as a man "foully commaculated with the papistical enormity" (31.27), "a huge *catholicam*" (31.28) who adds "and Elizabeth" (31.33) to the *paternoster,* making use of "*papisticorum bedorus,* of Papistian beads" (31.31) (the "stolen" gift of strung agates to the queen). As Duncan-Jones points out, the "insipidity of the convention of the loving beadsman is effectively counteracted."[36] To call Leicester a Catholic, however, contains another irony.[37] During this period the queen saw Leicester as forward in his opposition to the marriage of d'Alençon and in his political hopes for a Protestant league to weaken the Roman Catholics in France, Germany, Spain, and the Netherlands. He may have been England's leading anti-Papist, certainly so in the eyes of his English enemies on the continent. Yet Rombus is made to resolve both his idealistic amatory and political quarrels with the queen through the picture of him as worshipper, as Bacon would have had all of Elizabeth's impetuous courtiers,[38] and idolator to boot, a slave to passion for his mistress and for the state his mistress embodies. Furthermore, in singling out the lord of the manor at Wanstead as correct idolator, a thorny problem in religious controversy in Essex is momentarily solved.

In keeping with official Elizabethan propaganda designed for the queen by Sir Henry Lee, Sidney, and others, idolatry of the queen especially among the powerful peers of the realm must be publicly demonstrated, often on former Roman Catholic saints' days.[39] Here, on a real or symbolic May Day, the day of regal judgments,[40] Sidney, notably by use of the ironic mask of Rombus, had once again successfully made the point that the tilts and pageants and all the former saints' day celebrations were designed to make. Master Robert of Wanstead, the Earl of Leicester, has dutifully worshipped Elizabeth as love object and as queen of England. And Astraea, the goddess of justice, has returned. Thus, through his court entertainment, Sidney has made his public point by indirection. Let us for a moment turn to Sidney's ironic (and hyperbolic) style, here in a letter of advice to the queen, concerning the courtship of d'Alençon.

Advice to the Queen (1579)

In Sidney's most serious political moment, when his uncle, Robert Dudley, the Earl of Leicester, apparently had him write a public letter to pressure the queen to terminate negotiations for marriage with the Duc d'Alençon—"A Letter to Queen Elizabeth Touching Her Marriage With Monsieur"—Sidney's witty and courtly—though pedantic—persona sets up distinctions and then undercuts them, most noticeably in his description of the French duke's personality. For example, his smooth "voice" juxtaposes d'Alençon's imagination as well as his personal education as prods to incite aspiration to power, but then undercuts the whole concept of such a desire: "he, both by his own fancy and by his youthful governors embracing all ambitious hopes, having Alexander's image in his head, but perchance ill painted" (52.19). In miniature this ironic procedure is a kind of rug-pulling. The reader is made to expect, by a courtly voice controlling rather majestic language, an observation about those hopes and the antithetical function of inherent imaginings as opposed to princely training—the reader is enticed onto the rug by splendid words—but then his expectations are overturned by an ironic aside about blurred portraits of Alexander and intellectual dullness.

A similar ironic undercutting, containing a reference to Ajax's huge shield in Homer, appears at the end of the letter: "And if he grow king, his defence will be like Ajax' shield, which weighed down rather than defended those that bore it" (56.30). Here the notion of unwieldy and unbearable weight undercuts the notion of kingship and lively national defense. Thus, although the work as a whole remains politely indirect about supposed flaws in the character, health, and person of d'Alençon, verbal irony delivered by our letter-writing persona pictures Monsieur as an ambitious lightweight.

Sidney balances his ironic attacks on Elizabeth's suitor with equally subtle hyperbolic images of the queen as a virtually unapproachable object of erotic worship. Undoubtedly a frank letter by contemporary standards, Sidney's letter to the queen resembles more a poem of warning and eulogy, like Spenser's "April" or "November" in *The Shepheardes Calendar* or Ralegh's *The Ocean to Cynthia,* because, while it is apparently candid and even intimate, it conveys its message poetically by means of indirection, by metaphor and complex words. If Sidney had tended to fashion a debile picture of d'Alençon by means of understatement, he opposed it to an idolatrous picture of the queen. Thus, in the words of his courtly persona, the proposed match could only have appeared faintly absurd.

The number of manuscript versions of Sidney's letter, one showing up in a seventeenth-century commonplace book under the category of "Advice,"[41] attests, I think, to attention given to the form as well as to the content of the work. Besides taking a negative stance in a real or imagined marriage crisis and a positive one on the queen's rule, the letter becomes a model of tactful indirection. Lack of tact was to cost John Stubbs his right hand in the controversy following his *The Discovery of Gaping Gap* (1579) on the unsuitability of the French king's brother. That so many versions of Sidney's work exist may even indicate the queen's approval of its circulation. Elizabeth was wise to recognize two opposing views of every major administrative problem—such as the disposition of Mary, Queen of Scots, or the founding of a Protestant League, or her marriage—in order to appear to be choosing among pieces of advice rather than generating public policy on her own. If some policy failed she could shift some of its blame from her by favoring its opponents. In this case, she received a letter from Sir Thomas Cecil favoring and one from Sidney opposing the match, and neither writer seems to have suffered for it.[42] Which view she came to favor is unclear, because she "tabled," in a sense, d'Alençon's proposal, after accepting it.

The wide distribution of Sidney's letter, however, creates an interesting problem for the editor at a crucial moment. At the end of an elaborate argument about the political worth of such a match, notably concerning its unlikelihood of bringing together factions in England, the recent Oxford edition reads: "So that if neither fear, nor desire, be such in him as are to bind any public fastness, it may be said that the only fortress of this your marriage is of his private affection: a thing too incident to your person, without laying it up in such ivy knots" (53.3). As if Sidney's final reservation confused his editors, many variants of the final words of this passage exist,[43] the more plausible ones having "slight knots" for "ivy knots." "Slight," however, as Duncan-Jones has pointed out,[44] seems to be a gloss on what ivy suggests metaphorically. Sidney constructs this letter around several familiar metaphors, of disease in the human and the body politic, the sun and the homonymous son as metaphor for kingship as well as lineage in reference to the need for a male heir, eyes that dazzle through love and authority, and the metaphor of the ship of state on turbulent seas. Here "ivy" seems more like Sidney, as does, "laying up," an archaic phrase for "twisting yarn to form a strand,"[45] rather than the more clear "tying up," an occasional variant.

In these words, Sidney's persona sets up the political disadvantages of Monsieur antithetically. As the groom he could neither bind up the English factions through common fear nor common desire. Then Sidney's persona suddenly introduces the question of "private affection," tacking on the final phrase "without laying it up in such ivy knots." "Ivy knots," placed at the very end of the sentence suggests that d'Alençon's private feeling, even a marriage based on that feeling, is far too slight, delicate, untyable, breakable. The ivy knot metaphor, echoing the denial of his power "to bind any public fastness," suggests a light person. If d'Alençon seems less than ordinary, however, what an extraordinary picture Sidney the courtier-letter-writer gives of the queen in this citation. Like the unapproachable Laura of the Petrarchan sonnets, men's love is a trophy, something she enjoys from too many people—"too incident to your person"—to make it worthwhile to add the duke's, especially by the restrictive bond of marriage contract ("knot").

Clearly Sidney intends this public letter of advice to picture the queen as that remote love object, attractive, awe-inspiring for the courtier, youthful and beautiful certainly, as well as unquestionably fertile, although the queen was forty-six years old at that time. To promote such a hyperbolic image of the queen, Sidney adopts the mask of the courtier-lover, proposing to make "the true vowed sacrifice of unfeigned love" (46.13) in an epistle "only for your eyes," though secrecy could hardly have been his intention. He considers "the perfections of your body and mind" (53.9). He likens slander of the queen to "blasphemy" (55.32). Finally he suggests on successive occasions that the happiness of having children must constitute the truly "blissful" excuse for marrying. Since, however, the question of looking for an heir and controlling factions in England were crucial to the argument of the letter, Sidney gradually allows the concept of producing children to vanish by expansion into a metaphor for engendering loyal subjects. When offspring is first mentioned, Sidney's persona speaks of "the bliss of children: which, I confess, were a most unspeakable comfort" (51.7). Here, we think strictly in terms of the joys of immediate family.

When he next mentions children, Sidney places them in the equivocal political light of possibly indifferent, fickle or estranged successors to the crown, returning to the bliss of having them only as an afterthought or concession: "Virtue and justice are the only bands of the people's love. And as for that point, many princes have lost their crowns, whose own children were manifest successors; and some that had their own children used as instruments of their ruin. Not that I deny the bliss of children." (54.27). Direct offspring do not tie up the bands of people's love. Good citizens are the true progeny of "virtue and justice." As Sidney the courtier has boldly stated early in this letter, "your inward force (for as for your treasures, indeed the sinews of your crown, your Majesty doth best and only know) consisteth in your subjects" (47.16).

The final word in the piece, the complex word "posterity," however, expands into the concept of "blood lineage," children and children's children, "simply those people who follow you in England," and also "loyal subjects and children of loyal subjects" who make England a stable commonwealth or state free from civil war between religious factions. The idea of the queen bearing children thus gradually dissolves in favor of rearing the good children of loyal subjects. The letter ends, "Lastly, doing as you do, you shall be as you be: the example of princes, the ornament of this age, the comfort of the afflicted, the delight of your people, the most excellent fruit of all your progenitors, and the perfect mirror to your posterity" (57.4). Landing squarely on "posterity" is part of a strategy to move the queen—and Sidney's many other readers—from contemplation of actual offspring to the contemplation of all subjects, from peasant to courtier, as the queen's metaphoric children. Subjects are children. The word "posterity," even in the context of "progenitors," suggests the political progeny of Elizabethan England as well as actual sons and daughters. "Posterity" thus informs the work as a whole. It forces us to go back and understand Sidney's cryptic remark that he has a choice of successor already, probably in Scotland, but that son of Mary Queen of Scots is, in his opinion, a good subject, although not a direct offspring, and not, oddly, the offspring of a loyal subject. Eliza must become the mirror to all her subjects and future generations of subjects. The final word of the whole piece sends us back through the whole argument to recollect that thought.

Irony can be defined in terms of the power of ending, the power of delaying final interpretation until the last word is out, a word, perhaps, that forces the reader back to the very beginning of a text. Here "posterity" forces us to reconsider Sidney's courtly voice's reiterated concept that the queen's power chiefly resides in her loyal subjects. Of course, Sidney, the courtly adviser, has, on a dangerous subject, said the right thing. He was not exactly a flatterer because an inflated idea of the queen, for various reasons, was considered by him and some of his friends sound public policy. Like the towering statues of a physically short Caesar Augustus, the idea of Eliza the goddess of rule and of love seemed an expedient piece of propaganda after a century of political disturbance.

Traditionally, Sidney was thought to have fallen out of favor with the queen in part because of this letter. It was even thought to have contributed to his purported "rustication"—his being sent away from court to the country, in his case, largely to Wilton. Having reexamined the evidence, Duncan-Jones asserted that, as in the case of Cecil's letter, "there is no evidence that any disfavor followed the advice."[46]

Like any prince, Machiavellian in the best sense of the word, as we have seen, the queen encouraged promulgation of opposing views of future decisions, as long as they were polite, so that she could appear to be selecting between sets of loyal advisers rather than operating according to a headstrong and possibly fallible monarchic "will and pleasure," the claim that sometimes marred her father's public image. Sidney himself writes Leicester from Clarindon within a year of the composition of the letter—perhaps at the height of its circulation—that he is much missed at court but would be a "very unpleasant company keeper"[47] because of a heavy cold which has taken away his voice. He remarks that he is "so full of the cold as one can not heere me speake: which is the cawse keepes me yet from the courte since my only service is speeche and that is stopped."

That Sidney's "only service is speeche" may indicate that he would like bolder service, a common complaint among Elizabeth's courtiers, but the queen was wise to keep her best speakers at home, and Sidney contributed to that maneuver as propagandist. As in the case of the Augustan artists, Elizabeth's poets, kept at home—or guiltily away from home—did her the greatest service among her contemporaries and her posterity. Sidney's and others' words in their perennial appeal, did her image the ultimate propagandistic favor. Sidney's works, however, were preserved because he had more to say, in this case, his development of the paradox of progeny. He dismisses with gentle irony the direct progeny "of the Jezebel of our age" (48.6), the son of Catherine de Medici, and he opposes the notion of possibly ungrateful children with that of the good subject. Let us now look at the tone of Sidney's angry persona—his version of the "heartless threatening Thraso," who forces us, rudely, to explore the paradox of the simultaneity of fame and slander in the life of his uncle, the Earl of Leicester.

Naming and the Blatant Beast (1584)

At least since the world read Horace Walpole's praise of the *Defence of the Earl of Leicester* in a letter to George Montague,[48] this work has always been taken to be in Sidney's own angry and self-glorifying voice. An editor of the Oxford series, Duncan-Jones, asserts that "Walpole's perverse praise suggests the actual unattractiveness of the work" (125), a quality she feels results from Sidney's spending more than half his ink in his answer to *Leicester's Commonwealth* listing forbears of the family of which he is again the heir. Walpole, who elsewhere set in motion the critical debunking of Sidney's formidable literary reputation, admits he praises this work for its "vehemence" and "warmth" largely in relation to Sidney's ability to clear "up the honour of his lineage."[49] Here the great eighteenth-century antiquarian endorses Sidney for his recalling the antiquity and honor of his own race. The "warmth" Walpole refers to probably arises from Sidney's once giving the lie, later openly challenging the nameless author of the unnamed *Leicester's Commonwealth*, apparently a Roman Catholic polemicist on the continent, possibly the Jesuit Robert Parsons, to a duel.

Memory of Sidney's giving the lie to the Earl of Oxford over the use of a tennis court in London, or his letter to his father's secretary Edmund Molyneux saying he will "thruste" his "dagger" into him if he has leaked the contents of confidential correspondence to his father, seemed to bear out the theory that Sidney could have simply boiled over in this last "official" piece of his prose, although a look at the holograph foul papers in the Pierpont Morgan Library also attests to Sidney's taste for studied revision (see fig.).

I argue that while Sidney's defense of his uncle may appear vehement or unstudied, behind that angry mask lies an essay on slander and naming that develops with wit a paradoxical theme concerning the effects of fame. Personal notoriety produces simultaneous enfranchisement and imprisonment for the individual. On the surface, the persona of the angry man, Sidney's version of Terence's comic bully, reiterates his monstrous speech act, the resounding formal challenge. Inside, we discover a disquisition on public honor and dishonor, what Edmund Spenser was to call, in book 6 of the *Faerie Queene*, the Blatant Beast, the ultimately invincible opponent of the Knight of Courtesy and courtly honor: libel and slander. An elementary paradox resides in the fact that naming oneself provides a sense of identity, yet once one's name becomes known it becomes a target for obliteration by those who have not been named—the nameless slanderer. That barking beast can transform any name into a means of dishonor and annihilation of identity.

No work of Sidney is more superficially indirect than the *Defence of the Earl of Leicester*, simply because in responding to a purportedly slanderous attack one must avoid repeating the original argument and thus perpetuate the insult. No real substance turns up in Sidney's

P. 1 recto shows occasional heavy editing to shift his semantic drift. (Pierpont Morgan Library MS. 1475.)

angry attack on the polemicist who produced the pamphlet, *Leicester's Commonwealth,* nor, as we have seen, does he mention its title. Were he to mention its content, it would involve repeating its purported libel, such as, that Leicester might have murdered his first wife, Amy Robsart, by having her thrown down a staircase at Cumner Place breaking her neck in order to clear the way to marriage with Elizabeth, or that he planned to engineer a coup d'état if Elizabeth married Monsieur. Moreover, because the source of the libel remains unknown, no substantial contact with its writer can be established.

Sidney's persona makes clear at the outset of his work that names are all a hidden slanderer needs in his victims. To a name that is well known, one can successfully attribute any brutal or seditious act as long as one hides one's own name. At his most indirect, Sidney takes such slander to be mere rhetorical exercise, like the ones he loved in the second Sophistic era in Greece. He states "that if the author had as well feigned new names as he doth new matters, a man might well have thought his only meaning had been to have given a lively picture of the uttermost degree of railing" (129.4). Sidney's persona ironically suggests that the unnamed *Leicester's Commonwealth* might be taken to be a mock philippic, a "lively picture" or demonstration of that most suasory genre of, for example, Cicero on Mark Antony—verbal abuse. It would lack all content, if only the names were not real and substantial ones like Dudley and Grey.

Throughout this third formal defense of his career, Sidney's persona develops in his own outpouring of rage a metaphoric image of a monster who damages with his mouth, his teeth, his tongue, a tongue that can name all names but the name of its owner. Thus the violence of libel is indirectly connected with the violence of biting, swallowing, regurgitating, and spitting but its operative remains unknowable. Anonymous vilification of a well-known name is "odious to all estates, since no man bears a name; of which name, how unfitly soever to the person, by an impudent liar, anything may not be spoken, by all good laws sharply punished, and by all civil[50] companies like a poisonous serpent avoided" (129.9). This slanderous tongue now belongs to a metaphorical venomous snake. This image of poison or horror or damage from a mouth constitutes an emblem of backbiting in the piece.

By means of his reiterate metaphor, Sidney creates a picture of an invincible protean monster that cannot be identified, while it identifies by slander all the great courtier-advisors. It is a vomiting glutton or gluttonous vomiter. Thus Sidney's persona suggests paradoxically, that it is high praise for a courtier to be slandered because slanderers, when they wish to attack a good sovereign like Elizabeth or Caesar Augustus "do first vomit it out against his councillors" (129.23), their troubled advisors. Wolves attack "the truest and valiantest dogs" (130.9) first. But "the more the filthy impostume of their wolfish malice breaks forth," the more we know the courtier-advisor like Dudley, Grey, Sidney, or any "name" courtier is worthy.

The rule of the sycophant is "backbite boldly, for though the bite were healed, yet the scar would remain" (130.31). He asks if the slander did not come "from the mouth of some half drunk scold in a tavern" (131.12). The slanderer will pour "out all his flood of scolding eloquence" (134.5) "of false invective which a poisonous tongue could have spit out against that Duke" (134.7). The very excess of anger in Sidney's tone masks a consistent argument about the fragility of notability, and its inevitable decline into notoriety.

How can the name of that duke be reinstated, given the existence of such a protean and dangerous mouth? Simply by an elaborate listing of the names of the famous and infamous members of the well-known houses of Dudley and Grey, the most infamous being Leicester's father, Northumberland, who was beheaded in 1553 for the treasonous placing of Lady Jane Grey on the throne in London. In other words, even the name of a known traitor will help substantiate the validity of a family name. A name might not survive the poison of slander—or even the scars of backbiting—but it can be fortified somewhat by the application of the feeble antidote of reiteration. A listing of its achievements and failures may return a name to the state of being real and substantial, not just another toy of professional invective. Thus for 2,500 words or so, Sidney's seeming "vainglorious Thraso" (96) traces the successful and often tragic holders of these names in a sequence of generations that produced the line of the Dudleys and the Greys.

Our angry persona follows this elaborate trip through Leicester's and his own family tree with a rowdy giving the lie to the anonymous slanderer and an impossible request that he who would remain nameless might answer him within three months, choosing a "place . . . as a servant of the Queen's may have free access unto" (140.32). Leicester's defender has maintained throughout, however, that the writer of the slanderous tract is a continental polemicist who chooses to remain nameless, and thus clearly unavailable for a public appointment.

Perhaps the most surprising three names that Sidney's persona produces in his catalogue of advisors are those of "Gaveston, Earl of Cornwall, Robert Vere, Duke of Ireland, and De la Pole, Duke of Suffolk" (130.1) (supposedly traitorous courtiers of deposed rulers,

Edward II, Richard II, and Henry VI) who make up a list of perhaps the most infamous names in English history up to Leicester's day. Sidney implies, as we have seen, that when an envious "beast" cannot safely bring down the central name of the hereditary monarch in question, it must begin by destroying the lesser names, the advisors intimate to that person.

The counsellor of a ruler is always fair game for a slanderer, but the slanderer, consciously or unconsciously, cannot resist proceeding to destroy the name of the ruler as well. Envious slander naturally escalates seeking more and better names, as a wolf, once he tastes blood, must have more and supposedly richer blood. Sidney's persona says of Gaveston and the others: "It is not my purpose to defend them, but I would fain know whether they that persecuted those councillors, when they had had their will in ruining them, whether their rage ceased before they had as well destroyed the kings themselves, Edward and Richard the Second, and Henry the Sixth" (130.3). Having chosen the words "persecuted" and "councillors," Sidney has at least brought those advisors' guilt into doubt. He has also reminded us of the line of England's deposed rulers up to the age of Queen Elizabeth, and how they may have all been victims—their leading courtiers once destroyed—of the blatant beast.

Leicester, as Queen Elizabeth's lover and close councillor on foreign and domestic policy, received more criticism, often libelous attacks from anonymous sources, than Gaveston or perhaps any other courtier-advisor in the history of the English monarchy through the early romantic era of Walter Scott. Yet Elizabeth continued to support her "Robin" or "Lobbin"—nicknames connected with Dudley—throughout his career. Just before Leicester's death he was appointed to command the army at Tilbury to rebuff Philip II's long-cherished invasion of England, an attack Leicester and his party, and such propagandists as Ralegh, Spenser, and Sidney, long predicted. In what is perhaps her most openly emotional speech, Elizabeth, on this occasion at Tilbury, seems to reflect two ideas Sidney developed in his official works, one, that her chief inward force comes from her subjects, and, two, that her most valuable, and most vulnerable, subjects are her good courtiers. Thus she announces to "my faithful and loving People . . . my chiefest strength and Safeguard lies in the loyal Hearts and Goodwill of my Subjects."[51] Warning the "tyrranical" Parma, Spain, and other princes of Europe that though she has "the Body but of a weak and feeble Woman," she has "the Heart and Stomach of a King, and of a King of England too," she then turns the army, with a round justification, over to her much-slandered courtier, Leicester: "In the mean time, my Lieutenant

General shall be in my Stead, than whom never Prince commanded a more noble or worthy Subject." At the moment of Leicester's sudden death at fifty-four or fifty-five, the queen was apparently still considering him for the post of lieutenant-general of England and Ireland.

In his *Defence of the Earl of Leicester*, Sidney shrewdly chooses not to answer any specific criticism of the earl, but to present a disquisition—under the guise of angry rebuke and challenge—on the nature of slander and the susceptibility of all names, and of the utter license of the anonymous name-caller who is free to turn the benefits of fame into corrosive poison. Thus he proves his worth as a propagandist in a period of heavy controversy, but he also examines on the other side of his angry mask, the nature of naming and fame as instruments simultaneously of honor and dishonor, identity and annihilation of self. At an early moment in the piece, his angry persona mysteriously attributes the efficacy of our unknown slanderer to his "purification" through inhalation of "the air of Italy" (129.25). Would Sidney here be criticizing or, indeed, libelously slandering himself the culture of that great land of artists he made every effort—over all disuasion—to experience?[52] I think not. "Air of Italy," I suspect, represents rather the atmosphere of the home of rhetorical ability in philippic and in eulogy of the practitioners, ancient and modern, on that sophisticated peninsula, the land of words that create and destroy. Words are only as good or bad as their intent, and human nature is everywhere the same, just as fire burns alike in Greece and Persia.[53]

As we have seen, Sidney, in his official works, contributes to the development of conventional political ideals in extolling the Cult of Eliza and the Leicester faction. He also criticizes our assumptions and leads us by ironic control of content, style, and tone into new understanding of our inevitably paradoxical existence. In my continued search for the most plausible reading of Sidney, I will rely on clues about his works that are given by the author and his contemporaries, ultimately returning to the problems that recent critics have discovered concerning syntactical and structural antitheses and the irony of vanishing distinctions. Sidney adopted masks in his works—personae that allowed him to expose by serious jest what this Renaissance artist found to be life's mysteries. But all is consistently tempered by his own self-irony concerning the young man who, in Elizabeth's reign, set out on that adventure.

4
Astrophil's "Tragicomedy of Love . . . Performed by Starlight"

Recent critics have often equated Astrophil with the historical Sidney,[1] thus denying negative capability—or high fictive achievement—in the sonnet cycle. They draw logical inference from topical references in the text to Sidney at jousts, at court, on public service, or from references to his politics or to Penelope's appearance, even to the names, "Phil," "Philip," "Phip," "Rich," and to his Penelope's marriage to a supposed tyrant. The autobiography latent in Sidney's adopted personae remains overt, and it leads us into reexamination of his whole era of sentimental medievalization and consolidation of royal and aristocratic power.

History looms large behind this set of poems, but Sidney uses history for a highly selective purpose, one in keeping with his sometimes harsh condemnation of historiography in his *Defence of Poetry*. The actual Philip Sidney was living in an unusually confined—little short of incestuous—world of aristocratic, property-oriented in-marriage about which we know a great deal, a knowledge reinforced in limited ways by the poems themselves. Critics as diverse as Lanham and McCoy are sorely tempted to impose the reductionism of biographical and psychologistic interpretation on the cycle.

In his second poem, for example, Astrophil laments that

> Not at first sight, nor with a dribbed shot
> *Love* gave the wound, which while I breathe will bleed.
>
> (2.1–2)[2]

We understand that Sidney himself was slow to learn to love—if he did love—Penelope Devereux.[3] In 1576, Walter Devereux, the first Earl of Essex, had expressed a wish on his deathbed that Sidney might marry his thirteen-year-old daughter, Penelope, unquestionably the model for dark-eyed, blond-haired Stella, with the odd warning that "the Breaking of from this Match . . . will turne to more Dishonour then can be repaired with eny other Mariage in *England*."⁴ Devereux's hyperbolic language may suggest that he suspected strong attraction between the two sometime playmates.

At any rate, six years later, that daughter, younger sister of a man who was now one of Sidney's close friends and junior admirers, Robert Devereux, second Earl of Essex, was now being married off to Robert, Lord Rich, by the help of her now stepfather, Robert Dudley, the earl of Leicester, and possibly Sidney himself. Economics motivated all concerned parties.

Sidney, Leicester's nephew, and now and then his heir, probably suffered grief over these negotiations, because the historical Sidney and Penelope Rich seem eventually to have had an affair of sorts. But, as he implies throughout his works and even actions, if one inevitably creates fiction out of one's own life, out of what one knows, one must be highly selective for a peculiar dramatic purpose. As Ringler once said, "we are immediately struck with how much of his biography he left out of his poem."⁵ What he replaces for the history he so often condemns in his *Defence of Poetry* for its inability to teach, is a consciously crafted tragicomedy, largely in one poetic voice, to implied listeners, a drama that begins with the delayed explosion—"mine of time" (2.3)—of his idealistic persona's passion.

Astrophil claims Cupid's scattered golden arrows—"dribbed shot"—did not hit him, rather a circumstantially too slow recognition of Stella's worth. Given Stella's chastity, all Astrophil has left is his art, his painting of the lost lover's tortuous nether world, his consolation prize, which takes its own natural form of which he is proud. It is designed

> To make my selfe beleeve, that all is well,
> While with a feeling skill I paint my hell.

(2.13–14)

While history may provide his cue, in other words, Astrophil's anti-Petrarchan notion that love did not occur "at first sight" does not merely comprise an attack on the supposed hyperbolic lies of other poets. It helps paint a "skilled" picture of a passion that is slow to move and therefore more solid, more valuable to Stella. His love is neither sudden nor light. Nor is Stella's lover concerned with the true-to-life commercial world of arranged in-marriages. Sidney emphasizes that history, especially biography, lacks "universal consideration" (88), and it does so especially in characterization and "poetic form."

By selection, distortion, and conscious imagination, Sidney creates in Astrophil, a peculiarly self-conscious persona out of a precise tradition. This "busy loving courtier" descends from the *adolescens* of the Roman comedy Sidney extols in his *Defence of Poetry*. If Sidney ridiculed the historian with his "mouse-eaten" (83) particularity, he equally scorned the notion of the poet's "furious" lack of control (121) that might lead, according to modern Platonists, to a concept of poetry as autobiographical primary process thinking. Tradition led Sidney also to adopt a peculiarly Renaissance form for his sequence, the one that came to dominate the Elizabethan and Jacobean stage: tragicomedy.

The first commentator on the cycle, now called *Astrophil* or *Astrophel and Stella*,[6] the dramatist, pampheteer, and novelist, Thomas Nashe, insists that we read Sidney's *canzoniere* as a "tragicommody of love . . . performed by starlight."[7] In fact, this friend of Samuel Daniel and other members of Mary Sidney's circle at Wilton opens his preface to the bootleg 1591 edition with the announcement of the pristine hero of that drama[8] in relation to a recent success on the stage, quite possibly John Lyly's tragicomic *Midas*: "so ends the Sceane of Idiots, and enter *Astrophel* in pompe."[9] Of course, Nashe, like Spenser, employs "Astrophel" as a pseudonym of Sidney, later twice mentioning Astrophel's death, but he emphasizes that the work is a dramatic construct inviting "idle eares to the admiration of his [Astrophel's] melancholy"[10] as a means to a particular affect: the purging of the reader's own melancholy by fashioning an idealist caught up in a tragicomedy of his own making. Much of the drama, of course, unfolds internally, lit up or darkened by the variable "starlight" of the beloved Stella's ambiguous presence, but, as we shall see, those impressions tell a peculiar tale of trial and redemption.

How does one win an unwilling audience ("idle eares") to wonder at a hero's internal disorder ("admiration of his melancholy") but by a gripping drama, as Nashe says, on a "paper stage streud with pearle."[11] Sidney, I argue, designs this tragicomedy, though it plays itself out on mere sheets of paper and is delivered largely by one voice, to win the reader to experience Astrophil's own love melancholy and its cure.

Astrophil, a self-conscious version of the young lover of Roman comedy, provides us with a thoroughly dramatic vehicle for the catharsis of *maninconia*[12] Guarini later ascribed to tragicomedy. When he seems to be speaking lyrically to the moon (31), Astrophil is directly condemning Stella's "ungrateful" chastity with doubts about his venture. When he is giving Edward IV ironic formal praise for giving up his crown for Lady Elizabeth Grey (75), he is implicitly pleading with Stella that the world is well lost for the thrill of sexual passion.

A disembodied lyric voice appears only once in song 8, and it reincorporates itself by that poem's close. We always overhear him speak directly to second parties or we hear him talking to us, and the form of his tale follows the roller coaster rises and descents of tragicomedy. Thanks to his virtues and faults we can empathize in the peculiar emotive way we respond to that peculiar dramatic form. Renaissance tragicomedy resembles elegy, normally opening with an inexperienced and idealistic figure who suffers reversal where all seems lost in life and love, only to be relieved—in an elaborate scene of discovery and self-discovery—by the tearful happy realization of self-development and spiritual resurrection.

When Nashe speaks of the structure of Sidney's work—"The argument cruell chastitie, the Prologue hope, the Epilogue dispaire"[13]—he evokes a drama where the plan or *argomento* of chastity on both sides takes the natural form of a story of hope on Astrophil's and Stella's part leading to a catastrophe. Following that "fall," the "Epilogue dispaire" comprises an internal grand recognition scene where Astrophil survives the depths of melancholy brought on by his offense to Stella in "broadcasting" their adulterous passion. In Astrophil's self-examination, his gothic suicidal imagination gradually metamorphoses into the euphoria of idolatry of his beloved, now contained by the poetry itself and possessed by its author as his door prize.

Nashe, in fact, suggests the elegiac ending of the work when he introduces Sidney's persona as "Deare *Astrophel,* that in the ashes of thy Love livest againe like the *Phoenix.*"[14] The Phoenix image, traditional to sonneteers from the day of Petrarch's several conceits, forms the central image of the final poem of the *canzoniere*. Nashe's image, which suggests that one resurrects oneself, rising from the burnt-out remains of a lost passion is a paradox central to the work as a whole. One is left with an education and a literary property, a sequence of poems that stages that bitter, but fruitful, young man's experience, one designed to purge or burn off the general reader's own love melancholy.

Arthur Marotti and others have taken Astrophil's references to his coterie of "close friends, clients, and family members"[15] for signs that Sidney's own context is narrow and constrained by the dictates of immediate power-relationships, but Sidney universalizes the contrast between those listeners in keeping with his theory of medicinal reader response in his *Defence of Poetry*. The apparently closed context of the *canzoniere* is, I argue, an affective device used by Sidney to create

Astrophil's Tragicomedy

a sense of intimacy for the broadest possible set of readers. In fact, I propose that Astrophil's own admitted search for poetic fame creates an ironic parallel to Sidney's own exoteric project.

The Prologue

Astrophil's initial sonnet, in giving us our first impression of its hero, serves as a miniature of the whole tragicomedy. It is a self-portrait, but of Astrophil, the self-conscious lover, inevitably placed by himself at center stage. Forms of the first person singular appear no less than seven times in this poem:

> Loving in truth, and faine in verse my love to show,
> That the deare She might take some pleasure of my paine:
> Pleasure might cause her reade, reading might make her know,
> Knowledge might pitie winne, and pitie grace obtaine,
> I sought fit words to paint the blackest face of woe,
> Studying inventions fine, her wits to entertaine:
> Oft turning others' leaves, to see if thence would flow
> Some fresh and fruitfull showers upon my sunne-burn'd braine,
> But words came halting forth, wanting Invention's stay,
> Invention, Nature's child, fled step-dame Studie's blowes,
> And others' feete still seem'd but strangers in my way.
> Thus great with child to speake, and helplesse in my throwes,
> Biting my trewand pen, beating my selfe for spite,
> 'Foole,' said my Muse to me, 'looke in thy heart and write.'
>
> (1.1–14)

Soliloquizing intimately to his audience of his anxiety to express the truth of his heavenly love, the "busy loving courtier," Astrophil, never fails to remind us that he seeks to seduce Stella by courtly procedure. First of all, he produces a love poem designed in part to arouse Stella's curiosity about her sexual attractiveness and its victim. In one sense, her interest and desire for flattery will cause her to "take some pleasure" of his "paine" of passion. But in another, Stella may experience an entirely unreprehensible aesthetic pleasure in his artifact. The "pain" of unfulfilled love, after all, is the only known source, the split atom, so to speak, of poetic energy. This somewhat sadistic "Pleasure might cause her reade, reading might make her know."

Once she recognizes that he is suffering, a first stage on the road to seduction has nearly been travelled: arrival of pity on the part of the beloved—"Knowledge might pitie winne, and pitie grace obtaine."

When Astrophil goes on to speak of seeking out proper terms to produce that essential emotion, however, we make a broad shift from the pathos of the lover's ecstasy and pain, to the irony of poetic plagiarism.

A hard-working craftsman admits his presence in the work, seeking "fit words to paint the blackest face of woe." One reading of this line suggests search for the means of constructing a blackened self-portrait designed to make Stella agreeable to advance. Sidney's persona seems to admit that one never seduces by begging but by showing skill, intelligence, and a certain distance, if admiring. That is, demonstrating good genes. Therefore he must create a verbal portrait of love melancholy for his "star," an image true to psychology and "fit," formally speaking, to produce poetic worth. But he undercuts such would-be skilled "sincerity" in his very self-consciousness about the process of fabricating a poem out of others' words, "painting" with a quill on the "face" of a page in ink—what could be "blacker"?—

> Oft turning others' leaves, to see if thence would flow
> Some fresh and fruitfull showers upon my sunne-burn'd braine.

Astrophil, at some distance now, undercuts both pathos and ecstasy by rhetorical rug-pulling. He maneuvers us onto the carpet of expectation of heart-thrilling tragicomedy; then he pulls us off our feet. All we now have now are the interior spaces of the plagiarist at his dusty and clerkish task. Anxiety to produce good poetry tempts Astrophil to take his "plumes from others' wings" (90.11), and though he supposedly goes on to look in his heart, the words he finds in this case are conventional.[16]

The final line, "'Foole,' said my Muse to me, 'looke in thy heart and write,'" points up Astrophil's paradox. He wants to be simple and sincere but in the heart one only has the source of groans at Stella's flickering image. The heart is non-verbal. His need for the rhetorical devices of the Petrarchan tradition rather than the non-language of the heart becomes explicit in his reference to the inspiring "Muse," perhaps the most artificial—and ultimately unbelievable—of all poetic conventions. If Astrophil has a "Muse," it is Stella, but, in this case, we find the simulacrum of a schoolmarm, Calliope, correcting his approach to writing, an inherited artificiality stepping out from the fog of the myth of the Castalian streams of Parnassus.

While the "grace" Astrophil would, hopefully, "obtaine," furthermore, suggests both heavenly blessing from the worshipped beloved and also, of course, sexual gratification, two other ambiguous images cause paradoxical aspects of his plight to surface. First of all, turning leaves in order to allow rain to cool a brain dazzled by Stella—burned by his "sun"—suggests that his relief ultimately lies in conventional poetic fabrication. The world of the young love melancholic placed under a leafy tree—a bower that admits his beloved and his coterie—provides outdoor imagery controlled by interior struggle, a symbolic version of the Wilton that appears so often in Sidney's works. He seeks actual and metaphoric shade. Magically the leaves above his head are pages from the poetic tradition, and also his own best copy. Throughout the sequence the outer heaven above his head and hell below his feet reflect by traditional rhetoric the movement of his interior ecstasy and despair. Outer is inner.

Astrophil's consolation is the poetic energy that the unworkable love affair creates, energy that leads him into expropriation of "other leaves" from the poetic tradition. Moreover, in suggesting that he is pregnant, even in labor, with poems produced by the action of his true love—"great with child to speak, and helplesse in my throwes"—Astrophil's hopeful prologue implies that the offspring of poetic procreation may ultimately be his only savior from despair. In the sequence he will end up with the poetic child so much "labor" helped to produce. But the affair will remain, in fact, sterile, childless, even perhaps celibate, in all other senses.

The Catastrophe

Witnessing Astrophil's staging of his own tragicomedy, we emote with the pain of unfulfilled desire and the conflict of the ecstasy of idealism with its abysmal sense of self-loss. We also grin at his genial parody of poetic ambition in the study and smile with his achievement. Early in the sequence, to a self-put question, "Art not asham'd to publish thy disease?" (34.5), Astrophil responds, "Nay, that may breed my fame, it is so rare." Thus he links the idea that his awful suffering speaks beautifully to his hope for a poetic reputation, a desire that proves liable to eclipse his regard for Stella's own feelings. Near the end of this drama he begs his love, "*Stella* thinke not that I by verse seeke fame" (90.1), when his boasting of the poems and, through the poems, of his shared love has come to endanger that relationship. The catastrophe of this tragicomedy, then, the educational fall of the hero, occurs, I argue, at the moment he produces a poem that demonstrates sexual bravado, the sorest of young men's temptations.

The braggart lover always scourges his woman by publicizing her real or imagined capitulation to his sexual advance. Astrophil proves dangerous to Stella's household by his wit in producing an erotic contemplation of her. Following his reversal, an extended scene of self-recognition orchestrates all the elegiac aspects of his suffering. Only the poetry remains. The story of this first English *canzoniere*, narrated by Astrophil, whether or not he consummates his love for Stella, leads to rupture. In the end, Astrophil is left with his precious poetic identity, not with his Stella.

As his Oxford editor, William Ringler, Jr., has suggested, in introducing a summary of the events internal and external to the cycle, "Aside from . . . slight inconsistencies, Sidney's work is more carefully structured than that of any other Elizabethan sonnet collection."[17] Ringler's "slight inconsistencies" concern the placement of the majority of the songs, especially those not in iambic, but he admits that

> the six songs in trochaic metres narrate the more important events of the sequence—the stealing of the kiss [ii], the night-time courtship at Stella's window [iv and xi], the climactic episode in which Stella admits her love for Astrophil but at the same time refuses his advances [viii], his lament at her refusal [ix], and his thoughts of her while absent [x].

I argue that the tragicomic catastrophe of this cycle lies in the very existence of song 10, Ringler's final event. Its aftermath, the recognition scene then develops a notion of the way poetry is generated and how it saves our hero.

Song 10, coming between Sonnets 92 and 93, hardly represents neutral "thoughts of Stella while absent." It takes those liberties with the decorum of Petrarchan complaint that have recently been recognized in Sidney.[18] The poem's sexual suggestion may, in fact, help explain its popularity. Widely circulated by Sidney in his time, we have more than one version and three melodies to sing it by, by John Ward, as well as the brilliant William Byrd and Robert Douland.[19] That it clothes sexual acts in terms of complex intellective activity, does not necessarily require us, however, to assume Astrophil is crowing over consummation of his joys.

A poet can and always has fabricated poetry out of graphic fantasies of contact with a celibate beloved. In fact, only there do sexual matters work to perfection. And young poets, like all young men, have a disruptive tendency to kiss and tell, even to tell they have kissed when they have not. This written or sung speech act ironically provides the apt, poetical cause for the fall of our hero in the drama. The first five stanzas read:

O deare life, when shall it be,
That mine eyes thine eyes may see?
And in them thy mind discover,
Whether absence have had force
Thy remembrance to divorce,
From the image of thy lover?

O if I my self find not,
After parting ought forgot,
Nor debard from beautie's treasure,
Let no tongue aspire to tell,
In what high joyes I shall dwell,
Only thought aymes at the pleasure.

Thought therefore I will send thee,
To take up the place for me;
Long I will not after tary,
There unseene thou maist be bold,
Those faire wonders to behold,
Which in them my hopes do cary.

Thought see thou no place forbeare,
Enter bravely every where,
Seaze on all to her belonging;
But if thou wouldst garded be,
Fearing her beames, take with thee
Strength of liking, rage of longing.

Thinke of that most gratefull time,
When my leaping hart will clime,
In my lips to have his biding.
There those roses for to kisse,
Which do breath a sugred blisse,
Opening rubies, pearles deviding.

(x.1–30)

This assertive song from "thy" self-styled "lover," which, I argue, causes a row with Stella and, apparently, with her household, develops a central conceit of the sending of a "licorous" thought to her, a thought that is perhaps "liquorous" or "intoxicated," possibly "liking to lick," and certainly "lecherous."

In what high joyes I shall dwell,
Only thought aymes at the pleasure.

(x.10)

The thought is sent "to take up the place for me" (14), to "enter bravely every where" (20). Fantasy of aggressive sexual struggle with the beloved ultimately produces "glad moning," "joying," and "languishing." The following stanzas read:

> Thinke of my most Princely power,
> When I blessed shall devower,
> With my greedy licorous sences,
> Beauty, musicke, sweetnesse, love
> While she doth against me prove
> Her strong darts, but weake defences.
>
> Thinke, thinke of those dalyings,
> When with Dovelike murmurings,
> With glad moning passed anguish,
> We change eyes, and hart for hart,
> Each to other do imparte,
> Joying till joy makes us languish.
>
> (x.31–42)

These lines, short of the final stanza, all describe and imitate a love act in one kind of reading yet maintain the ambiguity—even generic ambiguity—that appealed so much to Elizabethan taste. The thought can always be read paradoxically as mere absent contemplation or "reading" of the beloved.

As James Finn Cotter put it, this described "sensual possession is seen not as an event outside the realm of poetry, but as an act of the creative imagination."[20] But it can offend, as Astrophil often does, the courtly code of secrecy and severe modesty. The final stanza appears in two versions, the following, preserved by Sir John Harrington and the Rawlinson manuscript in the Bodleian library, somewhat more openly suggestive than the one that usually appears in manuscript:

> O my thoughtes now thoughts surcease,
> These delights my payns increase,
> ["Ah," or] And I dy with too much thinking;
> ["Whearfore thoughts," or] Thoughte! therfore come sleepe wth me
> Till ["ye may" or] thou maist awaked be,
> At her lips my Nectar drinking.
>
> (x.43–48)

On the comic level, Astrophil is publishing a fantasy of sexual conquest that, in the dramatic context of these poems, gives Stella offense. What "delights my payns increase" than the erotic fantasy just indulged? Why else would such thought immediately be asked to "sleep with" the poet in substitution for Stella?

Astrophil also expresses, however, another kind of self-surrender in the dying and sleeping images—clearer in the standard version of this stanza—that suggests escape, even suicidal escape, from present frustrations. Thus the hell of the idealist lover haunts even his bawdy description of sexual ecstasy:

> O my thought my thoughts surcease,
> Thy delights my woes increase,
> My life melts with too much thinking;
> Thinke no more but die in me,
> Till thou shalt revived be,
> At her lips my Nectar drinking.
>
> (x.43–48)

Thoughts surceasing, life melting, the fantasy dying "in me," all suggest masturbatory orgasm but also another "dying"—the direct product of the self-neglect of the youth failing in love and career, to be averted only by the "nectar" of Stella's now improbable future kiss.

The Recognition Scene

The fact of this rash song seems to seal Astrophil's fate of separation from his star. What he suggests he has done in the following sonnets as a low "caitiff" (93.5, 94.10) or "wretch" (93.4, 94.14) is compromise Stella's honor through his very poetic cleverness. His offense "From carelesnesse did in no maner grow, / But wit confus'd with too much care did misse" (93.7–8). As we have seen, the young lover Astrophil cannot resist revelling in the ingenuity of his sonnets and songs nor can he resist basking in the critical regard of his "friends." His whole life revolves around his passionate love ("too much care") for Stella and its poetic product.

In the tight sequence of poems that follows this song, Astrophil's permanent separation from Stella on the grounds of witty indiscretion slowly dawns on him. Stella, at first, merely seems "vexed" (93.4), not lost, nor does he seem to notice the "*Argus* eyes" (xi.42) of her household. But when he loses all bravura, he indulges in two forms of poetic myth-making, one dark, one light. Astrophil purges his melancholy—and the reader's—through testing his poetic mettle in representing, first of all, panicky isolation in the nocturnal world then a euphoric identification with the daylight one. Thus the sonnets, dark and light, recognize that his consolation for the lost affair resides in his suffering and its poetic issue.

The dark (93–99) and the light (100–104) sonnets, lying in between the sexual fantasy of song 10 and Stella's peremptory reiteration of her rejection from a window in song 11, picture Astrophil's attempt at self-mastery through poetic investigations separately of nighttime landscape and a sunny sky. At first, morbid thoughts lead to his descending into a thrilling gothic world, what in the next great critical age John Dennis would call the "sublime," which creates in us a pleasurable sense of disorder and horror.

Sidney directly connects underworld imagery not with fear of mortality but with the operation of the mind of the love melancholic in frustration and despair, and thus our hero anticipates the graveyard imaginings of a Hamlet or Ferdinand on Shakespeare's or Webster's stage. Vertiginous panic designates the extreme limits of the idealist's sense of self-loss. Horror at the diabolic underbelly of existence marks his separation from nature, just as euphoria shows his identification with it. Night creates the separation, but then daylight transforms that world into a personification of his worshiped sun in the skies, and of his desire for her. Both modes provide Sidney's persona with poetic tours de force.

Lawrence Babb, in his study of Renaissance melancholy, *The Elizabethan Malady,* puzzles over the inclusion of lycanthropy, vampirism, and other forms of demonomania as symptoms of the experience of lost love, but Sidney makes the connection metaphorically and metonymically clear. The frustrated lover, possessed by his or her absent beloved, hates his or her bed, especially at night, because it is a reminder of who is missing. He or she rises and travels through likely landscape such as cemeteries and lonely woods. At daybreak, he or she goes to sleep in the crypt of a darkened bedroom. Missing the day means the moon with all its pulls on the psyche becomes the central planet. Pining and nausea cause him or her to appear bloodless, indeed ghoulish. His or her imagination dwells on the horrors connected with the demonology of lost things, to include haunted houses, rapid aging, dismemberment, or premature burial.

In the love melancholic's inferno, all is shady and silent. Sorrow has made the poet's "braine / So darke with misty vapors" that a "grief" must be called upon to "find the words" (94.1). Not only has the poet's world blackened to the point that he "can scarce discerne the shape of mine owne paine" (94.4) but he has "melted" into an indifference to death. He must do the complaining simply because

> . . . my poore soule, which now that sicknesse tries,
> Which even to sence, sence of it selfe denies,
> Though harbengers of death lodge there his traine.
>
> (94.6–8)

"Harbenger," since Elizabethan times a favored archaism of poetic diction, should, I believe, be taken in the sense of advance man or herald here, a "harborer," one who locates a "harbor,"[22] in this case in the train of elements of Astrophil's soul that cannot be heard. This procession of shapeless and soundless demons belongs to our hero's gothic imagination.

By means of a witty conceit, Astrophil presents a "train" of allegorical fellows, "joy, hope, and delight" who depart the company of his version of "everyman" Astrophil in his grief. "Sighs" will be

> Thanke-worthiest yet when you shall breake my hart.
>
> (95.14).

In an ingenious way, Astrophil is groping for death through heartbreak. The reader is chilled by comparisons of the blackness of night to Astrophil's thoughts which provide the central theme for four sonnets. In each, he connects the production of love poetry with the sufferance of regret, guilt, lack of entertainment, silence, tendency to tears, sighs, plaints, and the loneliness of night in his bedroom or out on nocturnal walks. He addresses Night as a goddess in sable mourning for the loss of her lover, Sun. She lacks that light as Astrophil lacks the light of Stella, which forces him to stay up and write and then sleep if he can during the day like the living dead.

Of course, divorce from his beloved Stella generates the energy source of poetic production, but, because, in his metaphor, the lover Sun also obliterates Night, as thoughts of Stella would destroy him, we are also reminded of his tendency to self-destruction. This landscape produces fellows who threaten to destroy Astrophil's mental balance. Ghouls appear:

> In night of sprites the ghastly powers stur,
> In thee or sprites or sprited gastlinesse.
>
> (96.10–11)

The lover himself becomes that oxymoron that he produces in ink, the living dead possessed by "sprited gastliness," moving across a panicky nighttime landscape joined by blood drinkers and other phantoms. Grief of lost love turns him into a monster who cannot bear the day, and wakes up only when "gastly powers stur" (96.10), at night. Hating the idea of rest that night beckons, a vampiric Astrophil calls out:

> But, but (alas) night's side the ods hath fur,
> For that at length yet doth invite some rest,
> Thou though still tired, yet still doost it detest.
>
> (96.12–14)

Panicked imagination produces thoughts now darker than night.

Astrophil's bed horrifies him not only because Stella does not lie in it, but also because it is "by my strange fortune staind" (98.3), by tears, but also, perhaps by blood and semen. Astrophil is invited by his bed to rest but is

> . . . constraind,
> (Spurd with love's spur, though gald and shortly raind
> With care's hard hand) to turne and tosse in thee.
> While the blacke horrors of the silent night,
> Paint woe's blacke face so lively to my sight,
> That tedious leasure marks each wrinckled line.
>
> (98.6–11)

On one level the poet's paper is physically tear-strewn and wrinkled, but the notion of painting his own face of woe with inky and wrinkled lines also suggests the terror of rapid aging. Then, like a ghostly spirit, his "eyes then only winke" when "*Aurora* leades out *Phoebus*' daunce."

Like vampires, Astrophil can only sleep in the day. Only when

> . . . that sweete aire, which is
> Morne's messenger, with rose enameld skies
> Cals each wight to salute the floure of blisse
>
> (99.9–11),

will he find his eyes "in tombe of lids then buried" (99.12). Separate from "each wight"—thus excluded from the human race—his night-tortured eyes are laid to rest in a crypt of eyelids only to arise, with his "ghastly" fellows, at nightfall. Throughout these dark poems, Sidney shows how the love melancholic generates delightfully horrific imagery.

The anxiety of separation from the world at night, however, leads to the ecstasy of identification with a diurnal world lit up in the following sonnets. In the first transitional light poem, Stella's tears become rainfall: "O teares, no teares, but raine from beautie's skies" (100.1). Her sighs "pleasing *Zephires* blow, / As can refresh the hell where my soule fries" (100.7–8). Since she becomes identified with paradisial nature itself, that nature can come again to "refresh" his molten "hell" of passion. As Astrophil becomes well, Stella, suddenly sick, is at one with the heavens. It is wet outside, as so often in his England.

> Nature with care sweates for her darling's sake,
> Knowing worlds passe, ere she enough can find
> Of such heaven stuffe, to cloath so heavenly mynde.
> (101.12–14)

The sky perspires—mists and rains—in identification with her masterpiece, Stella, in the poet-lover's euphoric imagination. Thus the roses of her cheeks have been "stolne from my morning skies" (102.4). They have blanched like her cheeks.

> It is but love, which makes his paper perfit white
> To write therein more fresh the story of delight,
> While beautie's reddest inke *Venus* for him doth sturre.
> (102.12–14)

If the image of Venus stirring ink for her son Cupid brings us close to a self-ironic view of our bookish poet's activities, and if Astrophil also seems too ghoulish in his obsession with her extreme pallor and his sudden health at the apparent price of her blood, the notion of writing on Stella is not gothic, but euphoric. The seemingly inanimate sky, actually animated by Stella, his star, provides the poet with his paper.

Thus, in both his dark and his light moods, the poet equates the action of the natural world with his internal response to Stella. Joyous humanizing of the operations of light nature replaces the panic of living in an indifferent or malevolent underworld. In such elementary myth-making he no longer dwells on his divorce from the visible world, but imaginatively engages himself in her processes, now identifying them with his own psyche in a state of desire. Instead of addressing himself poetically to Stella in a boat seen from a high window he calls on the Thames carrying her:

> I saw thy selfe with many a smiling line
> Upon thy cheereful face, joye's livery weare:
> While those faire planets on thy streames did shine.
> (103.2–4)

We have travelled from the wrinkles on the blackest face of woe to the smiling lines of desire for Stella. Inanimates join with natural forces to celebrate Stella. The boat dances to those watery lines. The winds "twine" (103.8) in her hair and "forst by Nature still to flie, / First did with puffing kisse those lockes display" (103.10–11). The euphoric lover relies on a figure of thought which contradicts what John Ruskin knew to be the function of nature,[23] but one that animates the world and poetically joins the reader to her operations in perhaps the most traditional of poetic schemata.

In the final words of this *canzoniere*, Astrophil resigns himself to separation from his beloved—symbolized by physical obstructions—and gradually accepts the consolation of poetic memories of Stella and their aborted affair. Song 11 and the sonnets through 108 are dominated by the image of barriers, ultimately a window through which he sees her in the final song. Astrophil is positioned permanently on the other side of some transparent medium that allows him only to see her, not to touch, directly related to the window of memory.

As he had first glimpsed her hair dissheveled by the wind from above,

> . . . from window I
> With sight thereof cride out; ô faire disgrace,
> Let honor' selfe to thee graunt highest place
>
> (103.12–14),

in permanent separation, he can now enjoy only the memory of her window image "glad (though but of empty glasse)" (104.11). Through the poetic joining of window glass and drinking glass, he suggests that having drunk to her with his eyes, his transparent surface is now without image. He has consumed the contents of the window. Later he rues the loss of her visual image on the other side of the window—"dead glasse" (105.3)—and delivers curses first to a page who seems to have dropped and extinguished his torch—possibly making it impossible to see Stella—then to the night (and its darkening of vision), then to the coachman who creates the distance between him and Stella. In the final sonnet he pictures "iron doores" (108.11) which keep him from his day.

The Epilogue

In his final words, Astrophil resolves his fate of separation from Stella in the image of his birdlike soul learning flight through the burning of his heart, an emblem for his tragicomedy. Thus he ends where Petrarch began:

> When sorrow (using mine owne fier's might)
> Melts downe his lead into my boyling brest,
> Through that darke fornace to my hart opprest,
> There shines a joy from thee my only light;
> But soone as thought of thee breeds my delight,
> And my yong soule flutters to thee his nest,
> Most rude dispaire my daily unbidden guest,
> Clips streight my wings, streight wraps me in his night,
> And makes me then bow downe my head, and say,
> Ah what doth *Phoebus*' gold that wretch availe,
> Whom iron doores do keepe from use of day?
> So strangely (alas) thy works in me prevaile,
> That in my woes for thee thou art my joy,
> And in my joyes for thee my only annoy.
>
> (108.1–14)

The esoteric image of Astrophil rising from incineration to his star is characteristically undermined by the humor implicit in the idea of clipped wings and the apprentice falcon's bowed head. Tragicomedy never leaves off on a strictly happy note but on an expiational one implying that all the tests and horror and incineration of the heart evinced one's true worth.

The Phoenix's rebirth on the ashes of despair emblematizes resurrection of Stella's memory in Astrophil's poetry and the poet's own concomitant flight from the charred remains of lost love. Through his persona of the "busy loving courtier," Astrophil, Sidney leads us into the heart and soul of a version of all idealistic young lovers. Like the astronomer of his *Defence of Poetry,* who "looking to the stars, might fall in a ditch" (82), star-lover's anxious passion for his sun and star takes an educational fall. In an early sonnet, our hero complains through a rhetorical question,

> For though she passe all things, yet what is all
> That unto me, who fare like him that both
> Lookes to the skies, and in a ditch doth fall?
>
> (19.9–11)

Far from the "mire / Of sinfull thoughts" (14.7–8), suggested by Astrophil's prim "friend," this "ditch" symbolizes the point of necessary descent into common sense of all idealistic lovers when they carry their assumptions and desires up against the wall of actuality. But Astrophil resurrects himself, as well.

While most ages dwell on the dangers of outward violence or hyperactivity in youth, Elizabeth's era seems to have been centrally concerned with youthful inactivity, melancholy, and potential suicide. Beyond the countless representations of the conventional pose of melancholic suitor to the Virgin Queen, Sidney, Spenser, and Shakespeare present universal images of the debilitating stasis of a passive form of madness that could either lead to suicide or other forms of self-violence, or to a comic redemption in poetic production where the festering soul of the hero or heroine is cauterized through artful expression of passion. Astrophil falls into that latter category.

An early, excellent editor of these sonnets and songs, Alfred Pollard, claims for Sidney large and original psychological achievement in the cycle, an innovation. What does he mean? That Sidney vividly portrays and accurately represents in some peculiar way aspects of youth in love? That through his dramatization he delivers new data and the means of analysis of a case of frustrated love? Pollard, like A. C. Bradley, seeks to show us that Hegelian inner conflict lies at the basis of Elizabethan dramatic characterization. But the analysis of inner conflict may lead us into a study of such complex psychic structures that we may be torn from the comic and universal aspects of a recognizable dramatic character. Sidney chose his hero from the poetic tradition for a particular end, a persona he adopted to educate us wittily about passion by fictional subterfuge. As critics and sociologists have shown, love melancholy and career melancholy have their conventional representation. Our ur-dramatic lover is the stock figure from Plautine and Terentian versions of Greek new comedy, *adolescens,* who also makes his way into the Greek romance plots that Sidney admired.

Love melancholy for Sidney's self-conscious version of *adolescens,* Astrophil, is a madness that he must sensibly survive. Overview saves him. His story leads us into its tragic and comical side—Astrophil in his confusion, nay, perhaps because of it, confounds unlike things in his interiorization of the world. *Adolescens* is always the most noble poet in his play, and he moves us—but the play is comedy, and he is a conventional butt, not some grand Dionysian or Christian scapegoat, but a stock comic character being initiated, "educated out" of his savagery—civilized in his mating.

Astrophil's Petrarchan ideal of true love, like the pastoral ideal of the collective society, must appeal to us if we are at all alive, but ideals create psychic strain for the faithful in their conflict with actuality, and in their poetic projection of self. Actually, humans, according to Sidney, share social interests and live by convention and decorum, whether Astrophil realizes this fact or not. Often he does not, and in the gap between life and his "great expectation" (21.8) extends that panicky lunar and then euphoric solar landscape that his brain lives in. Thanks to his extraordinary overview of all these processes, we find ourselves travelling with him. Posing as a "busy loving courtier" infected with the Elizabethan disease, Sidney erects a platform to demonstrate the nature of passionate love and development of the poetic imagination in what another persona, Musidorus, will call "these fantastical mind-infected people that children and musicians call lovers" (52). Madness, poetry, extreme youth, and true love combine for Sidney, as for Shakespeare, when his Theseus echoes him, to show the effects of life's most glorious dis-ease.

5
"Darknesse Cleare": Seven Levels of Starlover's Ambiguity

With the possible exception of the era in Athens of Aristophanes and of Aristophanes's, Xenophon's, and Plato's Socrates, no age revelled more in the pun and other forms of rhetorical ambiguity than the Elizabethan. Often such doubleness is employed for bawdy effect, to remind us of our bodies and their simple functions in the midst of intellectual or spiritual rhapsody, but Sidney's ambiguity has another ethical purpose in registering how career and love melancholy produces poetry. The "leaves" of Sonnet 1, indeed of all the sonnets, are ambiguous, suggesting both the microcontext of the ideal bower (trees) that shades the coterie of ladies, Penelope, Mary Sidney, Frances Walsingham, stern friends, curious acquaintances, and our melancholic hero, and the macrocontext of the literary tradition (others' pages)—the accumulated wisdom and technique of the ages.

Astrophil's conscious manipulation of his readers through verbal duplicity shows more overview than any other of Sidney's masks, though he is fixed in a specific egoistic character. Unlike the developed, indirect consciousness of the rhetor of his *Defence of Poetry* and the narrators of the two *Arcadias*, furthermore, his starlover is both candid and psychopathic. When Hazlitt compares Sidney's dazzling image to that of Hamlet in the mind's eye of Ophelia—"The soldier's, scholar's, courtier's eye"—he may have suggested more about Astrophil than he intended, because the soliloquies of this *canzoniere* lead directly into the staged *melancholia* of Shakespeare's idealists, Romeo, Hamlet, Troilus, and even, to a certain extent, Iago and Timon, and their corporate progeny on the stage of Chapman, Ford, Fletcher, Webster, and Middleton.

Unlike some recent detectors of slippage into autobiographic grousing,[1] however, I find in Astrophil nothing more than a well-wrought Renaissance mask, a tool for showing us a simultaneously coherent and dis-eased imagination. The very consistency of the poet's polysemous moves suggests Sidney's own distance from the analysis. Beyond the normality of primary meaning, double and treble signification in Astrophil's poem normally registers cries of the pain of jealousy, frustration, envy, and physical aggression, sometimes self-directed. On first acquaintance, we find a set of seduction poems in the tradition of the troubadours of Provence, precisely the kind of poetry Plato's civic-minded Socrates of the *Republic* would condemn, on second reading we have a perfectly civic-minded, classical warning about the dangers of idealism, depression, and aggression in youth, indeed, Elizabethan England's most "dramatized" social problems.

In order to demonstrate the melancholic Astrophil's rhetoric of involvement, I will impose on Sidney's works one more glossary of rhetorical figures.[2] Here I place in hierarchical order seven levels of ambiguity found in the sonnet cycle from verbal to narrative formulation, used to demonstrate a case history of the psychopathology of passionate, adulterous love. My seven categories, like Empson's,[3] do not pose as absolutes, but as tools designed to delve into Sidney's mine of Renaissance complication that is not so much compressed or concentrated as it is implosive. The purpose of such an exercise, thus, is not to categorize so much as to shed light on the causes (Astrophil's and Sidney's ulterior motives) and on the latent effects (in the reader within the story and without) of so many complex words and arrangements.

Since his art aimed to move the reader to the good in action (in actual life), ironic images of education, school, training and breeding, for example, appear throughout the sequence in all guises, from the appearance of the schoolmarms, "Studie" and "Muse," in the first sonnet to the burning and clipping of Astrophil's wings by "dispaire" in the last. Astrophil's means of instruction, unlike school training, involves catching up his reader in ambiguities that range from the word itself to the organization of the whole cycle. But if schooling teaches us nothing, life produces dangerous reversals for Astrophil.

Level I: Names

On the most elementary linguistic level, the narrator and central figure of the *canzoniere* presents us with a list of characters, a *dramatis personae*. In our day of astronauts and astrodomes, I think we can appreciate the Elizabethan joy in neologism, especially in nomenclature that joins two Greek or Latin roots to effect some *discordia concors*. Combined words instruct us in some new correspondence or difference in the universe of characters and things.

By a kind of word invention whose significance is made to be available only to the reader, Sidney had created a number of such yokings in naming personae in the *Old Arcadia*. For example, even when Pyrocles (fire and glory), the lover of Philoclea (love of glory), self-consciously adopts the name "Cleophila, turning Philoclea to myself, as my mind is wholly turned and transformed into her" (18), he is not playing on the significance of "love of glory" or "love of fire and glory" or "glory of love" but merely inverting the elements of his beloved's given name. In the revised *Arcadia* when Pyrocles adopts the name Zelmane (rare passion[4]), he is consciously borrowing a deceased lover's name, and unconsciously an identity, but he is not naming his disease. Pamela (all honey or sweetness) cannot know that her name mocks her sometime acid majesty. Nor can Philisides, whose name, as we have seen, combines "lover of star" with "Phil" and "Sid" and other echoes,[5] refer to such onomastic design.

Sidney's personae in the *Old Arcadia*, in other words, unlike the hero of his sonnet sequence, are not meant to be conscious of the meaning of their names. That the narrator of his sonnet cycle, however, is portrayed as the inventor or reinventor of his characters' names—including his own—helps explain the joy he takes in playing on the connotations of that set of pseudonyms, nicknames, and quibbles, but it also exposes his all-consuming envy, frustration, and urge for self-destruction.

> In a grove most rich of shade,
> Where birds wanton musicke made,
> May then yong his pide weedes showing,
> New perfumed with flowers fresh growing,
>
> *Astrophil* with *Stella* sweete,
> Did for mutuall comfort meete.
>
> (viii.1–6)

This stanza and a half opening song 8 contains one of three references to the "author" by name in the sequence, all in this song and the following one. And "Astrophil" returns to the first person singular in this song's ultimate line.

Like all mention of "rich," even, I think, in "most rich of shade," and of "Stella," as we shall see in a moment, naming himself involves the reader in ambiguity. "Astrophil," since it defines him strictly by his love *(philos)* of star *(astros)*, smacks of self-conscious, epistolary nom de plume, a seducer's weapon, as the diminutive of Philip, "phil," suggests self-deprecation. As readers, we must be aware of the possibility of conscious maneuvering on our self-ironic narrator's part, even in calling himself by name. For example, "phil" reminds us of the creator of Astrophil on the other side of the mask, as it does the bird his beloved keeps in sonnet 83, also named "Philip," but then, "Phip," warned of destruction at the "poet's" hands.

In this comic poem, "Astrophil" addresses the bird by two names that trace his decline in favor.

> Good brother *Philip*, I have borne you long,
> I was content you should in favour creepe,
> While craftily you seem'd your cut to keepe,
> As though that faire soft hand did you great wrong.
> I bare (with Envie) yet I bare your song,
> When in her necke you did *Love* ditties peepe;
> Nay, more foole I, oft suffered you to sleepe
> In Lillies' neast, where *Love's* selfe lies along.
> What, doth high place ambitious thoughts augment?
> Is sawcinesse reward of curtesie?
> Cannot such grace your sillie selfe content,
> But you must needs with those lips billing be?
> And through those lips drinke Nectar from that toong;
> Leave that sir *Phip*, least off your necke be wroong.
>
> (83.1–14)

When readers have joined in smiling admiration of a small, billing, songful, seductive version of Astrophil,[6] they hear that bird, that dangerous double, now knighted and quite visible, warned of destruction at the hands of our poet. The movement from admiration to envious rage is signaled by his alteration of the Christian name. The honoring of "good brother *Philip*" (83.1)—the correct form—decays into the contemptuous offer to strangle the rival, "sir *Phip*" (83.14)[7]—the lowly nickname of the knighted double. By extension, readers are given a taste of self-praise and of potentially violent, even self-violent ends. Brilliant poachers also risk their necks, and "sir *Phip's*" fate might predict that of our narrator, Astrophil.

"Stella," like "Pamela" in the *Arcadia*, creates a hearing problem for us, because it is a piece of Sidney's fabrication that later becomes a not uncommon Christian name. Since it is so often connected with the star and our great source of energy, the sun, the name Stella, which appears eighty-nine times, should force the reader to entertain the doubleness of an aristocratic young woman in an emotional bind, whose mundane activities, from singing, travelling, staring, blushing, and kissing, to caring for pet dog and bird, are carefully recorded, astronomically glorified by our idealistic lover making her loss occasion for self-annihalation.

The poet says

> . . . in *Stella's* face I reed,
> What Love and Beautie be.
>
> (3.12–13)

The heavenly Stella of the poet's making intensifies desire, while the earthly woman remains unavailable. Yet this quandary produces the joy of poetry, even in the creation of the name itself. As Rosalie Colie points out, "From the logos of Stella's name, especially when confirmed by the kiss of her mouth, all necessary words can be unfolded, in perfect measure and meaning."[8] We should not forget, however, that that name—the sole and direct source of so much conscious poetic brilliance—is of Astrophil's own invention. On each mention, "Stella" should remind us of poetic fabrication, and that Astrophil is capable of mining his pit of grief, and using such ore to shape new material in the anatomy of his woe. In other words, his object can dangerously "drop out."

By the surprise naming of the beloved "Stella" by her married name, "Rich," a structuring maneuver for three sonnets (24, 35, 37), Astrophil forces us to live with the paradox that the "rich" emancipator of energy and brilliance in our narrator, is supposedly the "poor" thrall to an abuser of a husband named "Rich." Thus an actual surname becomes subject to word game. Leicester bought Wanstead Garden from Lord Rich, and relations among the three families of Dudley, Sidney, and Rich were, apparently, ever cordial. But in the special context of this *canzoniere*, though Stella is "most rich in . . . everie part" (37.12), she "Hath no misfortune, but that Rich she is" (37.14). The poet enjoys such riches from afar—a heavenly distance—and nothing at hand, a hell that, in certain well-recognized senses, he shares with his rival:

> Rich fooles there be, whose base and filthy hart
> Lies hatching still the goods wherein they flow:
> And damning their owne selves to *Tantal's* smart,
> Wealth breeding want, more blist, more wretched grow.
>
> (24.1–4)

The rich, according to poor Astrophil, are normally doomed to the tantalizing death of wanting to accumulate more, even when the wealth Rich has been hoarding is Stella's body, but Rich's case—in this dramatization of rivalry—is worse, because he is said to remain ignorant of her worth. "Rich" grows "in only follie rich" (24.12), because he purportedly does not take into account the value of his treasure. The word play on "rich" is not merely paradoxical, however. The vehemence of such punning on his name suggests to us that Rich's supposedly crass ownership of Stella helps generate our poet-lover's attraction. In fact, the object of desire, wife Rich, in the word play, maintains her value in relationship to the value her husband Rich places on her. As René Girard has pointed out, dramatization of this kind of "mimetic rivalry" is commonplace in Shakespeare.[9] Our self-consciously poor (42.7) poet lives in a hell of envy and emulation, separated by an astronomical distance from his heaven. Because of this name's happy uses in creating ambiguity, Sidney risked using a well-known name, and apparently caused some consternation, post mortem,[10] but in the context of the poem, mentioning "rich" helps define his suicidal poverty.

Level II. Complex Words

The wealth of homonyms in the proliferating lexicon of English, as well as the variable spelling of his day without dictionary, yields for Sidney a quarry of ambiguous ore, one that he mines for various forms of double entendre. Through an accidental equation of sound, the pun assaults the logical underpinning of language, and instantaneously interrupts our primary sense in the syntactic flow. That perceived violence to the coherence of language may help explain why the spoken pun—from time immemorial—causes groans as well as smiles, but, with its Socratic background, it is also a most intellectual form of ambiguity, precious to Astrophil as to his savvy Renaissance fellows, Stultitia, Rabelais's Panurge, and Montaigne's homely, un-Christian persona, as an intellectual guage of his listeners' intelligence in the face of an extreme fallibility of language.

When, in his *Defence of Poetry*, for example, Sidney's rhetor emphasizes the need for storyline to move readers—in the case of Menenius Agrippa's fable of the parts delivered to the mutinous plebeians—he "cuts himself off" (93) with,

> In the end, to be short (for the tale is notorious,
> and as notorious that it was a tale).

(93)

"Tails"[11] are "in the end" and sometimes far too "short." Thus we disengage from our primary sense, and go back to recover piecemeal the residue of a subversive joke. Part of our groan no doubt derives simply from the mental fatigue of trying to avoid becoming the victim of verbal gamesmanship, even at the remote distance of reading Sidney. Of all rhetorical figures, the pun is the most cerebral—as we have seen, in Plato's works it is Socrates's favorite figure—and is always a means of intellectual upstaging that tempts us, at a loss, to pretend knowledge. But if we get the joke, we also smile with our punner's virtuosity in mocking the "ends" of his anxious theorizing.

When we hear in a late sonnet of the *canzoniere* that "lips *Love's* indentures make" (85.13), we experience the "painful mirth" of discovery that the notion of lips swearing contracts of love's allegiance must make room for the sense of (1) lips indenting (making impressions on) lips in a kiss and also (2) "love-biting" by the use of lips and teeth (natural dentures). In fact, we have recently been introduced to star-lover's tendency to such amorous violence when Astrophil, two sonnets earlier, swears "I will but kiss, I never more will bite" (82.14). The double entendre, "tale-tail" and the "treble entendre" of "indenture" function to bring us down to earth, reminding us of our fragile physicality in the midst of the bright rhetorical acts of the spirit or intellect, such as *narratio* and contractual promise of fidelity. Such "noble" primary meaning instantaneously implodes, forcibly reminding us of the idealist's straining for effects even in rhapsody that is conscious of its effects.

Sidney invigorates Astrophil's clever punning, on the whole, by restricting his word play largely to homonyms like "grace" or "joy" or "bless, blessed, blist," "death," or "hell," that reflect simultaneously his religion and his frustrated physical passion: "Knowledge might pitie winne, and pitie grace obtaine" (1.4). "Grace," as Lanham points out more than once,[12] semantically yokes the concepts of "mystical or last things" (heavenly beneficence) and "sexual gratification" (yielding to his advances). Of course "grace" at other times can also suggest (1) "her grace" (a title), (2) her gracefulness, (3) her "holy" words, and (4) his graceful verse describing her. "Grace," however, also suggests our hero's spiritual impoverishment, because his new religion in Stella can only be consummated in violence that denies words as well as spirit.

In our most actively dramatic moment of the cycle, he asks,

> 'Shall a heavenly grace want pitty?'
>
> There his hands in their speech, faine
> Would have made tongue's language plaine.
>
> (viii.64–66)

The narrator reverses the terms "pity" and "grace" of the initial poem at the moment of his attempt to add the force of fondling to his pleading. But the complex word "grace" retains its "heavenly" redemptive meaning in words which, as always, are far from plain.

When Sidney's contemporary, George Puttenham introduces the idea of punning as a step or level beyond onomastic word games—"when such resemblance happens betweene words of another nature, and not upon mens names"[13]—he immediately gravitates upon Sidney, chosing a passage of a poem from *Certain Sonnets* which plays on "live" and "love":

> And all my life I will confesse
> The lesse I love, I live the lesse.
>
> (27.39–40)

Puttenham chooses a passage that expresses cryptically a commonplace from Sidney's confessional poetry, that life without testing the extremes of passionate love becomes a partial death. These two lines are unified not only by the antithetical juxtaposition of "live" and "love" but also by the two-time echo of the first person singular "I" rhyme with its possessive, "my." Astrophil will take this particular sound reiteration (to include "I," "Aye," "Ay," "eye," and "high") much farther, as we shall see in a moment.

Here, however, in Puttenham's example, as when Astrophil jeers at other poets' speaking "of wot not what desires" (6.2), or when he states that they "(God wot) wot not what they meane by" (74.6) the notion of "divine fury," we enjoy tongue-twisters either to marry the concepts of life and love, or to mock the inanity of the cold-blooded erotic versifier. The poet is not punning exactly. Astrophil develops denser uses for homonymic ambiguity, however, that lead us into the rather disturbing realm of love's violence.

Sidney's use of the homophone shared by "I" and "eye" can balance a pair of "primary" senses that suggest star-lover's bitter schooling in passion:

> In her sight I a lesson new have speld,
> I now have learn'd Love right, and learn'd even so,
> As who by being poisond doth poison know.
>
> (16.12–14)

In the first line, "I" picks up a sense of "eye," since the "eye," belonging to the "I," causes his heavenly grief "in her sight." He is the victim of a single sense. The ego is subsumed by the visual organ, thus valorizing this ambiguity, but the semantic complexity of the use of this homonym only begins here.

Creating for "Rich" an icon of "hellish Jealousy," Astrophil later says he has "So manie eyes ay seeking their owne woe" (78.12). Throughout the sequence the "I" is "aye" (always) present, and it is through his "eye" that we experience his predicament. But the echoing monosyllable now contains a suggestion of the stated affirmative of "ay" or "ay, ay" as well as a reiterite cry of pain, "ay . . . ay," caused by the pangs of jealousy he shares with his rival, Rich. Astrophil suffers a similar plight as he does when he first warns that rival that he might be "(Exil'd for ay from those high treasures, which / He knowes not)" (24.13–14). Internal rhyme in "exil'd," "high," and "ay" reflect the permanent loss of Stella's heaven, I believe, with all the complexity that a monosyllable can generate.

The spelling of words that echo others when we read silently can actually lead us into missing ambiguous verbal play, discoverable only when we hear the words out loud:

> Fair eyes, sweet lips, deare heart, that foolish I
> Could hope by *Cupid's* helpe on you to pray;
> Since to himselfe he doth your gifts apply,
> As his maine force, choise sport, and easefull stay.
>
> (43.1–4)

Puns become the source of "groan-less" humor when they become both familiar and when we can live at ease with the two or more readings. Here, in the primary meaning indicated by the orthography, the "I," the ego, would "pray," offer a prayer, so that Stella might respond with the "gift" of a blessing or of heavenly grace. In a secondary meaning, however, the "eye," the sensory organ, would also "prey on" (devour) her body, his sensual food, as he was "looking," so to speak, for the gift of sexual grace. As sounded, the alternate readings maintain their balance, and cause an implosion of meaning that embraces teleology as well as, of course, predatory looks of desire that mark the limit of Astrophil's sexual fulfillment.

Level III. Oxymorons

Although, in the cause of right reason, John Hoskins would like to see Sidney's oxymoron ("Synoeciosis"[14]) providing a middle ground between "adjective" and contradictory "substantive" as in "*brave raggedness*"—"a meaning of neither precisely but a moderation and mediocrity of both"—his discussion leads to assertion of the violence of such yoked opposites in musical terms that deny such a rational solution. Hoskins depicts the dissonance of Sidneian oxymoron, such as *witty ignorance,* in typically affective terms: "This is a fine course to stir admiration in the hearer and make them think it a strange harmony which must be expressed in such discords."[15] Stirring admiration or wonder or shock in the hearer is certainly one of our love poet's goals, but oxymoron is also designed to lead us into a mystical land where the distinctions that words make are obliterated. They self-destruct, like the frustrated poet himself.

Hoskins concludes his discussion of Sidney's oxymoron by quoting the *Arcadia* on the nature of *concordia discors:* "There was so perfect agreement in so mortal disagreement, like a music made of cunning discords."[16] Clearly Sidney, at least in this case, gives his reader no easy exit from a paradoxical thought, or non-thought, or transcendent thought. Unlike our ambiguous name or complex word causing meaning to expand suddenly, the implosive jar of two-word paradox forecloses on semantic coherence. Thus it becomes the most compact verbal expression of the unrequited lover's nihilistic delusion. Denotation and connotation collapse with all difference. Ambiguity is never more tidy nor self-destructive.

> She heard my plaints, and did not only heare,
> But them (so sweete is she) most sweetly sing,
> With that faire breast making woe's darknesse cleare.
>
>   (57.9–11)

Darkness is by definition unclear. Clarity is not dark. But if we can verbally define a "darkness" that engulfs us, like the "darkness visible" of Milton's Chaos-Hades-Hell, it becomes in a sense, "clear." An obscurity is measured and clarified in the story of Astrophil's trip through the darkness clear of his own inferno. What makes that obscurity visible is his constantly reborn passion for his star and the poetry it produces. The emotional sense and the mysticism of love and its violence thus are made apparent by "strange harmony."

Astrophil the aesthete early condemns the workaday erotic poet's reliance on such paradox with the sardonic remark that

> Some Lovers speake when they their Muses entertaine,
> Of hopes begot by feare, of wot not what desires:
> Of force of heav'nly beames, infusing hellish paine:
> Of living deaths, deare wounds, faire stormes and freesing fires.
>
>   (6.1–4)

But though they are mined from the quarry of Petrarchan self-annihilation, these oxymorons serve a wide range of "strange" antithetical functions.

In the cycle, comical condemnation of the use of these terms to evoke the feeling of passionate love leads to consistent use of them to convey that otherwise inexplicable emotion by conscious paradox. We understand the state of "living death" as feeling never so vital yet never so deathly ill in the soul; "deare wounds" suggest to us the effect of lovers' glances and other sweet assaults that traumatize the soul; "faire stormes" evoke both our love of sublime disorder in nature and in ourselves in the internal "faire stormes" and tears that passion creates. If a scorned "freesing fire," finally, by negating its own substantive leads to a land beyond words, it helps describe erotic symptoms in antithetical terms, the scorching and bright light of idealization yet shivering of unfulfilled desire on the edge of contempt. Our search for antithesis, however, hardly exhausts oxymoron's semantic complexity.

Speaking of the fantasy land of erotic dreaming, Astrophil later calls on the god of sleep,

> *Morpheus*, the lively sonne of deadly sleepe,
> Witnesse of life to them that living die.
>
> (32.1–2)

Beyond the strange harmony of antithesis, we now read living death as the state of night dreaming when his beloved dominates his wandering imagination. As we have seen in the discussion of Astrophil's final poems in chapter 4, the paradoxical concept of the animated corpse suggests our blood-drinker raised from the dead when the pain of despair has finally killed all sleep, all seeming mortality. "Living death," in its deepest layer, suggests vampire.

At the very end of this *canzoniere*, as we have seen, we still hear in Sidney's elegiac oxymoron:

> That in my woes for thee thou art my joy,
> And in my joyes for thee my only annoy.
>
> (108.13–14)

The concept of joyful woe merely states for us the lover's otherwise inexplicable case, but the antithetical concept now expands into an ironic idea of the education he began with, in his picture of the operation of the schoolmarms, "Studie" and "Muse." Stella and the lover's regard for her has led our hero into a tenuous reconciliation with life's own joyful "annoy," into self-ironic repose. As Colie suggests in this regard, "his language provides examples of just the sort of thing he deplored in" the "straight talking sonnet."[17] But was Astrophil ever straight talking? There he complicated our response with the convention of anticonvention. Here he uses self-contradiction to explain the soul's education through love's torture and ultimate despair.

Level IV: Ambiguous Metaphors

When he employs metaphor, Astrophil strains to make it clear that he is "not saying that which is not"—that he is not jarring the reader with the *concordia discors* of patent fabrication or lie—but sculpting reasonable comparatives often by the aid of the terms of simile, "like" or "as." But, while he soothes us with the guise of rationality, he yokes an odd assortment of vehicles to his tenor of passionate love forcibly joining linguistic and erotic self-destruction. Beyond paradoxical images of the lover's plight, as pleader yet aggressor, contained in metaphors of love as war, and as hunting (venery as venery), and the sequence of body catalogues that convey wonder and worship with their glittering metals and gems, so contradictory to feminine softness, come two often juxtaposed metaphors, reading as opposed to eating beauty, that reflect, like the "eye," "I," "ay" pun, the extreme limit of his sexual contact in visual gratification.

Astrophil has warned us, in introducing Stella's name, that he "reeds" in her face "What Love and Beautie be" (3.13). But being satisfied with reading Stella is, of course, impossible. Astrophil must consume; otherwise he will starve. She is not a book; she is a beloved woman. But his nourishment will be her loss. Thus, in perhaps the most jarring reversal in the sequence of poems—not unlike the moment of near-rape of Pamela by the "goatherd," Dorus in the *Old Arcadia*—Astrophil sets up his reader for the rhetorical surprise of an "eating" metaphor delayed until the poem's final word:

> Who will in fairest booke of Nature know,
> How Vertue may best lodg'd in beautie be,
> Let him but learne of *Love* to reade in thee,
> *Stella*, those faire lines, which true goodnesse show.
> There shall he find all vices' overthrow,
> Not by rude force, but sweetest soveraigntie
> Of reason, from whose light those night-birds flie;
> That inward sunne in thine eyes shineth so.

> And not content to be Perfection's heire
> Thy selfe, doest strive all minds that way to move,
> Who marke in thee what is in thee most faire.
> So while thy beautie drawes the heart to love,
> As fast thy Vertue bends that love to good:
> 'But ah,' Desire still cries, 'give me some food.'
>
> (71.1–14)

Astrophil opens with the certitude that nature is a readable book and that reading Stella is sufficient. But the lover, banking on the possibility of satisfaction with reading of her beauty and also his own "fair lines" which translate that beauty, suddenly, as so often in the sequence, implodes in the fourteenth line, here, with the call for gratification in terms of consumption of food. If reading Stella is not satisfactory, if readers must consume her like food, the sequence itself is unsatisfactory since readers find the true idealized Stella only in our narrator's text. Stella remains Astrophil's invention and his only offspring from this "union."

Our narrator investigates metaphorically the nature of the "evidence" or offspring of their celibate relationship, the poetic lines. He also considers the destruction of those children. Describing how poetry is produced, he writes,

> *Stella*, the fulnesse of my thoughts of thee
> Cannot be staid within my panting breast,
> But they do swell and struggle forth of me,
> Till that in words thy figure be exprest.
> And yet as soone as they so formed be,
> According to my Lord *Love's* owne behest:
> With sad eyes I their weake proportion see,
> To portrait that which in this world is best.
> So that I cannot chuse but write my mind,
> And cannot chuse but put out what I write,
> While those poore babes their death in birth do find:
> And now my pen these lines had dashed quite,
> But that they stopt his furie from the same,
> Because their forefront bare sweet *Stella's* name.
>
> (50.1–14)

The image of masculine pregnancy and labor, which opens the sequence, develops into a vignette of birthing, postpartum depression, and infanticide.

This metaphor of infanticide has its "pathological" logic. In the absence of sexual intercourse, the poems must represent the only issue of his erotic ties to Stella. They are, as illegitimate children would be, dangerous accidental clues to his relationship with her. Such offspring that evidence illicit passion can be destroyed like unwanted "poore babes" either for the sake of protecting the secrecy of the affair, or simply because they do not sufficiently resemble their mother, that they have too much of their father Astrophil in them. Of course "putting out" or exposing infants is an elementary tragic theme. The lover's metaphor shows how idealistic love can lead to a kind of poetic savagery. It reflects the poet's urge to self-destruction by proxy.

Even if the aesthete Astrophil in his study is merely threatening to "dash" the lines or crumple up the poems, "each wrinckled line" (98.11), those "toyes" his "knowledge brings forth" (18.9), he is suicidal. On both sides of this relationship are produced and destroyed other incriminating "children," such as sighs our lover-poet hopes to see Stella trying to contain: "Sighs stoln out, or kild before full borne," or Astrophil's own tears destroyed by his grief:

> Nay sorrow comes with such maine rage, that he
> Kils his own children, teares, finding that they
> By love were made apt to consort with me.
>
> (95.9–11)

Here, a personified "sorrow" becomes a Herculean infanticide, protecting in this deadly way his children's honor from the dishonorable young man, Astrophil.

Level V. Allusion to Myth

Astrophil fabricates his verse—in the high Renaissance mode—out of the pagan myth of the Greeks and Romans. Conscious imitation of Catullus, Horace, Virgil, Ovid, and the love-poets (and sometimes scorn for the proverbial fabric of most medieval verse), reflects an urge to by-pass Biblical imagery that may seem sparser and less sensual and yet risked condemnation for blasphemy or heresy.[18] Embellishing love poems with Olympian mythography brings out our aesthetic poet's humorous vein early in the sequence but, as Colie points out,[19] Astrophil is free to create new mythographic monsters of his own to reach his mistress' ear:

> Some one his song in *Jove*, and *Jove's* strange tale attires,
>   Broadred with buls and swans, powdred with golden raine.
>
> (6.5–6)

Astrophil will soon be plagiarizing Ovidian "tales" and dressing himself up in strange "tails"—coccyx as well as penis—of bulls and swans to assault his earthly mistress, but he will gravitate on immortal victims as emblems to convey his sense of self-sacrifice.

Astrophil's extensive use of the image of a sadistic, naked schoolboy lord and rival, Cupid or Love, leads him into comparing himself with a sequence of brow-beaten or abused or raped immortals from Prometheus (14) to Atlas (51) to Ganymede (70)—indeed a probable reference to Sidney's post as Elizabeth's cupbearer. As Prometheus:

> Alas have I not paine enough my friend,
> Upon whose breast a fiercer Gripe doth tire
> Then did on him who first stale downe the fire,
> While *Love* on me doth all his quiver spend?
>
> (14.1–4)

To Stella's complaints, he says

> . . . find some *Hercules* to beare, in steed
> Of *Atlas* tyr'd, your wisedome's heav'nly sway.
>
> (51.7–8)

The word "heavenly" here picks up an echo of "heavy," heavy as the great globe Atlas must hold up. As Ganymede, his muse:

> . . . oft hath drunke my teares, now hopes to enjoy
> Nectar of Mirth, since I *Jove's* cup do keepe.
>
> (70.3–4)

These images suggest in part a noble victim and one that has humanity, indeed, the whole world on his shoulders.

Astrophil's central icon of self-sacrifice concerns the tyrant Phalaris of Agrigento, mentioned in his *Defence of Poetry* (90), who creates beautiful sounds by cooking human sacrifices alive in a bronze bull. Shrieks of pain were made musical. In fact, perhaps this was Phalaris's own fate. Astrophil's scalding bull turns out to be Stella herself. Astrophil insists he sacrifices himself in her, but poetry comes from the savage spectacle. In the analogy, Astrophil consumes himself in burning desire and then resurrects himself from the ashes of pain of his phoenix-like music. He wonders:

> That when the breath of my complaints doth tuch
> Those daintie dores unto the Court of blisse,
> The heav'nly nature of that place is such,

> That once come there, the sobs of mine annoyes
> Are metamorphosd straight to tunes of joyes.
>
> (44.10–14)

The cry of anguish, since it passes through Stella's ear into her heavenly and blissfully erotic consciousness, becomes melody.

Representing the instrument of torture, the scalding bull, Stella's "own voice oft doth prove" (59.6) those complex songs which he chooses to compare with groans. Astrophil writes:

> Wo, having made with many fights his owne
> Each sence of mine, each gift, each power of mind,
> Growne now his slaves, he forst them out to find
> The thorowest words, fit for woe's selfe to grone,
> Hoping that when they might find *Stella* alone,
> Before she could prepare to be unkind,
> Her soule, arm'd but with such a dainty rind,
> Should soon be pierc'd with sharpnesse of the mone.
> She heard my plaints, and did not only heare,
> But them (so sweete is she) most sweetly sing,
> With that faire breast making woe's darknesse cleare:
> A prety case! I hoped her to bring
> To feele my griefes, and she with face and voice
> So sweets my paines, that my paines me rejoyce.
>
> (57.1–14)

A cry of pain passing through Stella's ear, skin, or flesh to her soul—a kind of sexual intercourse—creates music. Stella reads one of his songs and turns the cry into music. When

> in piercing phrases late,
> Th'anatomy of all my woes I wrate,
> *Stella's* sweete breath the same to me did reed.
> O voice, ô face, maugre my speeche's might,
> Which wooed wo, most ravishing delight
> Even those sad words even in sad me did breed.
>
> (58.9–14)

This impregnation creates euphoria.

Level VI. *Descriptio*

These ambiguous stories within stories of mythical allusion, of course, always point us to the actual world and story of our lover-poet himself, which with Stella's final rejection near the end of the cycle, as we have seen, lead to withdrawal and internalization of all aspects of the outer world. "Astrophil's" *descriptio* and *narratio* are two forms of rhetorical ambiguity that cannot be separated. His pathological "mis-taking" the outer world for an expression of mood parallels his internalization of the narrative itself.

In one early poem, the narrator constructs symbolic elaboration of the workings of time, a poetic commonplace Puttenham calls "*chronographia* or the counterfait time,"[20]

> With how sad steps, ô Moone, thou climb'st the skies,
> How silently, and with how wanne a face,
> What, may it be that even in heav'nly place
> That busie archer his sharpe arrowes tries?
> Sure, if that long with *Love* acquainted eyes
> Can judge of *Love*, thou feel'st a Lover's case;
> I reade it in thy lookes, thy languisht grace,
> To me that feele the like, thy state descries.
> Then ev'n of fellowship, ô Moone, tell me
> Is constant *Love* deem'd there but want of wit?
> Are Beauties there as proud as here they be?
> Do they above love to be lov'd, and yet
> Those Lovers scorne whom that *Love* doth possesse?
> Do they call *Vertue* there ungratefulnesse?
>
> (31.1–14)

Instead of mere digits on a clock, Astrophil uses the image of the moving moon to convey nighttime. What time is it? Moonrise. We detect a description of the lunar landscape that catches the solitary lover's lycanthropic fancy. But when the poet suggests that the moon may be in love, and is his double—indeed that the court of heaven may be as corrupt as his sublunary one—we are led into an equation of inner and outer. The final three rhetorical questions lead to a surprise in the implosive "lunatic" inversion of the final line that suggests the unrequited lover's violent and paradoxical rage at the unresponsiveness—in fact, the chastity—of his star.

> Do they call *Vertue* there ungratefulnesse?

Astrophil really means, does he not, "do they call ungratefulness virtue in the heavens?" The botched word order betrays his moonstruck madness as his description of his star or sun betrays his blindness.

The cosmos does not strictly register the poet's mad interior moods but replicates Stella who dazzles him, as he says, and incapacitates his mind, leading him into nonverbal darkness clear. Ambiguous *descriptio* gives us a picture of Stella that cannot be seen except with the eyes of the blind. Her dark pupils, for example, convey obscurity. We hear the rhetorical question:

> When Nature made her chiefe worke, *Stella's* eyes,
> In colour blacke, why wrapt she beames so bright?
>
> (7.1–2)

Here the darkness serves as a veil in case: "They sun-like should more dazle then delight" (7.8) The poet's brain is "sunne-burn'd" (1.8) and his vision dazzled by those eyes as we have seen.

> *Stella's* joyfull face,
> Whose faire skin, beamy eyes, like morning sun on snow,
> Deceiv'd the quaking boy.
>
> (8.8–10)

Unless we imagine being snow-blinded on some winter morning, we cannot see her face. Blind Cupid's unwilling student and double must be punished by blinding.

Elsewhere Astrophil describes Stella hyperbolically in terms of a rock and jewel icon that gives us color and texture perhaps, but reflects the blindness, madness, and stupor of the worshipper. Her forehead, we hear, is:

> built of Alablaster pure;
> Gold is the covering of that stately place.
> The doore by which sometimes comes forth her Grace,
> Red Porphir is, which locke of pearle makes sure:
> Whose porches rich (which name of cheekes endure)
> Marble mixt red and white do enterlace.
>
> (9.3–8)

These semiprecious and precious stones and gems reflect Nordic aesthetical norms present even in the Mediterranean painting Sidney loved—but the metaphors also block our view of a real woman. What identifies Stella here is "rich (which name of cheekes endure)," her name, but only an ambiguous description, hardly applicable to cheeks.

Level VII. *Narratio*

In his *Defence of Poetry*, Sidney's rhetor emphasizes that without narrative, we do not really have poetry at all. Verse itself is "but an ornament and no cause to poetry" (81). He even supplies us with a "narrative" description of lyric song "when the lusty men were to tell what they did, the old men what they had done, and the young what they would do" (97). Without a "tale which holdeth children from play and old men from the chimney corner" (92) that can teach through "Ulysses in a storm, and in other hard plights" (90), we have no vehicle to generate the cherries of interest and rhubarb of self-discovery. Only through Aeneas's action, for example can his reader be trapped by identification and thus moved to adopt virtuous action:

> in the ruin of his country; in the preserving his old father, and carrying away his religious ceremonies; in obeying God's commandment to leave Dido . . . how in storms, how in sports, how in war, how in peace, how a fugitive, how victorious, how besieged, how besieging, how to strangers, how to allies, how to enemies, how to his own; lastly, how in his inward self, and how in his outward government.
>
> (98)

Only heroic narrative inculcates a desire to generate in ourselves heroic virtue.

Without marvellous and exemplary "when's" and "how's," poetry disappears, lapses either into philosophical "wordish description" (85), or monotonous chronicling of the "bare *Was*" (89). Poetry is fiction, and only by "feigning" (94) the impression of passing events, internal and external, can it catch and entertain our ear, thereby leading us into mental and moral health that leads to the good. Because he emphasizes that the events are invented by a poet who never affirms historicity, or even *vraisemblence*, however, he tempts us at the same time to see the flow of fictional events as an artificial construct of airy nonaffirmation.

It seemed revolutionary a few years back when Paul Alpers argued that *narratio* in Edmund Spenser's *The Faerie Queene* was little more than a figure of thought. Spenser "transforms his narrative materials not into parts of a fiction, but into stanzas of poetry, arrangements of words."[21] While Sidney's 108 sonnets and eleven songs are very different from Spenser in technique, syntax, diction, and substance, they do, like the nine-line stanzas of *The Faerie Queene*, resemble narrative. However, they remain, in their variable arrival after fourteen lines, an artful ordering of words—an end in themselves.

Alpers concludes his study of *The Faerie Queene* 2.4 with the remark that the "climax of the episodes is not an action at all, but a rhetorical scheme, a formal arrangement of words—precisely a stanza of poetry, and nothing else."[22] The same may be said of the climactic events of *Astrophil and Stella*, but I hope to emphasize the crucial importance of the concept of fable as a carrier, albeit artificial, of the reader's emotion. Sidney asks us to look for historicity, and for precise events, and yet, for affective purposes, he leaves us with the ambiguity of fictive quasi-narrative or negative history.

The most striking ambiguity in Astrophil's anatomy of woe concerns the status of the affair itself. Critics show no unanimity concerning an event of sexual contact or rejection that the reader has been made to anticipate, indeed the potential event, I would argue, that keeps readers reading. Sidney makes it clear in his *Defence of Poetry* that the reader is trapped into a kind of emotional favoritism in fiction. We read a love story in expectation of sexual contact between lovers as we read a heroic adventure tale in expectation of life-threatening action.

If supreme courts of this world plead that sex and violence are not intrinsic to fiction, then call them, like literary critics, love and death. Clearly the intrinsic emotional tension caused by expectation of love fulfilled or not, or half-fulfilled, or of the imminence of violence and death, or survival, keeps us reading. Without the impetus of narrative we do not have poetry or fiction, but essay, as Sidney reminds us on more than one occasion.

Sidney notes the effect of our emotional bias in narrative early in the sequence. Stella is showing no pity towards Astrophil's "be-clowded stormie face" (45.2):

> Yet hearing late a fable, which did show
> Of Lovers never knowne, a grievous case,
> Pitie thereof gate in her breast such place
> That, from the sea deriv'd, teares' spring did flow.
>
> (45.5–8)

In this poem, which ends with Astrophil begging to be read as tragedy, narrative fiction arranges our emotional response even more efficiently than actual human discourse and affairs. Clearly, Stella's empathy with the "lovers" directed her to seek for their happy union, as we seek the happy union of Stella and Astrophil. But do we actually find it in the moment that Sidney has led his readers to expect, a consummation of the affair? Or are we led to a vanishing point, the empty boast of our pathological poet-lover?

After all the tears and kisses and begging, Astrophil seems to imply, in the culmination of a final blason that he knows a fully naked Stella "Yet ah, my Mayd'n Muse doth blush to tell the best" (77.14). Are we meant to assume that the sexual contact we have come to anticipate throughout the sequence has occurred? Are we beyond maidenly or chaste matters, at least concerning our lovers?

In reference to song 4, where we seem to be placed on a bed in the night, in a home where Stella's mother resides, McCoy strenuously argues in favor of our necessary perception of a precise, even historical event of sexual contact. He says, dismissing Kalstone's and Ringler's "decorous" conclusions:

> if any further evidence is required that Astrophil is inside Stella's bedroom, the embrace of the penultimate stanza—"Leave to Mars the force of hands"—seems to provide it. The closeness of the scene and mood suggest that the conclusion's ellipsis is prompted by decorum of another, more courtly sort—protection of the lady's reputation.[23]

McCoy has certainly discovered an implied fact, yet he immediately notes that "there is still no change or development in their relationship." Given as we have seen, Astrophil's self-conscious tendency to brag in the most obvious youthful way in his songs, made known directly by him, I argue the event or nonevent remains ambiguous by design in spite of the boldness of its statement.

Inevitably, as McCoy shows, we, as readers, seek a clear solution and are frustrated. What, however, is Sidney's purpose in maintaining, as I propose, ambiguity about the fact of sexual consummation of his lovers? Clearly Sidney does not need to make us wonder about or even desire a certain outcome. I argue that he is making the point, through his dis-eased persona, Astrophil, that the lovers themselves and the reader with them must live on the edge of expectation of such an event in their narrative sense of the sequence of actual events of this affair, yet the sexual contact of the lovers will not ultimately prove to be so important. The event will not have, as McCoy himself points out, any effect on their doomed relationship, and this realization comprises our "medicinal," again implosive, discovery in the narrative. Astrophil, the willfull idealist, strains for a victory over Stella's chastity, I believe, with the reader, that remains all in the getting, and it puzzles our psychopathic lover as it puzzles us, as it later puzzles Shakespeare's Troilus. As with some modern detective novels, where the resolution of the action remains cloudy, we are tempted to say that the ending is a trope; yet the expectation of resolution of action kept us reading, and the ambiguity we discover in trying to work out the form of the ending contains a rather chastening lesson.

6
The Sonneteer's Mock Encomium of Self

Sidney's *Defence of Poetry* presents profound reading problems in part because it is both a formal oration and yet a work of "dissimulation" deriving from a tradition of wit in which the reader is entrapped by rhetorical maneuvers rather than "drawn by the ears" (111) by dialectical demonstration. Speaking of the similarities between Sidney's *Defence of Poetry* and Cornelius Agrippa's *De Incertitudine et Vanitate Scientarum et Artium (Vanitie of the Arts)*, A. C. Hamilton suggests that Sidney took Agrippa's mock declamation "as a work of irony whose concealed meaning was not the abuse of the arts."[1] But though he suggests that "Agrippa's influence upon Sidney is . . . even formative,"[2] he does not take the crucial step of recognizing in his *Defence of Poetry* a mock encomium itself, another genre naturalized from products of the glorious court of Henry VIII. The evidence, however, that Gregory Smith, Geoffrey Shepherd, Margaret Ferguson, and A. C. Hamilton[3] have collected relating Sidney's work to the *Vanitie of the Arts* and to Erasmus's *Moriae Encomium (Praise of Folly)*, cries out that we find a new approach to the character of the work. Tested for rhetorical efficacy, this *Defence of Poetry* begins to appear not only a mock encomium of poetic seduction, but, like Folly's construct of self-praise, also a "sermon" from a peculiar Renaissance self-ironic persona.

In Plato's *Symposium*, Alcibiades provides not only a metaphor but a justification of self-ironic procedure when he compares Socrates to a comic mask or bust of Silenus that, once broken apart, reveals figurines of the gods inside.[4] For Plato, as well as for Agrippa, Erasmus, Rabelais, Montaigne, and Sidney, the contemporary image of the reader of an ironic work engaged in the search for the ideal core of the onion would have been incorrect. They would have conceptualized a solid core not an ideal nothing beneath all the layers. But the process of locating that core is not a simple one, and it may be that the mask, frame, box, hollow bust, and onion images themselves, suggesting containers of truth—or nothingness—are misleading. These images for such a work tempt us to try to dent its surfaces of irony in order to excavate and mine truth, when the truth is literally on the surface. The truth is in the search for truth, or, shall we say, in our experience of the dialectic, the often self-contradictory *logos,* of the text itself.

In an effort to extract doctrine from his *Defence of Poetry* modern critics, from C. S. Lewis to Morriss Partee,[5] have sought to explain and resolve the seeming inconsistency of Sidney's "account of the poet as maker or ποιητής and the 'more ordinarie opening of him' as an imitator,"[6] but in the process of rectification of this paradox other inconsistencies appear. For example, critics discover an equivocal attitude toward the authority of Plato, or several positions regarding the status of moral exemplars, or unsteady use of critical terms such as "nature" and "love."

Frustrated perhaps by efforts to mine consistent critical theory from the work, two experts on rhetoric, who generally agree closely on the interpretation of Sidney's works, find themselves diametrically opposed on his *Defence.* Rudenstine remarks that the work is "public, carefully marshalled, consistent (in spite of its inconsistencies);"[7] Lanham argues that "this *Defence of Poesie* is itself a thoroughly rhetorical combination of fundamentally contradictory arguments which perplex us still further."[8] If we were to see Sidney as akin to the master praiser of folly, however, we would be released to accept, as I think we must, both of these seemingly contrary dicta. About the figurines of the gods, Rudenstine is correct—doctrine is solidly there—about the ironic mask, Lanham. The two critics are separately considering what Sidney's rhetor calls the "foundation" and the "superficial part" (100) of the work, which, as that rhetor states, must be carefully juxtaposed. Both readers fail to consider at length the seriously jesting side of Sidney, the ironic praiser of poetic persuasion, and thus they can hardly take the necessarily devious route to a coherent reading of the work.

In by far the most significant recent reading of the work, Margaret Ferguson takes Sidney's *Defence* to be ironic, but not coherently so, because it is—she claims—a product of the pressure of defending one's own poetic profession in a hostile Elizabethan cultural environment.[9] For Ferguson, self-interest causes the work to blur, thanks to rebellious urge and cultural paradox. While my extended argument will closely follow the *topoi* Ferguson examines, my demonstration of the development of the persona of the rhetor as would-be love-poet intentionally failing to defend himself will cause our conclusions to swerve. Her point of departure is the supposed real and potential unsureness of the conclusion of the *Arcadia,* both *Old* and *New.* In chapter 10, I propose putative solidity to that ending in Sidney's conceptualization of the *persona* Evarchus' *alazoneia.* Ferguson's version of Sidney's critical text is thus "defensive," like McCoy's and Helgerson's;[10] mine is apologetic in the broadest sense. We agree, however, on the nature of Sidney's ventriloquist self-justification.

In interpreting my proposed "apology" I have no fear that I will be accused of hearing voices; Sidney's tonal variety in his *Defence of Poetry* is readily apparent to recent critics.[11] Sidney's protean persona includes the self-deprecating courtier of the exordium and peroration; the satirist exposing hypocrisy of philosophers and historians of the confirmation or the proof; the lyrical voice hyperbolically comparing poet to Creator of the narration; the baroque painter designing lurid *exempla* of the refutation; and the omnipresent advocate arguing with his lawyer-like "if that be denied me" (75), "may I not presume," (77) "truly's," (77) and "indeed's" (78) or his "neither let this be jestingly conceived" (79), "I think (and think I think rightly)" (99) or his "undoubtedly (at least to my opinion undoubtedly)" (118), even to placing himself in a courtroom: "yet think I, when this is granted, they will find their sentence may with good manners put the last words foremost, and not say that poetry abuseth man's wit, but that man's wit abuseth poetry" (104). Like Folly, the speaker or rhetor seems to approach the author's own voice at one moment, only to drift into a caricature of the breezy sophist at another; and he is always pretending to know less than he does. How can we rely on any of the voices we hear from a critic who hides behind a repertory of masks and "nothing affirms, and therefore never lieth" (102), who is so poetical or fictive that we tend to relate ideas in his critical remarks more to the "voice" in question than to presumed authorial position? How do we locate the figurines of the gods that such ironic procedure seems to promise?

Clues lie in the relationship of the work to Latin compositions of the court of Henry VIII and to the culture of the turn of the sixteenth century. Although ironic declamations existed in Plato, Lucian, and elsewhere in classical and medieval literature, the scale of such a work as *Praise of Folly*, Cornelius Agrippa's *Vanitie of the Arts*, or More's *Utopia* suggests a need for formulation of a new category of prose composition, specifically a Renaissance category. What I call the "Platonic monologue" provides dialectical examination of issues by a single voice that ranges, like Folly, Agrippa's rhetor, or Hythlodaeus, from something akin to authorial spokesman to unreliable *nuntio* or narrator. Such a work is the product of tension between the rigidly compartmentalized structure of the classical oration and the free association of a Protean persona who transforms all matters that come to mind into instruments for the uses of praise or denigration in the circumstances of the moment. In other words, though the rhetor confines his argument to the patterns required by sophistic training for formally consistent orations, that argument so confined often becomes mock sophism, dazzling rhetorical displays that ironically conceal, behind all the verbal devices, superior knowledge. Tension is maintained in tone and genre by the comic delivery of serious, often tragic, speculation about human nature. Sidney produces a yoking of opposites, a *concordia discors,* a truthful lie and a serious jest.

The reader of such a work must follow the rationalization and limited arguments of the changeable rhetor as one would a dialogue where different speakers represent divergent points of view, each with good reasons, but good reasons cloaked in logic colored by the rhetoric of self-love. As the doctor, Eryximachus, praises medicine in the name of Eros in the *Symposium,* but with good reasons, so Sidney's rhetor, "now slipped into the title of a poet," praises passionate lyric, but with good reasons that seem casually to go beyond his own limitations as a love sonneteer. What remains after the dust of self-generated controversy settles in the reader's mind is an understanding of the problem of poetry, its ontology, and a suggestion of synthesis of divergent positions, which must, as in a dialogue, remain unstated. Pull the ears of your asinine, grinning listeners, and they will rebel. The one rhetorical move that the player who delivers a mock encomium cannot perform is to "affirm." Like Plato's Socrates on the edge of asserting the immortality of the soul to the fanatic Apollodorus, Sidney's persona culminates his argument by slipping behind the ironic mask and forcing readers to taste their own conclusions. No wonder this maneuver has baffled recent polemicists.

When Sidney's rhetor speaks of Erasmus's kind of work in his *Defence of Poetry,* he first places it in the context of mock declamations where "a playing wit can praise the discretion of an ass, the comfortableness of being in debt, and the jolly commodities of being sick of the plague" (100). Here the plan would be rhetorical exercise, like those academic performances in early and late antiquity which provided training for defense lawyers. Erasmus speaks of such mock *encomia,*[12] and Agrippa, in *Vanitie of the Arts,* actually provides us with a praise of an ass's dumb discretion immediately preceding his conclusion. The difficulty of such an oration lies in showing the good and pleasant and intelligent as dwelling in the inherently bad or unpleasant or dull. This kind of work does not exhibit the many-levelled irony of *Praise of Folly* because it neither turns on itself nor on the listener. For example, if one praises the advantages of the thirst of a victim of plague because it is only for water which is generally in abundance, one provides an example of pure skill in argumentation at a disadvantage. One is exercising ability at sophistry. But if one says "cockroaches make good pets for the poor," one is turning the irony back on the speaker as ostensibly a person who fashions himself or herself free from the suffering of the poor, but also back on the implied callous listener, calling attention to anything from pest-ridden housing to the starved affections of the indigent.

Sidney's persona, however, recognizes that larger ironical purpose when he points out that Erasmus—and Agrippa—"had another foundation than the superficial part would promise" (100). In fact, he defines this larger purpose, perhaps in reference to Erasmus's work, as we have seen, when he describes the satiric author "who sportingly never leaveth till he make a man laugh at folly, and at length ashamed, to laugh at himself, which he cannot avoid without avoiding the folly" (95). Self-irony is exhibited in the sporting or jesting, but its main purpose is to inflict a knowledge of one's own limitations on the reader. Such a rhetor teaches the reader to know by teaching him or her to know how little he or she knows so far. Thus he traps readers into laughing at their own affectation of knowledge.

That Sidney was fond of the form of such works is indicated by his praise, in his *Defence of Poetry,* not of the works themselves so much as their ironic genre. Thus he reserves admiration for the "foundation" of *Praise of Folly* and *Vanitie of the Arts,* which contradicts the implications of their "superficial part," or for the manner of such related work as the *Utopia* of Thomas More whom he praises for his "way of patterning a commonwealth . . . though he perchance hath not so absolutely performed it" (87). By considering separately the form and content of such works, Sidney is calling our attention to the rhetorical frame, which creates a gap between the speaker's explicit position and the author's implicit one; for example, in *Utopia,* the gap between Hythlodaeus's affirmative attitude, and More's own, toward divorce, euthanasia, or enforced witnessed body inspection of fiancés, or in *Praise of Folly,* the gap between Stultitia's and Erasmus's own view of the happiness of impoverished fools.

The need for such indirection, at least in courtly persuasion, in fact, is the subject of a debate between Hythlodaeus and More's own persona in *Utopia:* More's character in that work, responds to Hythlodaeus's claim that "there is no room for philosophy with rulers," with: "that is true—not for this academic philosophy [*scholastica*] which thinks that everything is suitable to every place."[14] "More" rebukes Hythlodaeus for failing to tailor his advice to his audience's limitations. One must learn to play a role adapted to one's moment on the stage, even if it turns out to be a limited one. "If you cannot pluck up wrongheaded opinions by the root, if you cannot cure according to your heart's desire vices of long standing, yet you must not on that account desert the commonwealth." Although Hythlodaeus's name suggests that he has "learned to talk nonsense," he suffers largely from a problem of delivery, not matter. He never learns "tactfully" to employ "the indirect approach." He dogmatically delivers his idealistic and polarized picture of a sane collectivism in a madly uncooperative world, the irony being that while the content of his words may on occasion be undercut by the frame, only his fanatical style casts him as Cassandra on life's stage.

More's ironic use of the authorial disclaimer in the frame story probably tempts Sidney to declare his "way of patterning a commonwealth" perfect, "absolute," and even if he "hath not so absolutely performed it." But the overly ardent voice of Hythlodaeus's praise of Utopian religious customs, for example becomes More's finest tool of irony, a voice that Sidney seems to echo on central occasions through his persona in his *Defence of Poetry.*

Sidney speaks of Erasmus's, Agrippa's, and More's work to show his admiration for the masterpieces of Henry VIII's court but also, I argue, to warn his reader of the pitfalls of responding simplistically to the words of his own *Defence of Poetry.* Allusions do not appear in so much abundance that they distract the reader acquainted with Erasmus's work, for example, but they serve as a gentle reminder of the rhetorical tradition Sidney is adopting.

Like Folly, Sidney's declaiming sonneteer has a repertory of hypocritical remarks and examples of hypocrisy in order to convey to the reader a sense of the omnipresence of human affectation and foible even in the fabric of his "argument." His initial emphasis on poetry's Greek and Latin etymology resembles Folly's own proud exposition of her own etymological pedigree.[16] His invention of Greek terms for his opponents, such as μισόμουσοι "poet-haters" (99) or φιλοφιλόσοφος "philosopher-lover" (91) recalls Folly's dependence on Greek coins such as μωρότατοι "most foolish," and μωρόσοφους "foolosophers"—as well as More's own μωρόσοφι (by way of Lucian)[17]—though she maintains overt disapproval of such pedantic practice.[18] The rhetor's inclusion and placement of references, furthermore, to Menenius Agrippa's fable of the parts and the stomach delivered to the plebeians (93),[19] to the sad fate of the philosopher kings (107),[20] to the claim of poets to make their subjects immortal (121),[21] and to his work as an "ink-wasting toy" (121),[22] all suggest direct debts to Erasmus's work that emphasize the instability of both. Even quotes from classical authors tend to swerve. Rhetorical techniques borrowed from Folly may seem almost ineffable, such as bizarre polarization of *exempla.* According to Folly's manner, Sidney's persona, for instance, exclusively presents alternately toddlers and moribund old men, or a faceless plebeian mob and a regal king David as examples in support of a theory of the morally salutary effects of poetry (92–93). This bizarre pendulum-effect contains a subtle warning to his best reader about the shifting groundplot of the work.

A more important warning to the reader, however, than specific borrowing from Erasmus is the Erasmian effect of the whole piece. Like Folly, Sidney's persona undertakes the task of defending directly or indirectly all aspects of his peculiar vocation. And while his persona is not that of an allegorical god of poetry, as Stultitia is of foolishness, he is a proponent and practitioner of his titular trade, a character who, as he says early in the work, "in these my not old years and idlest times . . . slipped into the title of a poet" (73). The kind of poetry he has produced, he reminds us on occasion, is sonnets, seductive or pseudo-seductive poems, such as we find in *Astrophil and Stella* and elsewhere in *Arcadia, Certain Sonnets,* and *The Lady of May*. His references to sonnets, arriving as they often do without warning, serve to remind us of his specific avocation, as Folly reminds us of her sex or her patchwork garb. The effect is one of surprise, calling us back to an original context in the midst of rhapsodic rhetorical flight. Thus, while attacking the concept of community of women in Plato's *Republic* he interpolates "little should poetical sonnets be hurtful when a man might have what woman he listed" (107).

The anachronism of placing sonneteers in Socrates's commonwealth jars us into recalling the rhetor's specific epideictic function, courtly flattery of young ladies in hopes of earning sexual favors. In the midst of reproof of the bookishness of English lyricists, he interjects a reference to the supposed context of such poems which "if I were a mistress, would never persuade me they were in love" (117). Of course, the reader cannot doubt that for Sidney, in all his variety, the lyric poem has other virtues than aid to seduction, but here he self-ironically portrays his rhetor as unbalanced by his obsession with his limited trade and its goals. The mention of lyric calls to his mind "passionate sonnets" (103), and to open his final curse on all poet-haters or μισόμουσοι in behalf of all poets, he comes up with the solemn imprecation "that while you live, you live in love, and never get favour for lacking skill of a sonnet" (121). Clearly Sidney's persona is not speaking for all poets here, but, in his egoistic bias, he is allowed to imagine that he is.

Because he is a sonneteer, or poetic seducer in his own self-ironic terms, Sidney himself holds a position of no strength in defending his art against the puritanic Gossons of this world. These polemicists, armed with the authority of Plato's *Republic*, scorn the abuses of poetry because it invites one to sensuality, and appeals to the passions, especially the sexual passions of unsteady youth. Of course, Sidney's implied audience is, by no means, the sheriff, the euphuistic hacks, and the puritan populace of the city of London, but a different kind of group, a coterie, primarily ladies, Lady Rich and Frances Walsingham—and his sister, the Countess of Pembroke, of course—among them. The ladies are the natural audience for this sonneteer—but they reflect the world of readers at large—and his references to them round out the elementary context of his work, the recreation of the persona of the "busy loving courtier."

In the midst of an argument about the power of poetry for good or ill, Sidney's persona remarks "truly, a needle cannot do much hurt, and as truly (with leave of ladies be it spoken) it cannot do much good" (105). By means of this aside, the sardonic rhetor "apologizes" directly to the ladies for belittling the needle's constructive powers, but he also casually creates a context for what he is saying. At another moment he indirectly chides women for sometimes not knowing where or how they are ill by comparing "poet-whippers" with "some good women, who often are sick, but in faith they cannot tell where" (98).

The male persona in defilade reprimands his female coterie. Or he compliments them indirectly on the power of their beauty: "We are ravished with delight to see a fair woman, and yet are far from being moved to laughter" (115). At the close of the work, like Folly, he returns to his elementary context which provides his ironic frame and, consumed with egoistic desire, "conjures" the ladies to believe poets "when they tell you they will make you immortal by their verses" (121). Sidney then allows his sarcastic rhetor to sound the death knell on that immortality to be gained, suddenly no longer in the context of banter with a coterie of ladies, but in the dusty spaces of the world of publishing, and books.

"Thus doing, your name shall flourish in the printers' shops; thus doing, you shall be of kin to many a poetical preface; thus doing, you shall be most fair, most rich, most wise, most all." Since sonneteers do not generally dwell on their ladies' wealth in the heat of self-immolation, we probably discover in this bathos another reference to Lady Rich—"most rich"—and to some of the circumstances in which Sidney "slipped into the title of a poet." In the writing of *Astrophil and Stella*, Penelope was always "most fair" and "most Rich" for the seductive, or rather pseudo-seductive, quasi-seductive, self-destructing poet.

No more than Erasmus, however, does Sidney restrict himself to one context in his encomium. As Folly only occasionally appeals, in her role, to the laughing crowd of people that Holbein the Younger has drawn for us, Sidney's rhetor only occasionally makes excuses, correctives, compliments, and appeals to the ladies. This closing moment, for example, provides merely a framelike ironic reminder that our sonneteering rhetor would like the drift of his sonnets believed. The dramatic relationship between sonneteer and lady is only Sidney's point of departure for his rhetorical flights.

In the opening to his *Defence of Poetry*, the exordium, Sidney shows us indirectly how to read his praise of poetry by creating a parallel between the reader's relationship to his work and his own rhetor's relationship to the praise of horsemanship and horses of John Pietro Pugliano. His susceptibility in this circumstance involves another play on his first name, φίλος ἵππος "lover of horse." Sidney's jesting introduction has traditionally been taken to be little more than an attention-getter along the lines of the remotely relevant joke that the banquet speaker employs before opening more serious discourse.[23] Recently, however, critics[24] have discovered serious arguments behind this jest. I suggest it actually provides an elaborate warning to the reader about how to approach the body of Sidney's fictive apology.

In the second-hand description of Pugliano's "praise of horsemanship" that opens his *Defence of Poetry*, the narrator offers two separate observations about his instructor's motives that will eventually help us understand the nature of Sidney's persona and his own biased "instruction." The rhetor typically dissimulates when he proposes alternate but opposite reasons for the commencement of Pugliano's encomium: He was "either angered with a slow payment, or moved with our learner-like admiration" (73). The effect of such a procedure is to leave the reader in doubt about a character's motives, as one always is, in actual life, until one makes sense of the speech at hand. In other words, Sidney is allowing his reader the luxury of omniscience neither here nor elsewhere when one tries to gauge the intentions of his own persona. Given some guidance, life does not offer such certainty, and Sidney is conveying an experience that contains a lifelike lesson of sorts for his reader's benefit.

This particular distinction, like so many in Sidney, I argue, collapses into two joined parts. We conclude Pugliano had both prods. From some of his choleric language concerning the flattery of courtiers, we understand he might well be angry with late remuneration from our courtiers, but he is also filled with enthusiasm about his subject, horsemanship and horses. This source of inspiration brings our attention to Sidney's second comment about Pugliano's motivation: "that self-love is better than any gilding to make that seem gorgeous wherein ourselves be parties." Such perversion is applicable to all humans, he implies, especially to Sidney's persona in his present circumstance of defending love poetry against all assault.

Sidney's method of presenting Pugliano's defense of horsemanship is a special form of oblique indirect discourse where we hear what we suspect to be some of Pugliano's resounding phrases, "masters of war," "ornaments of peace," "speedy goers," "strong abiders," etc., naturally translated from his native Italian, and one special term, *pedanteria,* which, in remaining untranslated, evidences Sidney's technique. *Pedanteria* is a key word because it shows where and how the self-loving praiser's logic can go awry, in this case, because of a mental confusion, brought on by self-love, about the connection between the part and the whole.

Pugliano says that skill in government is a mere pedantic acquisition in comparison to skill in horsemanship; yet horsemanship is a part of government. If government were a *pedanteria,* horsemanship would be a part or aspect or element of a pedantry. Pugliano, in Prague, performing the duties of Esquire of the Holy Roman Emperor's stables, would be serving the war-making capacity of an intellectual frippery. In a moment, we will see how his rhetor shows he has fallen into the same trap.

In case we have missed the drift of Pugliano's erring logic, Sidney's persona, later, in the context of "serving science," explains his error: "Even as the saddler's next end is to make a good saddle, but his further end to serve a nobler faculty, which is horsemanship, so the horseman's to soldiery" (83), ultimately to the end of virtuous action exemplified by "princes over all the rest." Here, the whole in relationship to horsemanship is, as before, "skill of government." Pugliano suffers from a typical and fundamental social disease.[25] He loses a sense of his own function in society through desire for what others have. In this case, he desires the power that his superiors, ultimately the emperor, properly enjoy insofar as they in turn, do not lose a sense of their own identity and rank, for example, in resorting to tyranny or abdication. Self-love lends such antisocial desire its strength and endurance as we shall see in the odd case of Sidney's rhetor.

In a letter of advice to his brother, Sidney warns that Italians, as rhetoricians, are "given to soe counterfeit lerning, as a man shall learne of them more false groundes of thinges, then in anie place ells."[26] Of course, sowing counterfeit learning is not exclusively an Italian vice of the Pugliani of this world. Each time we congratulate ourselves to others for being more than what we are, self-love will cause us to pass on "false groundes of thinges," as the love poet might in his obsession with seducing ladies through flattery.

In his comment to his brother, Sidney is primarily concerned with an audience that may, like brother Robert, or ladies who read sonnets, be influenced or tricked by sophistry. In this case he is concerned not with Italians who fool themselves so much as with their audience that has, in his opinion, a capability of being deluded. Similarly, in his opening passage, Sidney warns the reader to beware of sophistry when he remarks of Pugliano's discourse, "if I had not been a piece of a logician before I came to him, I think he would have persuaded me to have wished myself a horse." The horse, after all, had received the highest praise from Pugliano, and, like the object of praise of the sonneteers, the lady, the horse was described hyperbolically according to what sometimes were "false grounds of things": "Then would he add certain praises, by telling what a peerless beast the horse was, the only serviceable courtier without flattery, the beast of most beauty, faithfulness, courage, and such more."

We can imagine a horse's "courage," perhaps even "faithfulness," but if we do not become suspicious when we hear him described as the "beast of most beauty," we are in the grips of a sophist. We expect such a thought in a speech of praise, just as we expect to discover the announcement of a mistress' unsurpassed beauty in a sonnet, but if we have the capabilities of a piece of a logician, we rebel, even if our name and essence is Philip, horse-lover. No more than one lady or one kind of beast, human or otherwise, can be peerless in beauty, and which one is a matter of taste; we may, but we probably will not, agree, unless we are overwhelmed by "false grounds of things." The odd autobiographical quibble on philippian tendency to horse-love closes the argument. This warning applies, however, not just to the narrator but the reader of this defense of poetry.

Pugliano, moreover, had just claimed that the horse is "the only serviceable courtier without flattery." Here, though he is clearly using the example of the mute, supposedly ungreedy horse to criticize courtiers—present party of parsimonious Wotton and Sidney included—he is also presenting a false ground of the art of the *cortegiano* because the horse is no flatterer largely because he is, like Agrippa's ass, incapable of speech. The horse might well charm us with exaggerations of our good qualities if he could. He simply cannot flatter, nor can he respond or advise in any way that requires the use of words. He is admirably quiet, but only because he is, in human terms, dumb, a false ground of serviceability. Instead of praising the discretion of an ass on foolish bases, Pugliano has here praised the discretion of a horse in remaining mute.

When he defends his own poetic trade, Sidney's rhetor in his self-inflation, unlike Pugliano, only seems to be forgetting that love poetry with its supposed goal of seduction is hardly the whole of poetry, or that poetry is no more than a part of human wisdom, or of philosophy in the broadest sense. In other words, the rhetor exposes the validity of his opposition: The whole of poetry as well as the whole of which poetry is a part, human wisdom, or philosophy, becomes clear.

Most of the rhetor's examples of poetry, for example, come from narrative poems and fiction whose fictional stories are developed on the basis of an *"idea* or foreconceit" that appears to be philosophical not from love songs. In defending the antiquity of poetry, moreover, he mentions that "even among the most barbarous and simple" (76) of American Indians, there are poets who "sing songs, which they call *areytos,* both of their ancestors' deeds and praises of their gods." However, he then seems to portray such poetry as merely preparatory for the introduction of the sciences and philosophy among them: "If ever learning come among them, it must be by having their hard dull wits softened and sharpened with the sweet delights of poetry (76)." Elsewhere he allows philosophy to be a superior teacher in proudly pointing out that the poet, "for instructing, is well nigh comparable to the philosopher" (99), though the latter lacks the power to move the unwilling. Typically, in the midst of responding in kind to attacks on sonneteers by arguing philosophic obsession with "love" he refers to "my masters the philosophers" (104). If his tone is murky and sarcastic, his meaning is clear. φιλοσοφία, love of wisdom, like government for the expert horseman, is the whole of which any poetry, including the most expert love poetry, is part.

Sidney, the serious jester, here, and elsewhere, openly warns the reader to be careful both of the inflationary effects of self-flattery and of being fooled by arguments of others—especially those of his rhetor—that have in some way been affected by self-flattery. All rhetoric is seductive, not just that of the passionate sonneteer. What he then proceeds to produce, his *Defence of Poetry,* in part shows the effects of the self-flattery of Sidney as love-poet, but in such a way as to warn readers of the fallibility of his arguments, and to trap them into experiencing poetic problems for themselves. He asks us not to believe what we hear but to know what we think. As in his picture of Pugliano, when Sidney bases his arguments on false grounds of things, he lets us know that his rhetor, the sonneteer, has exaggerated or dispensed with logic if he has done so, and he almost always has, but with discretion.

7
The Anti-Platonic Platonic Monologue

Perhaps on the pretext of Gosson's taunt that Plato "banished" the poets from his ideal commonwealth, Sidney's persona, throughout his *Defence of Poetry,* maintains a bantering, jesting attack on Socrates, Plato, Plato's works, and Platonism in general. Part of his reason for doing so no doubt results from Sidney's own abhorrence of abstraction and his doubts about the virtues of pure contemplation. For Sidney, unalloyed cerebral activity, much like self-love, can cause one to forget one's role in an immediate social structure, and even tempt one to love death or suicide, the ultimate self-exemption from social function. All forms of monastic life are dangerous. Transcendent meditation is a dream interrupted by *eros.*

Among philosophers, however, Sidney clearly holds Plato above all others in brilliance. He is mentioned twenty times in the text and Socrates twice, as opposed to Aristotle, for example, who is mentioned only ten times. And the rhetor displays a knowledge of eight to ten dialogues.[1] In fact, the only thinker Sidney seems willing to juxtapose to him is Paul, who, he takes pains to point out, is a student of Greek philosophy and poetry and thus likely a Platonic. Unlike the case of Paul, however, the rhetor consistently finds himself faulting Plato and his thought. These attacks expose a sequence of seeming contradictions, the first being that the only effective attack on poetry, in the *Republic,* must take poetic form to be convincing; the second that the love that generates all poetry must simultaneously combine lust with restraint; the third that the poet is at once an inspired prophet yet imitator. Before he leads us into these Platonic mysteries, however, Sidney's sonneteering persona jousts with Plato and his perfectly valid reservations about the immorality of sonneteering as a seducer's aid, as a stirrer up of passionate excess. Thus he initiates a failed preventive war against Platonic severity.

The rhetor's most open dismissal of Plato's moral argument takes the form of *ad hominem* attack. He portrays the philosopher as personally deficient either because he is boring, incompetent or, in fact, immoral himself, most notably as an "advocate" of promiscuous homosexuality. In eulogizing the simplicity and rhetorical efficacy of Menenius Agrippa's speech to the Roman populace, for example, our praiser of poetry first scoffs at "far-fet maxims of philosophy, which (especially if they were Platonic) they must have learned geometry before they could well have conceived" (93) them. Here the orator refers to the *Harmonics* of Aristoxenus, which gives a unique account of the lectures of Plato.[2] Straining his audience with an introductory survey of geometry, Plato loses the attention of all but one of his listeners. For those familiar with this anecdote, Sidney's self-irony lies in the fact that it is Aristotle who remains to hear his master out on the subject of the good. Here Plato is a dull lecturer, except insofar as he "moves" Aristotle to remain in his seat. He does not interest all, but his reasons make their "passionate" appeal to the nonpareil among philosophical students.

Secondly, the rhetor makes Plato's incompetence manifest by pointedly referring to his supposed unsuccessful political career as adviser to the king of Syracuse, "where Plato could do so little with Dionysius, that he himself of a philosopher was made a slave" (107). Here Sidney's persona takes doubtful evidence about Plato's sale into bondage to the ambassador of Sparta as a certain sign of Plato's inability to turn his political thought into action, at best a weak line of "historical" argument, but wittily delivered. Indirectly, of course, he reminds us of the need for courtly indirection. Naturally Socrates's tale of difficulties with the democratic regime in Athens are touched on, to Socrates's moral "shame." The rhetor announces that "many cities banished philosophers" (107)—that is, not poets—though at another moment Socrates's trial and condemnation to hemlock or exile are taken to be atrocious examples of history's failure to teach virtue (90).

On the moral level, Plato's *Phaedrus* and *Symposium* are made to be more reprehensible than seductive heterosexual poetry because they "authorize abominable filthiness" (107). Here the rhetor intentionally mistakes a Socratic concept of love that was demonstrably restrained and unphysical in both dialogues—the central image being Socrates's rejecting Alcibiades's advances with ridicule in the *Symposium*—for the "abominable filthiness" of promiscuous homosexual activity, a predictable jeer. The word "authorize" is comic, like "banish," because it projects an image of Plato as moral arbiter, a schoolmaster and censor with prescriptive power over his students. The rhetor's *ad hominem* argument is clearly sophistic because it seeks to prove the assumption that because a man is immoral, he cannot recognize immorality. All this jousting forces us to conclude that only a combination of the persona's passion and Platonic restraint makes us all that walking human paradox: a passionate fool, *rationis capax*.

However the reader takes these anecdotes about Plato's and Socrates's lives, the rhetor's arguments so far are clearly directed at the person of Plato and do not touch on Platonic thought itself. The reader is armed by his or her awareness of the rhetor's tendency to attack the character of his opponents, and knows that his epideictic purposes—here of denigration—carry him to illogical and slanderous extremes, but for an ulterior good. His attacks on Plato's matter, however, are more subtle in their sophistry and they leave exposed, ultimately, not only a sense of the superiority of both philosophic ideas and poetic form, the necessary and inevitable clash of *eros* and moral stricture, but also the "contradictory" moral and ontological definitions of the poet as *vates* and craftsman, some of our many glimpses of the figurines of the gods in this Platonic monologue.

Popular Philosophy

Late in his *Defence of Poetry*, the rhetor pictures himself cornered in argument: "[N]ow Plato's name is laid upon me, whom, I must confess, of all philosophers I have ever esteemed most worthy of reverence, and with good reason: since of all philosophers he is the most poetical" (107). This remark is ironic both because the reader well knows that it was hardly late in the work that the name of this philosopher was "laid upon" him by Gosson and the others, and because he is claiming that Plato is essentially a poet. Therefore Sidney's persona can argue that Plato, like Pugliano, makes the elementary blunder of failing to recognize the whole of which he is a part. In banishing poets, Plato mush banish himself.

Early in his *Defence*, the rhetor had presented Plato as a creator of pure fictions who borrows the names of his contemporaries: "wherein he feigneth many honest burgesses of Athens to speak of such matters, that, if they had been set on the rack, they would never have confessed them" (75). Alcibiades, Parmenides, Eryximachus, even Socrates and Aristophanes, the rhetor argues, simply could not have known what Plato would have put in their mouths because Plato was a creator of fictions of a special sort, that is, a philosophical poet in the rhetor's use of the term. Yet Plato, he argues, attacks and banishes poetry from the ideal commonwealth in his fictional *Republic* as if he were unaware that his kind of work was an example of that larger enterprise, poetry. Thus Plato, according to the rhetor, dismisses his own foundation, the whole of which he is a part.

Momentarily, Sidney's persona successfully dissolves the distinction between philosophy and poetry and sophistically exalts the latter not only by proposing that the ideal philosophical form is fiction, but that poetry subsumes the best philosophy.

Sidney's rhetor exaggerates the poetic element in Plato by emphasizing his fictional superstructure at the expense of the analytic philosophy internal to the speeches. But later, as we have seen, he will yield a superior, even an all-encompassing moral role to philosophy in his mock skirmishes with Plato over the abuses of passionate lyricists. The reiterate failed attack and the unblemished return of philosophy exposes a paradox. Plato "feigns" because without the delightful indirection of a story about certain fictive creations named for well-known "burgesses of Athens," he would not be read. Poetry may be a questionable tool in its appeals to the passions, but to make that very point to the broadest audience, Plato must adopt poetical form. The best "*idea* or foreconceit" (79) ideally adopts fictional guise. The best philosophy is exoteric.

Restrained Lust

In the midst of further bantering, Sidney's persona admits he would "rather justly construe than unjustly resist" (108) Plato's moral authority. Here he hints that he may have unjustly (unfairly) resisted Plato, when he could have justly (properly) understood him. He admits what the reader has already found to be an elementary aspect of the work. Plato's dialogues have been unfairly interpreted in order to produce material for attacks on the thinker who, according to Gosson, would have "banished" poets like this "busy loving" sonneteering persona from the ideal commonwealth.

As the omnipresent, frowning Stoics were Stultitia's constant enemies, Plato, because of his consistent religious position, remains the steady frowning opponent of Sidney's rhetor, the passionate lyricist, who continually reacts to that threat. The rhetor's attacks take open forms but also more subtle ones, especially in the ethical realm, where we find Plato's moral strictures on controlling passion juxtaposed to the rhetor's valid insinuation that passion in humans is not only inevitable but also our only motivator to the good. Since the rhetor is allowing both sides of the argument to be exposed, he may pretend to be on the offensive when he is actually taking a defensive position. But our paradoxically requisite combination of hot passion and cold reason, our need to hasten slowly in seeking the good, remains exposed.

Because his fundamental ironic mask is that of the poetic seducer, Sidney's persona—not surprisingly—repeatedly returns to, yet, in all but one case, avoids meeting head-on the Platonic argument that bad lyric panders to our desires and seduces us to passionate excess. The civic Socrates of the third book of the *Republic* argues that poetry is immoral, a go-between to antisocial passion. Since it is part of Sidney's tradition of wit that an argument humorously dismissed be allowed to reconstitute itself in order to haunt the rhetorician, as Stoical reproof haunts[3] Folly, Sidney's "passionate" persona must dismiss this accusation on a sequence of occasions by various means that extend beyond the mere *ad hominem* attack. The first retort—it reappears—involves a separation of poetry from poets, implying that the poetic endeavor in the abstract could be entirely good; its practitioners simply happen to be panderers to egoistic emotion. The rhetor states, "I speak of the art, and not of the artificer" (89) immediately after mentioning his most moral "right poet" Dante. That he makes use of the proximity of mention of a Christian poet in refusing to discuss the passionate abuses of poetry helps load his argument.

In the context of *La Vita Nuova* and *The Divine Comedy*, poetic abuse of the sexual passions seems a remote enterprise. Not so much as a logician but as a legal rhetorician, as we have seen, he later reformulates the notion of ill use of the good in chiasmic reversal of word-order: "And not say that poetry abuseth man's wit, but that man's wit abuseth poetry" (104). Of course, Plato's Socrates of *The Republic* has already concurred with this argument in allowing lyric poets of the so-called "Pindaric"[4] mode of heroic and institutional eulogy to remain in his ideal commonwealth and removing or retraining praisers of potential sexual partners and of the antisocial passions. Of course, Sidney's rhetor, the love-poet, cannot allow this "banishment" or enforced rehabilitation, and Sidney leaves it up to the reader to discover modest self-incrimination in his "rhetorical" retorts. Here as elsewhere, Sidney demonstrates through his persona the divergence between rhetoric and logic that Plato emphasized and Aristotle minimized. Plato's logic is dismissed by rhetoric, but the eternal debate between the positive and negative moral uses of poetry becomes exposed in the process.

Brilliant rhetoric, which only borders on logic, can dismiss Socrates's moral argument only momentarily. As if realizing Plato cannot be "banished" on such feeble grounds, Sidney's rhetor produces a second argument: "Whatsoever, being abused, doth most harm, being rightly used (and upon the right use each thing conceiveth his title), doth most good" (104). If we claim that poetry is harmful to the morals of its audience, we must remember that that which does most damage or injury is also capable of doing us the greatest benefit. Therefore poetry does the most good. This argument is a false syllogism that parodies Socrates's favored method of cornering an interlocutor by concession and definition. Think of the plague whose salutary effects were previously praised by an imaginary rhetorician, or debt. Most good does not necessarily come from what produces most harm. But since the idea of complementary extremes is presented in witty antithesis, it is adequate for the opportunist rhetor. Plato frowns on.

In the context of the abuses of poetry by men who produce "passionate sonnets" as well as elegiac and heroical works that pander to antisocial passions, the rhetor presents his most positive answer to Plato by means of a play on connotation and denotation of the word "love." Dialectical in type, it asks what is the matter with that particular passion when Plato and other philosophers have "spent a good deal of their lamp-oil in setting forth the excellency of it" (104). Witty concentration on the cost of lamp oil may divert the reader from recognizing the fact that Plato was not praising the kind of love to be found in the passionate sonnets of the *canzoniere* that express Astrophil's desire for sexual "food" (71.14). Philosophical examination of the spiritual love of god, and institutions, and beauty, and the good, all the higher rungs of the ladder, so to speak, are suddenly collapsed into the elementary level of ordinary *eros*—human sexual activity. Since rhetoric and wit and self-drama will always try to dominate our mock-serious argument, however, Sidney then allows his "sonneteering" persona a self-image as victim in the apostrophe, "Alas, Love, I would thou couldst as well defend thyself as thou canst offend others" (103).

Paradox endures, however, underneath the veneer of wit. This declaration of victimization, like, Desire's erotic plea to Stella, implies a truth moral arbiters cannot deny: Yearning for passionate physical love is inevitable in all humans, and silencing sonneteers will have no effect on this fact. Plato's Socrates in the *Republic* was a fanatic, for a moment, in the cause of social ideals, but personal ideals of passionate love have not, therefore, been killed off. Sidney does not fatalistically accept immorality in love so much as he explores love in its positive and negative aspects. Love, like poetry (and social "reform") is potentially very good and very bad, most generative and most destructive. Sidney's personae, in the mass of his literary works, choose to educate lovers and other idealists, guiding them through to the other side of pitfalls created by circumstances and conventional mental attitudes—

often Platonic ones. We should not live without the Platonic social ideal of self-restraint nor that of spiritual love, yet ideals tempt us into self-annihilation.

In the passage that marks the end of the debate with Plato himself, the sonnet-making rhetor ultimately accepts Plato's denunciation of the purely seductive sonnet, if such a poem exists. In his lawyerly way he admits that the claims that some poetry can train the mind "to wanton sinfulness and lustful love . . . is the principal, if not only, abuse, I can hear alleged" (103). The philosopher, the lover of wisdom, like Socrates or Plato, rightly comprehends and even properly judges poetry and poets. Notwithstanding the rhetor's comic lending of Gosson's term "abuse" to Plato, and his grudging tone, philosophy thus regains its status as without peer in the realm of ideation.

If Plato, however, is finally allowed his moral point, he is not allowed to do away with sexual passion. In fact, the bantering and quibbling has led us by design into entertaining both sides of a dialectical investigation of the uses of poetry and of the necessity of both passion and restraint. Sidney's rhetor uses the same self-ironic method to lead us into entertainment of the contradictory definition of the poet as "inspired" prophet yet craftsmanlike imitator. To do so, he must first dismantle, sophistically, the Platonic notion of the artist as at second or third hand to "forms" or "ideas" or "daimons" directly available to the philosopher.

Prophetic Craft

Sidney's persona implicitly attacks the epistemological argument from Book Ten of *The Republic,* and elsewhere in Plato, that the poet is a mere imitator of imitations found in nature of ideal patterns. The rhetor sets out, on the other hand, to show that all other arts imitate nature, too, and that philosophy is, in fact, twice removed from the ordinary physical world in its abstraction or generalization based on an imitation of actual nature. His virtuosity in quibbling is on display as he sets out to use the term "nature" seventeen times in a variety of compounds, contexts, and meanings in the space of 227 words of prose (78). His shifting use of the term "nature" arms his argument that poetry only is creative, other sciences and arts but mimicry. The quibble on this word as on "love" provides, in this case, essentially false grounds of argument, yet "internal" dialectic leads us ultimately, with the collapse of his argument, to entertain a definition of the poet as both a prophet—in the two senses of seer and scourge of the tribe—and a craftsman struggling to approximate an elusive *vraisemblence.*

Once the rhetor has categorized the lawyer, historian, and grammarian as mimics of nature (here, human nature) in recording man's judgments, acts, and language, the word "nature" reaches its purest semantic drift, when we read that "the rhetorician and logician, considering what in nature will soonest prove and persuade, thereon give artificial rules, which still are compassed within the circle of a question according to the proposed matter" (78). Here the "nature" that provides those clues to means of proof must be cognition or reason itself. Thus the "rhetorician and logician" cannot be "limited" by imitation of the action of "reason," except insofar as they do not dream up "forms such as never were in nature." To say that logic and rhetoric are limited by the "circle of a question," furthermore, serves only to remind us that their discursive form, while less affecting than the centrifugal "circles" of fiction, is more accurate.

Proceeding to tie the physician to the study of the "nature" of man's body, Sidney's rhetor then attacks Plato's presentation of the metaphysician as a builder "upon the depth of nature." His juxtaposition of the physician and the metaphysic is a sophistic connection based on the root of the two words, not etymology—does a metaphysician oversee physicians?—but the rhetor would also have us see a special distinction. The physician creates an immediate anatomy of the human body. A philosopher or metaphysician, such as Plato, however, anatomizes other analyses of bodies in the universe "in the second and abstract notions." Here the rhetor has seemingly turned the tables on Plato's Socrates, for example, who can now be seen as an imitator of nature to the second degree, when he would have excluded poetry from his ideal commonwealth, at least partially, on the same grounds.

Sidney's *persona*, now testing like a new Icarus the heights of sophistic eulogy, proceeds to praise the poet as a creator of new forms, ideas, and "fore-conceits," improving nature by his divine "inspiration," all of which suggest that he, like Plato's god, is the creator of the *daimons* or perfect patterns which Lady Nature imitates or ignores in her "brazen"—both brash and Bronze Age—fashion. At this moment of rhetorical flight, Sidney's persona defines the poet as prophet. In the ethical sense, that prophet leads and draws men and women to an understanding of the nature of moral worth, as for example, in creating an ideal Cyrus "to make many Cyruses" (79) of humanity. Improving human nature belongs strictly to his ethical art.

In the context of soothsaying, his maker sets him "beyond and over

The Anti-Platonic Platonic Monologue 123

all the works of that second nature: which in nothing he showeth so much as in poetry, when with the force of a divine breath he bringeth things forth surpassing her doings" (79). This "inspiration," or godly blowing up of the "balloon" of the poet, like Virgil's sibyl, allows him to be "lifted up with the vigour of his own invention" (78) and "grow in effect another nature" (78). As seer, furthermore, if he is not predicting the near future, he is developing, like Isaiah, a prophetic image of the perfection of first Edenic and last apocalyptic things.

With the burden of creating this crescendo, however, capped by indiscretion and even heresy in his concept of the poet's invention of a world to rival God's, the authorial persona collapses. His raising up of the poet over the philosopher comes to a halt. The concept of the inspired poet is now replaced by an opposite image of craftsman, no longer creator of new worlds but duplicator of old ones, even of what we now call poetic conventions. Having interpolated "neither let this be jestingly conceived" (79) in mid-argument and "neither let it be deemed too saucy a comparison" (79) and adding "with no small arguments to the incredulous" towards the tail end, he falls back on mere reiteration, then admission of his sophistic use of etymology.

> But these arguments will by few be understood, and by fewer granted. This much (I hope) will be given me, that the Greeks with some probability of reason gave him the name above all names of learning.
>
> Now let us go to a more ordinary opening of him, that the truth may be the more palpable: and so I hope, though we get not so unmatched a praise as the etymology of his names will grant, yet his very description, which no man will deny, shall not justly be barred from a principal commendation.

"Poesy therefore is an art of imitation" (79). This transitional moment allows the rhetor to move on as he says to a usual definition of poetry as artful *mimesis*. Thus he undermines his previous argument that poets are essentially creative rather than mimetic "actors and players, as it were, of what nature will have set forth." But the reader can hardly forget the force of that eloquent panegyric of the poet's prophetic function. And the rhetor's avowal that he was only speaking of the names given to poets, such as ποιητής, *vates* or "maker," cannot obliterate our memory of his brilliant exposition of the poet's vatic energy and essence. Such a collapse of rhetoric has exposed both notions of *poesis*, prophecy and craft, and merged them.

In this passage, which has always been of central consideration in studies of Sidney's *Defence of Poetry*, therefore, we find an attack on

Plato's epistemological definition of the poet as an imitator of an imitation of forms. Yet, we also find agreement with Plato's two divergent ontological definitions of the poet, first of all as "inspired" radical creator and secondly as "skilled" recreator of likenesses. No more than Plato does Sidney seek a simple resolution of these two opposed ideas. In fact, Sidney's rhetor juxtaposes them, on one other occasion, in order, I believe, to allow us readily to perceive their apparent contradiction.

When expounding a theory of the development of poetic craft through "art, imitation, and exercise" (112), Sidney's persona reminds us of the poet's "inspiration" that led the ancients to say that poetry "was a divine gift, and no human skill" (111). Then he adds the proverb *"orator fit, poeta nascitur,"* arguing for a poet's vatic "inspiration" from birth. On the one hand, our poet must go into rigorous training; on the other he or she must already have arrived, *ab ovo.*

The source for the idea of the creator of a second nature blown up "with the force of divine breath" is the *Ion,* in which dialogue, as Sidney later points out, in spite of its obvious irony, Plato "giveth high and rightly divine commendation unto poetry" (108). This commendation is exactly what Sidney's rhetor has performed in presenting the poet as inflated like Apollo's sybil with "divine breath." But Sidney's persona appears uncomfortable with this definition apparently because it pictures the poet as mere agent or medium of divine prophecy. A balloon can be *inspired* or blown up, but Sidney's poet must also be a conscious craftsman, expert in producing controlled expression. He must not only look in his heart and write. He must also be free to range quite rationally "within the zodiac of his own wit" (78), not will-lessly creating inspired babble like Plato's frenzied would-be poet. Therefore, he argues at this late moment that he cannot agree with Plato's theory of involuntary divine fury, "since he attributeth unto poesy more than myself do, namely, to be a very inspiring of a divine force, far above man's wit, as in the forenamed dialogue is apparent" (109). Here Sidney's persona dissimulates in ignoring Plato's jocular animadversions on uncontrolled poetics. By disavowing a theory he has already presented in full, however, he ends up, like the reluctant referee, "affirming nothing" and forcing us to decide on our own. Sidney's own tolerance, even love, for contradictions and complementary ideas manifests itself everywhere in his works, but here, as always, he leans toward an ethical solution.

In the peroration, when the rhetor lightly spoofs the Florentine neo-Platonic Landino for believing that poets are "so beloved of the gods that whatsoever they write proceeds of a divine fury" (121), the rhetor's main objection to the theory of inspiration rests on moral grounds. Whether or not Plato ever sincerely presents a theory of inspiration, that idea posits a poet with no will of his or her own. Divine *efflatus* involves no more self-control than automatic writing. The gods speak through a "will-less" intermediary. Sidney's rhetor cannot accept the concept of a poet without free choice any more than Sidney could accept a Calvinist reading of human predestination at the expense of freedom of will. Therefore, in the midst of his panegyric on the inspired poet he remarks that our "erected wit maketh us know what perfection is, and yet our infected will keepeth us from reaching unto it" (79). If there were no remedy, he would never have broached the problem, and his solution, paradoxical in form, emphasizes the essential morality of poetic production, whether we see it as controlled prophecy, or as unfantastic mirroring of human nature.

Plato's alternate theory of the poet, as a creator of true likenesses, comes from the *Sophist*, in which Plato's Socrates makes a distinction between icastic imitation of nature and fantastic imitation of mere wishful appearance or impression—of chimera. As with the concept of inspiration, Sidney returns to this theory several times, and he again leads us to an ethical conclusion. The first mention of the poet's mimetic function, as we have seen, is strategically located in the climax of his hyperbolic praise of the "inspired" poet's ability to create a "second nature." In distinguishing what the unfantastic imagination produces from the fantastic, the rhetor says that the true idea of the poet "is not wholly imaginative, as we are wont to say by them that build castles in the air" (79). If the poet mirrors, he must not create mimetic versions of agreeable fantasy. If he necessarily avoids the bog of particularity, he must also avoid the airy insubstantiality (and perhaps immorality) of impulsive wish-fulfillment, of "castles in the air."

The rhetor's solution leads him into espousing a concept of true mimesis as the creation of general or universal likenesses to life that are ultimately bound by their moral uses. Thus he brings about an uneasy marriage between Plato and Aristotle allowing the poet to be a true imitator of "universals" not of "particulars" or of pure "fantasy."

> But now may it be alleged that if this imagining of matters be so fit for the imagination, then must the historian needs surpass, who bringeth you images of true matters, such as indeed were done, and not such as fantastically or falsely may be suggested to have been done. Truly, Aristotle himself, in his discourse of poesy, plainly determineth this question,

saying that poetry . . . dealeth with καθόλου, that is to say, with the universal consideration, and the history with καθέκαστον, the particular. (87–88)

Like Plato's Socrates, Sidney's persona constantly forces the reader to consider moral and religious themes in his exposition. The universal in this passage connotes what causes good action as opposed to what causes bad or futile action. His sophistic rhetor immediately produces the prime popular example of bad action among Socrates's followers, Alcibiades, about whom "the particular only marks whether Alcibiades did, or suffered, this or that." Sidney's informed reader would know that the historical Alcibiades was a central problem for the readers of Plato, since this supposed capricious traitor to Athens and mutilator of sacred statues was taken to be evidence of the failure of Socrates to teach. Indeed Alcibiades's behavior became a major justification of Socrates's condemnation as a seducer of youth.

By mentioning the perhaps futile search for a historical Alcibiades, however, Sidney is also suggesting also his other image, the positive of the negative, the brilliant, ingenuous, and often misunderstood student of Socrates found in *The Symposium* and in *The Lives* of Plato's follower, Plutarch. Thus the rhetor indirectly fashions an example of a universal or general goodness in the "poetical" image of Alcibiades of Plato and Platonists, so like Xenophon's Cyrus who was supposedly designed by "fore-conceit" (79) to make Cyruses of his readers.

Sidney's rhetor is so concerned with defining the creation of likenesses in terms of ethical teaching that he may, when he actually comes to employ Plato's own words, find it necessary to perform outright obliteration of that philosopher's distinction between true and false imitation. Speaking of the abuse of poetry, he says: "For I will not deny but that man's wit may make poesy, which should be εἰκαστική (which some learned have defined: figuring forth good things), to be φανταστική (which doth, contrariwise, infect the fancy with unworthy objects)" (104). While I think Plato would also conclude that true likenesses lead us to the good and mere appearances to the bad, he would have arrived at that conclusion by means of a considerably more complex epistemological route. "Good" and "unworthy" things, here, more than "substantial" and "insubstantial," suggest morally beneficial or harmful images, what so centrally concerns Sidney's rhetor in his dialectical development of notions of the poet.

Hazard Adams, the great Kantean critic, has remarked that the apparent concept of radical creativity of the imagination or fancy in

Sidney's *Defence of Poetry* has only seemed "to anticipate a Romantic concept of the creative imagination," because such an idea would be "based on an epistemology unknown to Sidney and his contemporaries."[5] But Sidney's rhetor consistently uses the term "imagination" in his *Defence of Poetry* to indicate that genial capability—or, if you will, "compartment of the mind"—that apprehends as well as creates. Thus he speaks of the distinctions of the moral philosophers lying "dark before the imaginative and judging power" (86). Not unlike the early Romantics, he is trying to effect a reconciliation between the two Platonic definitions of the poet as prophet and as imitator of nature. It cannot be an accident that Sidney has his rhetor place in direct and obvious juxtaposition both theories of Plato, of whom, we hear, as we have seen, "the wiser a man is, the more just cause he shall find to have in admiration" (109).

As Erasmus will occasionally speak directly through his "inspired" simulacrum, Folly, shocking us into recognition of serious intent, I believe that in this rare moment we hear the cautious, habitually indirect voice of Sidney himself describing the appreciation of Plato's works as an achievement that must come with time. Normally we must go to the "fore-conceit" of the whole work, the idea and structure of the Platonic monologue, to find Sidney's authorial presence, but here he speaks directly to his actual audience for a vanishing moment, predictably only to return immediately to feverish sophistry, as we have seen, in adding: "especially since he attributeth unto poesy more than myself do, namely, to be a very inspiring of a divine force" (109). Shifting back into the self-ironic sophist suddenly, Sidney's persona shows us how to handle irony by pretending not to recognize it.

Sidney's rhetor closes his *Defence of Poetry* with a complex jest that includes a kind of critique of Neoplatonic—normally "white magical"—thought, as it makes that set of ideal concepts most gorgeous. The critique is not new to his defense. Earlier in the work, in order to resist the Platonic idea of poets, as Gosson put it, as "fathers of lies,"[6] he writes: "But the poet (as I said before) never affirmeth. The poet never maketh any circles about your imagination, to conjure you to believe for true what he writes" (102). With a seeming quibble that the poet "nothing affirms, and therefore never lieth" (102), he dismisses the concept that poetry purports to create likenesses, at least in some "particular" or "believable" way. On moral grounds, the poet never fully suspends his reader's disbelief just as he never entirely relinquishes his own will in the process of feigning. Sidney's persona has already rejected the concept of the poet as duplicator of facts in his debate with the putative historian. But while he is in the process of defining poetry as fiction, he is also disavowing the notion of the *vates*, the magical prophet, of Neoplatonic lore, who makes "circles about your imagination," who "conjures" like the black or white magician in a state of will-less prophetic effusion. The poet is the imaginative creator, in the likeness of his maker, of unfantastic fictions. He is neither pure imitator of nature nor pure prophet, but both, an inspired maker of likenesses or a mimetic inventor of fictions.

When we return, at the close, to the jester of the introduction, however, not surprisingly, we find the rhetor vigorously making circles about our imagination as he recalls his local purpose in the oration as genial seducer: "[S]ince, lastly, our tongue is most fit to honour poesy, and to be honoured by poesy; I conjure you all that have had the evil luck to read this ink-wasting toy of mine, even in the name of the nine Muses, no more to scorn the sacred mysteries of poesy" (120–21). Here, the self-ironic "praiser of passionate lyric" calls upon, "conjures," the Muses by name to do his "hocus pocus" but provocative bidding. The sisters nine are constrained to help initiate novices into the esoterica of poetry, which for the sonneteering rhetor, famously includes seduction of the ladies as we have seen. And Sidney, as always, allows his rhetor to expose his own folly. Commonsensical observations about poetry are systematically juxtaposed to the improbable imaginings of Neoplatonic lore in order to point up the extravagance of the latter in all their glory.

A sensible Aristotle, in claiming in the *Metaphysics* that poets were the treasurers of ancient religion, no doubt in their creation and memorization of hymns to the Gods, is sardonically juxtaposed to the Neoplatonic Bembo, who claims they introduced all civilization into the world—"first bringers-in of all civility"—an extreme claim that leads to allegorical exegesis of hieroglyphics and the evocation of a misty age of philosopher priests. Scaliger, who urges stronger "emotive" beneficial moral effect for readers of Virgil than of philosophers, Sidney's rhetor's claim throughout, is juxtaposed to the Neoplatonic Clauserus and his extremist argument that all knowledge "and *quid non?*" is veiled in Hesiod and Homer, an ancient truism that Plato himself ridiculed in the *Ion*. "*Quid non*" here serves as a warning to the reader to doubt such an all-inclusive claim, but the reader must also look beyond the shadow of sarcasm to a dearly held Neoplatonic ideal of developing readings of all radical creation, human and divine, nature and poetry. Sidney's rhetor finally juxtaposes his own sensible suggestion that poetry can be "written darkly," as Sidney conceals references to Queen Elizabeth and her politics in *Arcadia*, to Landino's claim that poetry proceeds from the divine fury of the author.

In fact, the rhetor maintains his comic effects at the expense of Neoplatonism to the last word of his *Defence of Poetry*, poking gentle fun at astrology, Egyptology, the search for audible heavenly harmony in the cosmos, and allegorical interpretation of the pagan myths. He curses you with clumsy sonneteering in love, and death without epitaphs, if "you be born so near the dull-making cataract of Nilus that you cannot hear the planet-like music of poetry; if you have so earth-creeping a mind that it cannot lift itself up to look at the sky of poetry, or rather, by a certain rustical disdain, will become such a mome as to be a Momus of poetry" (121). But all these popular enterprises of esoteric Neoplatonism remain magically intact. Their dazzle makes its way through the clutter of Sidney's sardonic mask.

As the praiser of poetry, Sidney has shown both his immersion in Platonism and his resistance to it. But even here on the edge of satire of Neoplatonism, his *persona*, as Erasmus's Folly did before, warns the reader to be wary of being led by the ears. Thus he says that he does not wish unto poetry-haters the "ass's ears of Midas,"[7] reminding us of the pricked up ears of Folly's audience. We mortals, like skill in poetry, "must not be drawn by the ears" but "gently led" (111). We need to be warned not to believe what we hear. Poetry is what Sidney has coaxed us to make of it. His fundamental quarrel with Plato concerns philosophy's inability to move the unwilling reader, as we will find in the next chapter. Neither the schoolmaster nor the philosopher with their penchant for leading by the ears can be depended upon to perform such an exoteric task, and Sidney's persona disavows such an intention even at the height of his theoretical exposition.

8
Retroactive Reading

The clearest doctrine to be derived form Sidney's *Defence of Poetry* concerns the poet's corrective, curative, and educational function, notably in tragedy where by means of "sweet violence," the poet stirs "the affects of admiration and commiseration" (96)—but that doctrine, of course, also applies to dramatic aspects of his *Defence of Poetry*. On several occasions, Sidney's rhetor returns to his argument about the exclusive ability of poetry—that is fictional narrative—to move the reader to virtue by means of a process that begins with delight, admiration and emulation and ends in painful instruction and self-commiseration.

What for Aristotle in *The Poetics* was a purgation of pity and fear in the audience, for Sidney, is a process of entrapment based on identification of the reader with relatively admirable characters and their words in difficult choices. I call this process "retroactive reading." Our "admiration" and identification with what are essentially authorial personae lead to our "commiseration." The reader is engaged by the flow of poetic narrative in a learning experience like life where assumptions about the fictive world impinge upon the cold fact of error and affectation. Once we realize we have, in a sense, been seduced by a mask, our medical cure has taken, and we must go back and reinterpret and reevaluate the experience.

As we have seen in his *Defence of Poetry* Sidney demands a special relationship with his reader. He is didactic but not directly so. We learn an ambiguous truth: that language and reality diverge—that we must be skeptical of the claims of words to contain truth. Sidney traps us into going back and realizing how we were fooled when we naively accepted as correct or comprehensive what we had heard from a limited central voice whose observations we shared. By means of reminding us in his *Defence of Poetry*, Sidney gives us an explanation of a strategy that he employs in the *Arcadia* and elsewhere in his works.

If, as in *Praise of Folly*, repetition validates an argument, one might ask why readers have not widely recognized Sidney's principle of fictive entrapment through identification. I believe, in part, he obscures his experiential notion of fiction's affects by the seemingly static implications of the visual terminology that Sidney's rhetor employs, a critical vocabulary that has tempted some recent readers[1] to overlook the emphasis on experience and process suggested by another set of terms for "motion" and "medicine."

One metaphor for learning, "seeing," seems to be in conflict with another, "moving" or another, "being cured" of error. The rhetor's critical vocabulary—reflecting then-current language of art criticism on the continent—sometimes seems entirely "visual." The terms, "perfect picture," "image," "possess the sight of," "illuminated," "figured forth," and, again, "picture" (85–86) are all used in a single passage of Sidney's *Defence of Poetry* to describe what is, in fact, the moving effect of poetry on the reader. Critical language growing out of appreciation of the dominant art form of every era—sculpture in fifth-century Hellas, painting in the Renaissance, music in the romantic age, architecture in the modern—tends to control the lexicon of the literary criticism of that period of time. Like "form" and "plastic" in Greek high criticism, "theme" and "motif" in the nineteenth century, "structure" and "tension" today, a set of visual terms invade the lexicon of Sidney's rhetor's critical statement about fiction, because painting resided, I argue, at the apex of Renaissance arts. Its criticism, in Vasari and others, had such a huge influence on the language of critics of all other liberal arts. Because of his "visual" terminology, we may be tempted to see Sidney's concept of the process of appreciation of poetry as no less static than our visual apprehension of an allegorical figure in a Neoplatonic composition of Veronese or Titian.

Paul Alpers has pointed out, however, that while "we ordinarily understand speaking picture to mean a picture that speaks . . . Sidney does not attribute to poetry any formal analogies with painting, nor does he think poetry is vivid because it renders the visual experience of external objects."[2] Fiction brings about psychological effects by sending the reader through difficult experiences whose ultimate lessons he will re-member in the way he recalls the lessons of actual existence. The creation of "many Cyruses" (79) of his readers is a psychological process best exemplified by our response to heroic narrative such as *The Aeneid,* in which a central figure enjoys our empathy, if not always our assent, in fearfully complex circumstances. Thus Sidney's rhetor suggests we actually re-member for ourselves Aeneas's own straits: "Only let Aeneas be worn in the tablet of your memory, how . . . in obeying God's commandment to leave Dido, though not only all passionate kindness, but even the human consideration of virtuous gratefulness, would have craved other of him" (98). The persona's extraordinary emphasis on the difficulty of Aeneas's choice shows Sidney's preoccupation with the moral effects of fiction. If the identification implied by wearing Aeneas in the tablet of our memory creates lively knowledge in us, it is in our experience of Aeneas's difficulties, not in static approval of his ultimate responsibility for immediate family and the household gods.

We begin by admiring Aeneas's recounting tales of Troy to an enamored Dido and her court but end up swallowing a bitter pill in the love and rejection of that queen, passionate love in general, and in her suicide that results in large part from Aeneas's familial and sacred imperatives. Wonder ends in remorse and self-pity. Remembering Aeneas's difficulties in our actual lives is produced by a learning process that is not ultimately pleasant, if rewarding. The "tablet" of the reader's memory has now written on it a terrible rejection of "passion," "kindness," "humanity," and "gratefulness," all in the name of fearfully civilized conformity to the demands of higher social responsibility. What began in admiration resolves itself in commiseration with Aeneas's choices and self-commiseration through our identification with him.

Because, for Sidney, poetic truth lies in such bitter discoveries, his rhetor resurrects the Lucretian image of sweetened medicine[3] to make his point. Poetry strategically entices the reader into "swallowing" truth, which suggests actually being moved to seek the good in one's own behavior. His rhetor, of course, implicitly attacks the philosopher and the historian as schoolmasters, like Rombus of *The Lady of May*, or the *canzoniere*'s schoolmarms, who frighten or bore auditors who are fundamentally unwilling to be good or wise, who refuse to be "led by the ears" in the name of the universal schoolchild's freedom to avoid education. Thus he says that poets must "delight, to move men to take that goodness in hand, which without delight they would fly as from a stranger" (81).

Later he remarks that if the truth had been "barely, that is to say philosophically, set out, they would swear they be brought to school again" (92), and they might become corrupted to the point of thinking "virtue a school name" (93). The rhetor's attack on historians and philosophers and their inability to move men to the good resembles the attacks of Folly and the orator in *Vanitie of the Arts* on the Schoolmen,[4] but Sidney, as always, has a purpose that transcends such bickering and rhetorical maneuver on the part of his defensive persona. Through repetition and increasing concision, he develops a theory of the ethical action of poetry or "delightful teaching" (81).

In his fullest statement, Sidney's rhetor says that readers "yet will be content to be delighted—which is all the good-fellow poet seemeth to promise—and so steal to see the form of goodness (which seen they cannot but love) ere themselves be aware, as if they took a medicine of cherries" (93). Medicine, as elsewhere, is a recurring image in Sidney's *Defence of Poetry,* once used in reference to doctors who lie when they administer poisons they claim are "good for sicknesses" (102) or when they "teach poison" (104), as we have seen. Here the poet is the truthful doctor. If bad medicine can kill a man, then the good medicine of poetry can move a man to virtuous action. The truth of good fiction is good medicine for moral ills.

Sidney's persona's unmetaphorical statement of the poet's goal is "moving to well-doing" (90). "Moving," like "nature" or "love," provides for the rhetor a fund of meanings. "Move" must have a larger significance than simply "affect emotionally," since the poet is portrayed as drawing, leading and medicining his reader. The word implies process, the action of entrapment of the reader through various rhetorical strategies, above all, through the narration itself. Sidney's two examples of the curative function of fiction serve to explain this strategy of corralling his readers—here two audiences who desperately need to be reminded of their identity, the plebeians of Rome in tumult and King David of Israel in love with his neighbor's wife, Bathsheba.

The first example of fiction's medicinal action is the parable of Menenius Agrippa, the telling of "mutinous conspiracy" (93) of the parts of the body against the belly that Shakespeare staged in *Coriolanus*. The plebeian auditors are amused by a seemingly harmless fable only to discover themselves identified with the foolish members of the body in revolt. Sidney describes the audience reaction in his recurrent medical terms: "This *applied by him wrought such effect* in the people, as I never read that only words brought forth but then *so sudden and so good an alteration;* for upon reasonable conditions a perfect reconcilement ensued" (93; italics mine). Thus he implies that the moment of discovery in the audience results from the teller directing the guilty party to the analogy between fiction and his present situation. In North's version of Plutarch's Livian passage, " 'Even so,' quoth he, 'O you, my masters and citizens of Rome, the reason is alike between the Senate and you.' "[5] The audience is not allowed to maintain a comfortable distance or detachment from this "sweetened" truth but is ultimately tricked into personal error through identification with the protesters.

Again Nathan's parable becomes the strongest medicine for his listener specifically at the moment that David discovers that the fiction is really about his own errors. David finds, in effect, that he is not only the audience, but also the protagonist of the tale, the greedy rich man who expropriated the tenant farmer's lamb, as he took Bathsheba from Uriah. After causing David to cry out with rage and condemn his counterpart in the tale, Nathan says to David, "thou art the man."[6] Thus King David and the plebeians are directly identified by the creator of the fable with its central characters in a way that demands retroactive reinterpretation of the whole tale. Their error of not recognizing the limitations of their social identity in civil disturbance and tyranny is being cured painfully.

The medicine has been swallowed, just as Sidney's child has been "brought to take most wholesome things by hiding them in such other as have a pleasant taste, which, if one should begin to tell them the nature of *aloes* or *rhabarbarum* they should receive, would sooner take their physic at their ears than at their mouth" (92). The rhetor's ostensibly irrational jest about audial consumption here puzzles his readers into another paradoxical truth about human tendency to folly. The melancholic child in his abhorrence of medicine would prefer to take the rhubarb anywhere but in the mouth, even in the two ears, but then the tale as told is a delightful medicine which is ingested through the ears, and greedily. Listening up, the child will "swallow" a sweet tale that contains a painful learning experience his lips would have certainly known to avoid for its "painful" taste.

Sidney, here as elsewhere, may treat story line as if it were a rhetorical maneuver, a means to teach rather than an essential matter, but it is the leading means of teaching resilience and virtue to our unwilling and restless souls, of medicining the sick psyche. Of course, an ironically undercut speech of praise or denigration can perform the same function, as we have seen, but less well, because it lacks the sweetness of fable and full-blown characterization.

David's and the plebeians' experience in hearing the stories of Nathan and Menenius Agrippa constitutes an audience's tribulations through identification with heroes and heroines of epic and romance that are, in Sidney's case, authorial personae. A cure is brought about by subterfuge that at some point is fully evident to the audience. The listeners or readers in their curiosity and pleasure or rage are abruptly caught in the quicksand of their identification with erring characters and their words. They are thus made aware of their own faults, but not as painfully or harmfully as might happen in actual life.

In one of his many jests in his *Defence of Poetry*, Sidney's rhetor retells the historical tale of the faithful servant of the Persian King Darius, Zopyrus,[7] who had his nose and ears cut off in order to pretend to be in disgrace with his master and so win the confidence of the Babylonian king, his ultimate victim. In opposition to this story,

Sidney's rhetor praises Xenophon's fictional version of the pretended deserter, now Cyrus's servant Abradatas, which did not include in its narration such extreme measures as facial disfiguration. The "poetical Zopyrus," Abradatas, in other words, did not have to maim himself. The rhetor asks enigmatically "why you do not as well learn it of Xenophon's fiction as of the other's verity; and truly so much the better, as you shall save your nose by the bargain" (89). The rhetor addresses us as "you" because the reader inevitably identifies with the protagonist of heroic tales.

Beyond the irrationality of the idea of losing your nose reading, Sidney implies that learning by fiction—the experience of art—rather than by fact—actual experience—is less dangerous to one's person. His picture of artists who, out of curiosity, go to war and lose the arms they need for painting, in the *Arcadia,* makes a similar point.[8] Sidney's belief in the medicine of didactic fiction is so strong that he puts it nearly on a par with the medicine of worldly experience, and it is safer for your well-being, because you can incorporate it in the tablet of your memory without suffering the inevitable maiming of actual life.

I have suggested that narrative in Sidney's concept of delightful teaching is merely one of an array of rhetorical maneuvers designed to entrap readers and move them medicinally to see a particular and memorable truth. A description or a speech can serve a similar function as parts of the fable. *Descriptio* and *oratio* in the tutelage of *narratio,* converge, for example, in the opening to the revised *Arcadia* to deliver to the reader both a celebration of and yet a subtle warning about Neoplatonic, pastoral and Petrarchan idealism. Here we are seduced by a voice delivering a panegyrical description of an Arcadian seashore, soothed by speeches of love-complaint by two Neoplatonic shepherds, then surprised by the sudden event of a half-drowned man arriving on shore and the brisk narrative of his rescue from the sea, then from attempted suicide.

All three aspects of this opening tale are, I believe, gently undercut by the irony of the protean narrator and the designer, Sidney's Chaucerian narrator. Warnings in the text appear and cause the reader to go back and discover the inherent dangers in contemplation, idealism, and lover's despair—indeed in affected contemplation—the first case being the reader's own delight in esoterica, which provides for us a kind of delightful bait or gilding of the rhubarb of truth. The reader is invited to concur and identify with what proves to be strained idealism, yet by the sudden ending of the scene we are sent back through the text for a corrected revision as prescribed in Sidney's theory of retroactive reading. In fact, we ingest truthful medicine without the authorial admonishment we would reject as if we had been sent back to school.

Nothing in Elizabethan literature is more "deliciously" esoteric than the pre-Socratic and Neoplatonic allusion in the opening moments of this work, and Sidney's narrative voice carefully maintains stentorian heights of style in its delivery: "It was in the time that the earth begins to put on her new aparrel against the approach of her lover, and that the sun, running a most even course, becomes an indifferent arbiter between the night and the day, when the hopeless shepherd Strephon was come to the sands which lie against the island of Cythera" (3).[9]

Sidney's new opening to the *Arcadia* comprises an announcement of the time in Elizabethan high style, rhetorically, as we have seen, what Puttenham called "*chronographia*, or the counterfait time." With his "earth" and "love," Sidney's narrator takes a middle road in mythic elaboration for the special purpose of preserving the announcement's semi-allegorical nature. The reference to "Cythera" suggests the birth of the goddess of Platonic love, Aphrodite Uranus or Cytherea rising from the severed genitals of her father Uranus, near that island. The love that she symbolizes forms the basis of the concept in Renaissance philosophy of Platonic love and its beneficial contemplative qualities and its invitation to abstraction from the world. At this moment, a distant narrator has enthralled us with delicious mythographic and iconographic suggestion, which, in a moment, will require our "retroactive reading."

In this passage, as elsewhere in *The New Arcadia*—and, to a lesser extent, in the *Old*—Sidney ran the risk of writing in prose poetry of such concentration it requires the attention called for by the most ironic and hyperbolic Elizabethan poetry. Prose narrative in *The New Arcadia* must be read over and over with the care one takes with Marlowe's poetry. To this day, this stylistic maneuver has lost Sidney potentially some of his best readers.[10] But his extraordinary adoption of poetic language in prose remains in keeping with his rhetor's insistence in his *Defence of Poetry* that poetry's essence is not verse. Employing an apparel image, his sonneteer persona says sardonically that

> indeed the greatest part of poets have apparelled their poetical inventions in that numbrous kind of writing which is called verse—indeed but apparelled, verse being but an ornament and no cause to poetry, since there have been many most excellent poets that never versified, and now swarm many versifiers that need never answer to the name of poets. (81)

Here the love-poet takes a swipe at his courtier rivals, like Oxford, who are characterized as collecting like flies or bees, but he also announces his admiration for prose poetry. As in Sallust's occasional reversion to dactylic hexameter, the moment must determine the style. Furthermore, as in the case of all his other "private" works, the *canzoniere*, his *Defence of Poetry*, and the two *Arcadia*s, we must imagine Sidney himself delivering his texts, adopting a rainbow of personae for his coterie of ladies in the bower at Wilton. At this early moment of *The New Arcadia*, for example, Sidney moves on to deliver two other peculiarly ironic and hyperbolic poetic voices.

The speeches of Strephon and Claius enhance our delight in contemplation of esoterica, while they gradually expose their own excess and inapplicability. While Strephon (writher) obviously suffers from unsettling "remembrance" of Urania—using the term on seven separate occasions—he, at least, has discovered a contemplative nirvana well above his shepherd peers described by him as "bemired in the trade of ordinary worldlings" (3). While he shows an ungenerous condescension towards his fellows "medicining their sick ewes" (3), such an attitude about mundane matters seems inevitable in one's search for that transcendental love that is antithetical to all earthly functions. Thus we, for the moment, may ignore subtle internal and authorial warnings about his apparent social self-exemption.

Bursting into tears over his memory of her departure, his fellow, Claius (weeper), takes up the panegyric of Urania in a Neoplatonic vein, reproaching Strephon for reckoning "up only our losses" (4) and describing, albeit haunted by her memory himself, the good effects on them of Urania's inner and outer beauty, notably their acquisition of occult learning, esoterica inevitably relished, at this point in the narrative, by Sidney's reader. For example, Claius's explanation of the occult art of mnemotechnics and the "theory of places"[11] suggests that love for Urania, indeed, has raised his thoughts "above the ordinary level of the world" (5). In fact, when he points out that Urania has "thrown reason upon our desires and, as it were, given eyes unto Cupid," he glosses his own icon: "Hath in any, but in her, love-fellowship maintained friendship between rivals, and beauty taught the beholders chastity" (5)? Only divine or Platonic love, symbolized by an unblinded Cupid, knows no jealousy among friends and bars consummation and physical desire. If Claius gives us warning of his fallibility at this moment, it results from his version of melancholy, that, like Strephon's, grows out of memory of Urania's physical presence, a sense of loss that is inevitable but perhaps not so Platonic.

At this moment, however, as he "was going on with his praises" (5), the narrator has made the reader fully inclined to accept only the positive and curative nature of Platonic love and pastoral idealism. Our pleasure in the rewards of their love is reinforced by delight in identifying occult allusions that are in large part authorial. In other words, the mythological referents of "Cythera" and the name "Urania" are not available to the shepherds. Claius cannot be made to recognize the significance of his own name. And although Strephon rises above his fellows and Claius explains an aspect of the art of memory and the concept of "eye-opening" love, the majestic authorial voice has been largely responsible for thrilling us with Neo platonic reference which provides the sweetening for Sidney's medicinal strategy.

Claius's complaint is then suddenly interrupted by the arrival on shore of the naked and unconscious young man. When the shepherds first approach Musidorus's body, the narrator comments "they found his hands (as it should appear, constanter friends to his life than his memory) fast griping upon the edge of a square small coffer which lay all under his breast" (5). In effect, Musidorus's hands, in grasping the coffer for flotation, are countermanding a suicidal order from a brain infected by memory. We immediately refer to the "memories of Urania" that drive our melancholic shepherds to despair. Sidney's Chaucerian narrator suggests, quite positively that the life-organism does not listen to the brain in this "unnatural fray" (6).

The problem of suicide is a central one in the *Arcadia*, finding a dramatic culmination in Pyrocles's attempted suicide in Act V of *The Old Arcadia* and in Amphialus's attempt in the Third Book of the *New*. Sidney's narration connects its source with a sense (in this case, premature) of the sundering of an intense relationship, specifically with the memory of one's lost fellow in that relationship. Aggravated sense of loss which we have already seen in the shepherd's remembrance of Urania's departure causes an idealistic view of the partner and former times altogether, which invites self-destruction. This suicidal near-corpse arriving on the shore parodies their own plight.

At this spectacle, the shepherds overcome what reservations they may have had about "medicining" sheep or humans and run to apply first aid. The Chaucerian persona of the narrator delivers artificial respiration in a particularly earthy manner, "lifting his feet above his head, making a great deale of salt water to come out of his mouth, they laid him upon some of their garments and fell to rub and chafe him till they brought him to recover both breath the servant, and warmth the companion, of living" (6). This image of the shepherds' response to the arrival of a drowning man on the beach jars us.[12] The narrator's words undercut the abstracting melancholy of Strephon and Claius. In fact, at the scene's close, we find the contemplative shepherds consoling Musidorus for the loss of Pyrocles—we guess in unison—in homely terms—in diction and syntax—from the shepherd's life: he might be "as one that had lamented the death of his sheep, should after know they were but strayed, would receive pleasure, though readily he knew not where to find them" (9).

Ben Jonson once remarked that all Sidney's characters "speak as well as himself."[13] As in this case, I think he means less that they speak alike than that they continually communicate their personae in a better-than-average manner. Here the shepherds' emotional concern as well as their true plainness are admirably encoded in their words without use of Jonsonian dialect, catachresis, or silence. Sidney thus avoids caricature in his criticism of these voices. Unlike Jonson, he is not a satirist, *per se*.

The two shepherds are poorly rewarded for their sympathy and efforts:

> They therefore continued on their charitable office until, his spirits being well returned, he, without so much as thanking them for their pains, gate up; and looking round about to the uttermost limits of his sight [as the shepherd, Strephon, is first seen "casting his eyes to the isleward" (3)], and crying upon the name of *Pyrocles* [as Strephon upon the name of Urania], nor seeing nor hearing cause of comfort, 'What,' said he, "and shall Musidorus live after Pyrocles?' Therewithal he offered wilfully to cast destruction and himself again into the sea. (6)

Sidney's narrator then makes clear that the shepherds comprehend the lesson that a life-organism naturally refuses to self-destruct no matter what the memory dictates from the brain. Thus the persona remarks that this was "a strange sight to the shepherds, to whom it seemed that before, *being in appearance dead had yet saved his life,* and now, coming to his life should be a cause to procure his death!" (6) (italics mine). The shepherds pull "him back (then too feeble for them)" and "by force stickled that unnatural fray" (6). What Sidney has "argued" fictionally is that body and soul naturally reject any activity of the brain that denies the function of body and soul. The healthy organism rejects cerebral suicidal orders like those germinating in the shepherds' and now Musidorus's brain. After this second rescue, Strephon and Claius vigorously affirm the principle of social function, as they had once gloried in rising above their earthy professional duty in contemplation of their love for Urania. They are converted to their social function by Musidorus's near-suicide. When Musidorus challenges their natural prerogative to medicine his "dis-ease"—"what such right have you in me as not to suffer me to do with myself what I list?"—becoming "the more tenderhearted towards him" on the score of hearing him speak their native Greek, they reply that they were "bound by course of humanity to prevent so great a mischief." Yet they had nearly forgotten that "course of humanity" in their own indulgence in memories of Urania.

Sidney has here presented contemplation of beauty and its purported loss in simultaneously positive and negative aspects. At first we read what seems to be a round justification of contemplation of the lost beloved as a rung on Plato's Socrates's ladder leading to purer and purer forms of transcendental meditation culminating in apprehension of the oneness of it all. On the other hand, with the spectacle of Musidorus's attempted suicide in the brine—as Strephon seemed to be drowning in his own tears—we see such contemplation of beauty as a mortal disease—though a glorious one—whose symptoms are alienation from the world and self-destruction. Sidney is no neutral joiner of contraries here. We are actually provided with a positive, new, and synthetic attitude toward a mind infected by memory of an absent beloved.

No concept is more important than that of recollection, memory, or remembrance in this passage, and no concept takes on such radical new meaning after our experience of reversal in the flow of the text. Like all of Sidney's messages, I argue, this strategy reflects the policies of the Elizabethan censors, but it also conveys universal medicine for psychic imbalance. Having assumed that memories of Urania provided the right road to contemplation, we find that they cause distraction from social purpose and disorienting isolation from the world. Strephon has already admitted as much. In his first words, he said: "hither we are now come to pay the rent for which we are so called unto by over-busy remembrance—remembrance, restless remembrance, which claims not only this duty of us but, for it, will have us forget ourselves" (3). Not only does remembrance paradoxically cause the shepherds to forget shepherding, and their rank or position of shepherd, but, as Strephon soon points out, it, sadly, does not "grant us any holiday either for pastime or devotion, nay, either for necessary food or natural rest" (3). We connect Platonic love here with melancholic distraction rather than positive abstraction from the world. Such idealism invites suicide. As readers, we ingest, against our will, rhubarb to cure our own melancholy. In our "retroactive reading," we discover our joy in passionate idealism has been consistently undercut by means of a gentle ironic exposure of foibles and logical vagaries within the speeches themselves. This irony, barely visible on the first reading, now seems a consistent coding of the words in Sidney's complex "sweet" entrapment, and his "moving" and "medicining" of the reader.

A mild logical problem appears, for example, in reference to the art of memory and the permanence of places which cause it to function.[14] Strephon's complaint about his compulsion to return to the shore opposite Cythera has specifically to do with a sandy place. With all their erudition about the function of places in the art of memory, Strephon and Claius suggest specific locations on the shore that are proverbially delible: Urania's footprints in the sand. Thus in the midst of his "division" of the shoreline, Strephon extravagantly berates his fellows for leaving "those steps unkissed wherein Urania printed the farewell of all beauty" (3). And Claius asks how "we can miss such fancies when we see any place made happy by her treading" (4). Memory is based on slipping and sliding and obliteration of footprints on a beach. Such obsessive remembrance easily becomes suicidal remorse. Other foibles appear in the complaints.

Strephon may be a "writher" because he is excessive in his melancholy and his joy. Sidney's narrator introduces him, as we have seen, as "the hopeless shepherd Strephon" (3). He is without hope, but he is also "hopeless" at shepherding for the moment. Alliteration on "d" sounds toll out the euphoric and depressive extremes of his suicidal love melancholy: "where, viewing the place with a heavy kind of delight . . . and setting first down in his darkened countenance a doleful copy of what he would speak." His language is extreme in its repetition, for example, of the word "remembrance" which rings, like a bell, seven times throughout his speech. And he is excessive both in his contempt of the ordinary and in his idealization of Urania. Urania, as we discover when we first meet her in a portrait myopically "medicining" an injured lamb, is a mistress who walks on the ground. She is both an ordinary young woman in clothes and in occupation and yet very attractive:

> But the next picture made the mouth give place to their eyes.
> It was of a young maid which sate pulling out a thorn out of a lamb's foot, with her look so attentive upon it, as if that little foot could have been the circle of her thoughts; her apparel so poor as it had nothing but the inside to adorn it, a sheephook lying by her, with a bottle upon it. But with all that poverty, beauty played the prince, and commanded as many hearts as the greatest queen there did. (97)

Urania's sensual charm, however, is not merely registered by reference to the mouth-closing eye-opening courtly company attending a beauty show of eleven "painted" ladies, and in the authorial observation that her body adorned her dress. It colors Strephon's language. Strephon exposes his frustrated desire for Urania in "amorous" fallacy. He remarks, for example, "Yonder, my Claius, Urania lighted. The very horse, methought, bewailed to be so disburdened" (4).

Do horses lament relief from human weight? Strephon, however, might well bewail such disburdening in his own fantasy. His joy suggests to him an image of personified elements boisterously parading their love for her, when "the winds whistled and the seas danced for joy, how the sails did swell with pride, and all because they had Urania" (4). But for Strephon there is good reason for such rhetorical "inspiration": He is not merely hyperbolic; his desire, like Astrophil's, as we have seen is being transferred to nature at large in all this whistling, stamping, and swelling.

Strephon is a "hopeless" shepherd in part because he has forgotten his identity as shepherd and his joy in shepherding, his profession, yet also he has lost himself in melancholic obsession with the departed Urania. What such love lent him and Claius was a taste for the life of contemplation, which was not properly theirs. It belonged to the "great clerks" who, Claius later claims, with the delighted magnification of a double negative, "do not disdain our conference" (5). This desire for erudition of course subtly matches the reader's own taste for occult reference. Thus when Claius speaks, the reader inevitably falls in with his "sheepcote" imagery.

In speaking of how memory is a "racking steward," Claius states, "As well may sheep forget to fear when they spy wolves as we can miss such fancies." This is a conventional image, a time-honored pastoral trope. But that memories of Urania resemble murderous wolves contains a subtle warning about mortal obsessions. Furthermore, the simile suggests a comparison of Strephon and Claius to quite vulnerable sheep, the object of the trade Strephon and Claius are rejecting in favor of Neoplatonic philosophy. Claius says: "Certainly as her eyelids are more pleasant to behold than two white kids climbing up a fair tree and browsing on his tenderest branches" (7). Sidney is, by way of Claius, trying his hand at one of the most elaborate and hyperbolic traditions of lyric—dating back to *Song of Solomon* and beyond—with results that have seemed to most readers a classic of extravagance of allusion. But Sidney's persona subtly exaggerates in ways that lay bare a "medicinal" paradox for his reader.

Claius never escapes his rejected ordinary shepherding in rhetorical flight. He registers his attraction to Urania's blinking eyelids, but the matter of his hyperbolic imagery grows out of herding, his actual but almost denied profession. Thus we are warned that we can never escape ourselves and our surroundings. When we hear, "The two white kids climbing up a fair tree," we pause at the words "fair tree" because their source is ambiguous. Is not "fair" more the kid's thought than Cláius's? The tree is "fair" because it looks like food. The affective adjective in this image refers to an animal's consciousness, and the implicit comparison of Claius to beast points more to the demands of his body than his enraptured soul. Of course, shepherds should identify with their sheep in order to know animal husbandry.

Claius goes on to state "no more all that our eyes can see of her (though when they have seen her, what else they shall ever see is but dry stubble after clover's grass)" (5). Is not Claius now seeing her through the eyes of his hungry goat? Herders should look for greener pastures for their flocks, but perhaps with less immediate delight. His eyes have become hungry goats. If mistakenly read in earnest, such an image can even confuse a reader as shrewd as William Hazlitt. For the bathos belongs directly to the persona, Claius, and the humor to the ironist Sidney who has adopted the ulterior didactic purpose of forcing us into "retroactive reading." Claius is sensually taken with Urania, and his hyperbole deflates or implodes only gradually. Through affectation of love's idealism, Claius is made to expose gently his own desires and foibles. And he takes us with him by design.

Claius goes on, "no more all that our eyes can see of her . . . is to be matched with the flock of unspeakable virtues laid up delightfully in that best-builded fold." In comparing the structure of her body to a best-builded fold, Claius delights us with a homely, pastoral image for Urania's body. But though he insists that Urania has raised his thoughts "above the ordinary level of the world" (5), he remains, it would appear, on a lower rung of the ladder of love. Furthermore, his inflated language returns to sheepcote imagery that reflects his immediate functions and surroundings and the actual vocation he insists on denying. In our identification with Claius, we accept the conventional pastoral imagery only to discover that Sidney has been subtly parodying the uses of such imagery—as well as glorying in it—and having it betray our idealistic shepherd's actuality-bound imagination and denied sexual longing. Such imagery recreates a glorious and time-honored pastoral poetic ideal, one that returns to haunt us in the words of Shakespeare's melancholic Orsino; and Claius is another authorial persona.

As in his gentle parody of generally sound euphuistic moralism in Philanax's speech, or of book-learned sonneteering in the witty poem dedicated to Mopsa, Sidney causes the reader at some point to question the rhetoric of affectation in characters who have our undivided attention because their energy is genuine, their goals solid ones, and their voices seductive and highly communicative. Here we cannot ultimately reject Claius's sexual desire on moral grounds. Such longing is perhaps the controlling fact of life in *Arcadia*. Read pictorially, *Arcadia* is an invitation to sexual abandon. Claius's gentle fault lies in his subtle straining, his failure to recognize the place of his own desire and profession in his magnificent Neoplatonic and pastoral rhetoric. The reader, in discovering this inconsistency, enjoys as elsewhere a "medicinal" realization of the glory and abuse of idealism and modes of rhetoric in "retroactive reading." Claius's speech has entrapped readers in the splendor of idealism, and then released them to enjoy the ineffable humor and interior criticism the author has designed.

Through the subterfuge of adopting personae of narrator and character, Sidney requires us at some moment of discovery to retrace our steps through the delightful mire of seductive rhetoric, and Sidney's own theory of fiction in his *Defence of Poetry* supports this concept. We cannot achieve this reading if we see Sidney as a creator of set-pieces and exemplary characters. In fact, a reader's detachment or discontinuous movement through the text will frustrate Sidney's strategy. If we do not approximate the experience of his words being read aloud in an imaginary bower at Wilton, the honey at its surface may be our only sustenance, and we may be thereby "diverted" from an understanding of the text—our identity in the balance.

9
The "Unflattering Glass": Sir Fulke Greville's Theory of Reader Identification and Sidney's *Arcadia*

While Fulke Greville composed the later named *Life of Sir Philip Sidney*—probably between 1610 and 1612—on the model of a protestant saint's life of Sidney and a eulogy of Elizabeth used to criticize his supposedly fallen Jacobean age, the prayer book rhythms of his simultaneous panegyric and dirge also convey an urgent message about human identity and the function of Sidney's narrative. Greville says he will speak of his untarnished Elizabethan times "as men might easily discern in them (as unflattering glasses)" (7)[1] a picture of their own, but nonetheless implies that all artful narrative—like his pseudobiography itself—presents the reader with a mirror designed to disturb the "judicious reader's" sense of well-being.

Art mirrors us—like an unflattering glass—in a peculiarly didactic way, thus fashioning our goodness. The recognition of a disturbed reflection of ourselves in the world of the 1590 *Arcadia* produces virtue, according to Greville, by a complex process that I will discuss and show in examples from books 1 and 2.

When Greville speaks of Sidney's fiction, he points out two central and linking ideas about its action: It tells a story of momentarily characterless readers. Thus it reflects the image of the sick soul or "infected will" (79) in narrative action. This procedure requires a peculiar set of authorial masks. First he shows Sidney presenting, in the *Arcadia*, characters who suffer loss of identity in severe political circumstances, love relationships or ordinary social intercourse. Then he pictures Sidney beckoning his readers to lose themselves in identification with those characters.

In other words, we in the audience are made to experience life-like tribulations travelling through a labyrinth where we lose a handle on ourselves, by means of our undifferentiation, our melting into a sense of identity with fiction's would-be heroes and heroines, who, in fact, are experiencing themselves the disease of self-loss. Unlike the witch's glass of folklore, this mirror does not flatter on command. In effect, it disturbs us by picturing our own instability and insecurity, by holding up to us models of inner turmoil as our reflections.

Greville, in the context of Sidney's fable, for example, presents Basilius's loss of identity as ruler as the fundamental cause of chaos in Arcadia. He argues that Basilius's self-deposition is no harmless exchanging of roles, but a positive transformation of man into a dangerously double monster. He says that the Arcadian monarch's action is the product of "playing" with his "own visions" (8), cured only when he returns in the far future from his "dreams of humour" (10). What is the basis of those visions or dreams of humor but Basilius's notion that the king does not have a rank or position in society and family but is beyond all social obligation? He can, in those fantasies for himself, become whatever he chooses. Therefore, under the strain of the severe political circumstance of an apparent threat to the royal family's security (the prophecy), he allows himself to lapse into desiring for himself the contemplative life of shepherds. He feels he can "envision" himself out of a publicly active kingship, and the reader follows Basilius into a trap.

The ruler's self-exemption from office applies to Elizabeth's supposed moments of semi-retirement[2] as well as the Spanish king's tendency to retreat at sixty-three into a monastery, but Greville suggests that Sidney uses his characterization of the persona of Basilius largely for a more universal purpose.[3] Royal withdrawal from rank or position does not create a chain of command without a top: it creates levelling. Greville says Basilius can never succeed in his self-metamorphosis into shepherd; thus he becomes a monstrous *concordia discors* "to be justly censured as a princely shepherd or shepherdish king" (9), a nonruler creating a vacuum of power that brings about political disorders at home and abroad. He is living out, with his reader, the state's most dangerous Platonic fantasy.

Greville, therefore, presents his discussion of Basilius's struggles with his own identity from the point of view of the audience's own experience of his tribulations. He states that Sidney

> shows the judicious reader how he may be nourished in the delicacy of his own judgement.
>
> For instance, may not the most refined spirits, in the scope of these dead images (even as they are now), find that when sovereign princes, to play with their own visions, will put off public action, which is the splendour of majesty, and unactively charge the managing of their greatest affairs upon the second-hand faith and diligence of deputies—may they

The "Unflattering Glass" 147

not (I say) understand that even then they bury themselves and their estates in a cloud of contempt, and under it both encourage and shadow the conspiracies of ambitious subalterns to their false ends, I mean the ruin of states and princes? (8)

His view of the ruin that comes about when a sense of rank is lost suggests an elementary disease in the human political animal. Greville develops a picture that, in an unflattering way, reflects the image of his judicious readers ("most refined spirits") for their better understanding. These "refined" readers live in the "scope of these dead images." They will learn by experience how political disruption is "shadowed"—sheltered and screened from view—by self-burial at the top. In this case, Greville presents Sidney's persona, Basilius, as the means of an odd conversion in his audience. Readers must catch Basilius's disease of self-loss through fiction's inoculation in order to regenerate themselves. One must come down with a little of the disease to be rendered immune to the present contagion.

Greville continually hints at how the reader is made to absorb such wisdom. One regenerates oneself through a willing suspension of one's sense of difference from fiction's heroes and heroines. Reflecting Sidney's own dissatisfaction with pure philosophical statement in his *Defence of Poetry*, Greville remarks that "his [Sidney's] intent and scope was to turn the barren philosophy precepts into pregnant images of life" (10). If preceptorial wisdom proves barren in relationship to its audience, fecund images impregnate the largest possible audience with virtue through fictive narrations that are fables of self-loss. Greville is certainly in tune with Sidney's exoteric aims when he suggests that the end of such a poetical work is not "vanishing pleasure alone, but moral images and examples, as directing threads, to guide every man through the confused labyrinth of his own desires and life" (134). Greville apparently sees the work of fiction as effectively guiding all readers, like Ariadne's thread, through a maze of desire, which suggests the false turns and no exits of a middling hero or heroine in the circumstances of a confused sense of self. Sidney's fiction then becomes, for Greville, a model for life.

What is the process, however, of conveying that version of life to the reader? Greville orients his approach to this problem from the point of view of audience response and a peculiar travelling metaphor. On three occasions he defines the artist's recipient. He is, as we have seen, the "judicious reader" who is "nourished in the delicacy of his own judgement" (8). Or he is the "ingenious reader" enjoying "pleasant and profitable diversity both of flowers and fruits" (10). Or he is the "advised reader" who would have enjoyed a larger "field" to "walk in," had Sidney lived to complete his work (10). We must "walk in," or travel with the hero through his own difficulties. Greville suggests we actively suffer with the protagonist, "vicissitudes of sedition, faction, succession, confederacies, plantations, with all other errors or alterations in public affairs" (10).

"Vicissitudes" is a central word in Greville's *Life of Sidney*—as are "error" and "erring"—naturally, because his work narrates Sidney's own difficulties, Elizabeth's, and also those of the self-announced friend of Sidney who outlived him for at least another generation of extreme political turmoil. Greville's version of Sidney becomes an exemplar, suffering as a genius not "possessed of any fit stage for eminence to act upon" (24); and Greville paints his own self as curiously out of synchrony with the Jacobean age in which he prospered. This pseudohistorical work—with its admittedly panegyric design—implies reiterate struggle with the vicissitudes of a sense of self-loss in both its inherently admirable male figures, if not in its heroine, the incomparable Virgin Queen. But in the specific context of his discussion, *Arcadia,* what are these specific "vicissitudes" but those suffered by Basilius—and Sidney's reader—on the king's becoming a princely shepherd or shepherdish king? They consist of: Cecropia's sedition; the rebels' faction; Philanax's real and Amphialus's would-be succession; the confederacy of Cecropia, Artesia, Clinias, Anaxius, and others; and the enemy "colony" in Amphialus's island "plantation" in the incomplete book 3.

Employing an image of wheels cutting into terrain, Greville introduces his own work with reasons for escaping into the "safe memory of dead men": "The difference which I have found between times, and consequently the changes of life into which their natural vicissitudes do violently carry men, as they have made deep furrows of impressions into my heart, so the same heavy wheels cause me to retire my thoughts from free traffic with the world" (3). Greville suggests that through his own art, readers can prepare themselves for experience of the world without the damage of cutting furrows in their souls. Such experience comes through emulation of the Sidney of his own artifact, *A Dedication to Sir Philip Sidney,* so that readers might better "row and steer their course in his [Sidney's] wake" (22).

Greville, therefore, revives the Dantesque image of the soul as a ship in his description of Sidney's purpose in fiction. Greville states that Sidney's

> purpose was to limn out such exact pictures of every posture in the mind that any man, being forced in the strains of this life to pass through any straits or latitudes of good or ill fortune, might (as in a glass) see how to

set good countenance upon all the discountenances of adversity, and a stay upon the exorbitant smilings of chance. (11)

Through his mirror and travel images, Greville "poetically" argues that the fable of Sidney's "Arcadian romances" (8) does other than provide good and bad examples, as if pictorially. The reader, in his or her own success or failure with fortune, must be able to make immediate reference to the exact situation in the action, dialogue, or soliloquy of a central protagonist by means of memory in life's traffic.

In his hints at the psychology of teaching through heroes in a variety of plot situations, Greville is suggesting the foundations of English Renaissance narrative, to include *The Faerie Queene* and *Paradise Lost,* in which the reader is sent through the difficulties of "the state of favour, disfavour, prosperity, adversity, emulation, quarrel, undertaking, retiring, hospitality, travel and all other moods of private fortunes or misfortunes"[4] (10–11).

To experience a "mood" we must identify with the agent in the straits of an uncertain sense of self: with the princesses who, in their courtship, "descend from the inequality and reservedness of princely education" (8) thanks to Basilius's pastoral experiment, or with Musidorus and Pyrocles whose degree as princes is first disguised in alias, then lost in shepherd's clothing and Amazon's garb, respectively. The mirror image does not flatter us.

Greville's glass image recalls Sidney's own metaphor in his *Defence of Poetry* of the reader wearing Aeneas's difficulties in the tablet of his memory. The *tabula rasa* of our being is filled not only with the vicissitudes of experience, but those of our experience of others' experience in the form of fiction. We recognize ourselves in the mirror of fiction, and, as with actual experience, we wear that impression in our memories of the loss of identity of a whole sequence of protagonists in the *Arcadia,* "transformed in show, but more transformed in mind" (69).

Undifferentiation can arrive when kings and princes dress up as shepherds "to play with their own visions"; when shepherds "promote" themselves to the title of "clerks"; when shepherds take on the courtly duties of educating princesses; or when citizens take on tyrannical power in collective violence, thereby creating leveling at home and preparing the state for foreign intervention.

Greville, in fact, describes the destruction of the disguised monster, the "princely shepherd, or shepherdish king" in terms of ritual human sacrifice at the hands of the *vulgus mobile* and foreign interveners, arguing that such "creatures of scorn seldom fail to become fit sacrifices for home-born discontentments, or ambitious foreign spirits, to undertake and offer up" (9). The image of offering up the monstrous king Basilius for ritual sacrifice, the destruction of the hereditary monarch as *pharmakos*—in a sense, predicting his versions of the fate of Charles I—symbolizes for Greville the terminal stage of political decline. The initial stage of this decline is Basilius's "humor" in removing his "pomp and apparatus from king, crown and sceptre" (9)—the undisguised symbols of rank in title, garment, and emblem of office. But the reader's most acute models of undifferentiation are, for Greville, apparently, the princes and the princesses, and the queen Gynecia. Here the motive for dissolving one's difference is passionate love, not a desire for security and the false scent of monarchic freedom.

Greville's sole direct mention of the disguise of Musidorus comes at a moment in which he predicts the trial presided over by Evarchus that reestablishes order in Arcadia. Here he seems to know the ending to the *New Arcadia* (1593), though he immediately refers to the work as unfinished (10). In this trial scene, he describes the foreign ruler, "sitting in a cloudy seat of judgement to give sentence (under a masque[5] of shepherds) against his son, nephew, nieces (the immediate successors to that sceptre), and all accused and condemned of rape, parricide, adulteries or treasons by their own laws"(9). He connects the disguise of prince Musidorus (masque of shepherds) with the crimes or near-crimes that have been committed or imagined. Disguise frees one of social responsibility. As to Pyrocles's transvestite disguise, Greville only refers to "effeminate princes" (13). Here he suggests that Pyrocles's disguise as an Amazon lady has altered his sexual identity. He is made female.

On the transformation of the princesses, however, he is more specific. Basilius's experiment has made the ladies "fraily apt to change the commanding manners of princely birth into the degrading images of servile baseness" (9). Although they may be victims of Basilius's disguise as a shepherd, Greville clearly implies that the princesses have descended into not knowing who they are. And we experience their vicissitudes in "all other errors or alterations in public affairs . . . and all other moods of private fortunes or misfortunes" (10–11) with them. The quest for self leads to erring by character and reader alike.

Musidorus's Eyes

In Sidney's revised *Arcadia*, we discover the operation of Greville's theory of audience-identification with the hero's sense of self-loss when we travel through the narrative of Musidorus's attempted rescue of his friend Pyrocles, following his resuscitation. Sidney's persona, Musidorus, in his sense of self-loss, provides us with our vehicle of identification. In our experience of book 1 of the revised *Arcadia*, we gradually move from Strephon and Claius to this suicidal young man rescued from the sea. And our inevitable second look at the text makes this transition clear. Kenneth Myrick, in his analysis of the shipwreck scene of the first chapter, suggests that the point of view of the men approaching the wreckage is rigorously maintained. He says that in Sidney's narrative technique the reader is "constantly moving forward in the company of some one of the *dramatis personae*."6

In this case, as I have suggested, there is a gradual shift from the point of view of Strephon and Claius to that of Musidorus in the search for Pyrocles's body. The "eyes" of the reader are ultimately controlled by those of the more than anxious Musidorus searching the sea and approaching wreckage for his beloved friend's body. To reflect Mudidorus's morbid thoughts about a single, potential, "priceless" cadaver, the text provides us with many corpses: "amidst the precious things were a number of dead bodies" (7). The boat itself suggests a cadaver, "a ship, or rather the carcass of the ship, or rather some few bones of the carcass" (7). Through these images, we experience Musidorus's self-destructive grief in searching for what he wrongly suspects to be his friend's corpse, as he says, "far, far too precious a food for fishes" (7). In Greville's terms, Sidney guides us through the confused labyrinth of Musidorus's desire. Thus, by employing a "novelistic" or indirect third-person point of view, he allows his persona of the narrator to be subsumed by that of the melancholic Musidorus.

As readers, we set out in the fishing boat from the beach gently identified with the two shepherds. We share their point of view. When eyes are mentioned, it is "their" (that is, Strephon's and Claius's) eyes. Then we see portions of the bloody scene from all three pairs of eyes. Suddenly we shift our point of view away from the general position of the shepherds and Musidorus to Musidorus alone.

If we take all references to eyes and sight chronologically from their near approach to the "carcass of the ship" (7–9), we can hear the shift in orientation to Sidney's third *dramatis persona:* "their eyes were full masters of the object", "they saw a sight full of piteous strangeness"; "they saw the mast"; "they saw a young man"; "Musidorus saw"; "one of the sailors described a galley"; "he had nothing wherewith to accompany Pyrocles but his eyes"; "casting a long look that way, he saw the galley"; "he might well see them lift up the young man"; "he saw the galley"; and "but the fishermen made such speed into the haven that they absented his eyes from beholding the issue." The eyes are now established as those of Musidorus.

We experience Musidorus's disorienting discovery of the friend he idolizes, fully alive, followed by his second separation from him. The hyperbolic picture of Pyrocles belongs to Musidorus and the superstitious seamen ("they") who mistake him for an avenging god:

> But a little way off they saw the mast whose proud height now lay along, like a widow having lost her make, of whom she held her honour; but upon the mast they saw a young man (at least, if he were a man) bearing show of about eighteen years of age, who sate as on horseback, having nothing upon him but his shirt which, being wrought with blue silk and gold, had a kind of resemblence to the sea on which the sun then near his western home did shoot some of his beams. His hair, which the young men of Greece used to wear very long, was stirred up and down with the wind, which seemed to have a sport to play with it, as the sea had to kiss his feet; himself full of admirable beauty set forth by the strangeness both of his seat and gesture, for, holding his head up full of unmoved majesty, he held a sword aloft with his fair arm which often he waved about his crown as though he would threaten the world in that extremity. (7–8)

If the opening of this passage registers the surprise and wonder of the fishermen not that of Musidorus—"(at least, if he were a man) bearing a show of about eighteen years of age"—the hyperbolic picture of his beloved Pyrocles places us solidly in Musidorus's passionate consciousness. Sidney's persona, Musidorus, loses himself in his beloved friend, and we travel to self-loss with him.

When Hazlitt complains generally about "metaphysical conceits"[7] in this particular passage, he takes what presents to us Musidorus's joyous response at the sight of his beloved Pyrocles to be the mere extravagance of Sidney's supposedly detached and declamatory style. As we have seen, to exemplify Sidney's excess in this short passage, he cites the description of Pyrocles's hair: "stirred up and down with the wind, which seemed to have a sport to play with it, as the sea had to kiss his feet." But in this quotation the central word becomes "seemed" because such a conceit conveys to us Musidorus's hugely emotional response directly, even when the length of hair is related to Greek fashion. And our response is, at this moment and several succeeding ones, determined by his own.

As in Strephon's "amorous fallacy" in his description of Urania's embarkation, an animate wind and sea making love to Pyrocles's hair and feet constitutes Musidorus's poetic projection in prose of strong feeling and simultaneous self-loss. In his grief and idolatry Musidorus has forgotten himself, and we experience that loss of identity with him. He does mend, however, and we recover with him.

Sidney proceeds in the narrative with the consolations of Strephon and Claius and the famous description of the picturesque scenes of Arcadia "enamelled" with flowers—all from Musidorus's point of view. The narrator, by indirect discourse, filters the events to the reader through Musidorus's consciousness, even semiconsciousness as the case may be. For example, the shepherds' "speeches, though they had not a lively entrance to his senses shut up in sorrow, yet like one half asleep he took hold of much of the matters spoken unto him." (10). The reader in this moment hears through Musidorus's clouded auditory nerves.

As a result of Sidney's indirect point of view, we apprehend the world in reference to Musidorus's own five senses. Thus when he gains his first sight of the Arcadian landscape, the author reminds us that the scene "welcomed Musidorus' eyes (wearied with the wasted soil of Laconia) with delightful prospects" (10). And the meadows are "enamelled with all sorts of eye-pleasing flowers" (11). To effect the identification of the reader with Musidorus for the moment, detachment must be carefully reduced.

Hazlitt once complained about this passage that "we have meadows enamelled with all sorts of 'eye-pleasing flowers,' as if it were necessary to inform the reader that flowers pleased the eye, or as if they did not please any other sense."[8] It is easy to quibble with Hazlitt's word "informs" by thrusting in a version of Sidney's own dictum: "The poet never lieth for he never informeth." Hazlitt seems to be looking for external factual content here, when Sidney is engaging his reader in his fable by emphasizing how soothing Arcadian flowers are on the eyes of Musidorus, in such sharp comparison with the emotional and physical desolation of Laconia.

"Eye-pleasing," which occurs in the first description of Arcadian landscape, in fact, remains part of a strategy of identification that takes up most of book 1, from the end of Greville's chapter 1 through a major political discovery midway in the book, and later. Near the end of the book, Musidorus again becomes Sidney's central persona, as we have seen, as an "awry transformed traveller" announcing his loss of identity in the song, "Come, shepherd's weeds" (105). In this early moment, the reader is consistently required to see through Musidorus's uncertain eyes, and if his eyes wander, he is reminded by the narrator to return to the fold.

If we take this landscape description in the context of Musidorus's reawakening to the world of sense, we no longer have the paradisial landscape, supposedly unique to Arcadia, that Lindheim and other critics suggest, but what seems so to Musidorus. Lindheim says of this passage: "Here and elsewhere in landscape description, one finds Sidney's idea of perfection in its purest form, i.e., depictions of 'what should be' undiluted by shrewd observations of 'what is.'"

We should remember, however, that Musidorus himself later counters Pyrocles's similar description of the Arcadian countryside with the sardonic observation: "But I marvel at the excessive praises you give to this country. In truth, it is not unpleasant; but yet, if you would return into Macedon, you should see either many heavens, or find this no more than earthly. And even Tempe in my Thessalia . . . is nothing inferior unto it" (52). Clearly for Musidorus, this "heaven" exists strictly in the mending eye of the beholder who has returned gradually from the hell of a suicidal melancholy and a bleak land and seascape where, in a sense, he intended to identify himself with an imagined corpse. Arcadian landscape only provided him with a restless resting place in nature—a Virgilian, hardly a medieval, idealized *locus amoenus.*

The reader proceeds with Musidorus through discoveries provided by the kindly, over-curious Kalander, Philanax's abrupt and erratic letter of advice to the king, and the steward's sentimental and biased tale of Argalus and Parthenia. The epic battle with the Helots that follows contains a typical *anagnorisis,* in which we discover something about ourselves in the "unflattering mirror" of fiction.

In telling his tale of insurrection to Musidorus, the steward consistently describes the Helots in revolt as upstarts attacking the "gentlemen" of Lacedemonia. A servant establishes worth in his superiors by overemphasis. The tale is melodrama and the teller colors all references to the Helots with affective adjectives and descriptive terminology that load the case sentimentally in favor of the aristocrats in general and Clitophon in particular. For instance, because of the "hate those *peasants* conceived against all gentlemen," they devise "*cruel* death" for "the *poor* young gentleman" (26), Clitophon (italics mine). The circumstances surrounding Clitophon's capture by the Helots, however, do not warrant such simplism.

As a citizen of a neighboring state, Arcadia, as we later find out, Kalander's son was involved in irregular fighting, guerilla-style, on the side of invaders against the native Helots in a losing battle. The steward allows only that he "chanced to be at a battle" but in fact he could have been readily accused not only of being a mercenary in disguise but also a spy. But Clitophon remains the hero of the steward's tale, and Musidorus must identify with him.

After his capture, Clitophon remains alive, according to the steward again, only because the mysterious captain of the Helots (Pyrocles in disguise) "seemed to have a heart of a more manly pity than the rest" (26). By this time the reader and Musidorus must be certain how they feel about "the rest." The steward's *roman larmoyant* has held the floor for some time. The rest are dangerous revolutionaries against the estate of born gentlemen that commit, under the command of the villain of the piece, Demagoras, "divers the most outrageous villainies that a base multitude full of desperate revenge can imagine" (30). As if we might fail to make the "villainous" connection, the steward reminds us again that the Helots—that "base multitude"—are "villainously cruel" (33).

The word "villain" is inherently ambiguous in the Elizabethan era. Clearly the steward is using the term both in the neutral literal sense that denotes the level the Helots occupy in the social structure, and in the figurative sense, which has pejorative connotations of barbarity. Only at the climax of the scene, however, will readers be forced to interpret the connection between the two senses of "villain," as they go back and make new sense out of the passage. As with Sidney's emphasis on Musidorus's actual vision, I hardly feel Sidney overdoes such affective terminology. Its persistence provides the reader with an authorial warning about the steward's oblique rendering of the tale of Clitophon. Thus when Musidorus calls for his armor after the steward's tale, the reader has been made to desire with him the slaughter of those cruel, base, and villainous peasants.

Crossing the Laconian border, the Arcadian aristocrats, with Musidorus, nearly take by subterfuge a city held by the Helots. Piers Lewis, while arguing generally that Musidorus in heroic action fights to "right wrongs and accomplish wonders" literally and figuratively for the aristocracy, makes an exception of this "stratagem,"[10] which turns out to be a Ulyssean trick, what in Virgilian warfare would be called a *dolus*. For one, it confirms the lie that these Arcadians are allies of the Helots. It wears military disguise against all rules of war, and its argument is delivered by a Sinon figure: "a cunning fellow (so much the cunninger as that he could mask it under rudeness)" (35). But the force of the steward's biased rhetoric cannot have lost its effect on us, and we inevitably support Musidorus when he proceeds, pumped up with the adrenalin of blind martial idealism, to engage a villainous captain of the Helots in hand-to-hand combat.

When Musidorus's helmet is removed by his opponent, however, instead of taking advantage of the success of his assault, that opponent prostrates himself: "his chief enemy, instead of pursuing that advantage, kneeled down, offering to deliver the pommel of his sword in token of yielding" (38). The reader, with Musidorus, is confounded by this reversal, and the confusion is encoded in Sidney's jerky prose: "Palladius standing upon himself and misdoubting some craft, and the helots that were next their captain wavering between looking for some stratagem or fearing treason" (38). The recognition that the enemy captain is Pyrocles follows. "'What,' said the captain, 'hath Palladius forgotten the voice of Daiphantus?'" What has happened? Both Musidorus and the reader have swallowed a pill of instruction, but what is the discovery? In part it has to do with politics, in part with language and the rhetoric of melodrama.

We have travelled, as Greville suggested, through a double sense of self-loss. Naturally the steward's rhetoric has simplified the problem of the Helots. It is true they are cruel. Revolution is cruel. But we are shortly warned that the Lacedemonian gentlemen had been more than cruel. They had imposed bondage on a conquered race, and the Helots had taken up arms under duress. Life is more complicated than melodrama.

Sidney's readers often take him up as an apologist for his own specific class,[11] but the effect of this passage comprises a justification of the principles of the English constitution, the parliamentary system, and the common law, that Elizabeth and her propagandists made singular efforts to revere. Nor is it an example of unwary Platonic or Utopian idealism in politics. The case of the Laconian "gentlemen" and the Helot "villains" remind us of the Celts, Angles, and Saxons, under Norman rule, made much of by Spenser and other Elizabethan political poets like Samuel Daniel.

As in his *Defence of Poetry* when his rhetor defends the pastoral mode for presenting "the misery of people under hard lords or ravening soldiers," (94–95)[12] and scoffs at would-be conquerors who strive "who should be cock of this world's dunghill" (95), Sidney defends the underclass or classless as "shepherd-knight" and self-conscious rebel, but also as defender of the English political system that supposedly protected the rights of the downtrodden better than any other kingdom: certainly better, supposedly, than the Papal state, Spain, Portugal, France, and the metaphoric tyrannies, Persia and Russia. In this passage, Sidney forces his readers to travel through the labyrinth of prejudicial desire only to discover their own misplaced sense of sovereignty. Thus readers come to see their attitude toward disenfranchised "villains" in a mirror that condemns all such prejudice.

Only following the recognition of Pyrocles does the reader fully absorb the relative nobility of the cause of the Helots. A surprised Musidorus—and reader—learn of problems in creating a foolproof treaty to establish the formerly "villainous" Helots and Lacedonian "gentlemen" as equals. A political principle emerges: that conquered peoples have the right, if not the duty, to revolt. As so often in Sidney, however, the lesson also concerns man's fallen language. Do not believe what you hear until you have gauged the input. Language in the steward's melodrama was obscuring aspects of the truth from the speaker himself as well as from Musidorus and the reader. Since we follow Musidorus, we experience his own surprise. In the moment of discovery we swallow the rhubarb of truth. The reader goes back and reinterprets the steward's bias. Having identified with what he took for the right and with Clitophon's cause, Musidorus finds he is largely in the wrong, but for admirable reasons, and so do we. Fiction has mirrored us, but without magnification, for our benefit, and Sidney's procedure has trapped us into seeing how to look in an unflattering glass.

The Icon of Cupid

Stephen Greenblatt argues that book 2 of the *New Arcadia* contains lapses in direction precisely because Sidney constantly mixes modes. He says:

> There are moments—particularly in Book II of the revised *Arcadia*—when Sidney does not seem fully in control of the shifting genres, and the result is confusion and finally tedium. Moreover, the work continually risks losing the reader's sympathy and patience by constantly blocking and baffling his response: tragedy without purgation, comedy without laughter, romance without wish-fulfillment.[13]

I have noticed no lapse in skill, but I would like to test Greenblatt's theory in a special case of shifting genre from tragedy, to epyllion, to chivalric romance, where we "see" the audience in action. But first, not to quibble with Greenblatt's formulation, I would like to substitute "she" and "listener" for "he" and "reader."

In recent chapters, I have investigated a private Sidney consciously adopting personae to entertain and instruct a female audience. In the actual world, the location for this activity was normally the remarkable manorial home in Wilton belonging to Sidney's brother-in-law, William Herbert, Earl of Pembroke. There Sidney's younger sister, Mary, to whom he dedicated the *Arcadia,* and Philip entertained a largely female coterie on occasion that included, among others, Penelope Devereux Rich and Frances Walsingham, soon to be Sidney's sixteen-year-old bride. There he probably read his private works, adopting a voice for each character. To create a fictional version of such a bower of poetry, Sidney returns scores of times in the *Old* and *New Arcadias* to the notion of an arbor, a largely "feminine" location suggested, at times, both by a woman's coiffure and a formulaic *locus amoenus* conjoining the beauties of art and nature, a place for oral delivery of private poetry.[14]

In fact, the central bower of poetic-recitation in the land of *Arcadia* belongs to Sidney's persona, Pyrocles, the "awry transformed traveller" now in disguise as Zelmane the Amazon. This transvestite persona uses his dissimulation in order to enjoy the company of the ladies, even when they go swimming in the nude. Following this particular episode in book 2, "Zelmane" leads Philoclea, Pamela, and Miso into "her" bower of poetry to tell their tales of love and passion to the somewhat recalcitrant group of lady "readers."

When the narrator first describes this place—through Musidorus's puzzled consciousness—the connection between Zelmane's hair—the cover for her mind, so to speak—and the bower as cover for poetic activity, is made explicit. In Musidorus's view, "Well might he perceive the hanging of her hair in fairest quantity, in locks, some curled and some as it were forgotten, with such a careless care and an art so hiding art that she seemed she would lay them for a pattern, whether nature simply, or nature helped by cunning be the more excellent" (68). "Zelmane" disappears to sing her first song "Transformed in show, but more transformed in mind," in "a fine, close arbour. It was of trees whose branches so lovingly interlaced one the other that it could resist the strongest violence of eyesight" (69).

In both cases, under "female" hair and treetop, art joins nature in performing an aesthetic and practical function. Our fictional coterie of Zelmane, Pamela, Philoclea, Miso, and later, Mopsa, presents and responds to the natural and artificial dreams of love germinating in the heads of the ladies, each picturing a woman losing herself in passionate love. Three genres of erotic narrative make their appearance in an *agon* of feminine narration and critical response, but loss of control of these genres, I argue, belongs to the female personae, not their auther, Sidney.

Among the extraordinary set of stories within stories in book 2, often concerning a woman's loss of identity in love, therefore, we find Sidney drawing and redrawing the reader through a maze that symbolically represents separate generic versions of passionate love and its vicissitudes as told by a set of three female authorial personae. In our travels, we experience a sense of déjà vu because we remember similar events and images just told by another female voice. Our response is certainly "blocked" and "baffled" but for our own good. In each case the speaker brings her own bias to a tale of rejection of a father and adoption of a love, and each presents to her audience a suitable icon of love to match the nature of her tale.

At no point in the framed narrative of the *New Arcadia* are we made more aware of Sidney's manipulation of masks, nor of concepts of audience response, and the generic shifts show what they must say about love: love is psychic; love is emotional; love is physical. On descending levels of consciousness, Philoclea sends us through a tragedy of Petrarchan idealism and the barbaric terrorism that reflects its metaphoric violence. Pamela's keeper, Miso, travels with us through an ironic epyllion of Ovidian desire and possessive jealousy. Her daughter Mopsa sends us through a farce of a romance that reduces love to mere consumption, like the satisfaction of a desire for food, now available, now not.

Philoclea's seemingly impossible love (her "heterosexual" desire for what appears to be another woman, Zelmane) as well as her father's ineffectual interference in her love life, inform her recounting of the hopeless love of Tiridates and Plangus for Erona and Erona's unrequited passion for Antiphilus ("against love"), and perhaps even her revulsion at the idea of a provocative, adolescent, iconic Cupid. Philoclea's voice delivers an artful tale of thwarted love's consistent transformation into atrocity. Before she ends her narration with a reference to one of her own rhetorical maneuvers, she speaks of the kind of violence engendered by love that predicts her own ordeals in the captivity episode of book 3. As we experience Erona's and Philoclea's vicissitudes in love in this narrative, we never travel far from consideration of an icon of Eros (see figure) as a mischievous boy whose weapons are military hardware and whose very nature combines provocation with sexual immaturity.

From the first, Philoclea announces that her version of herself, Erona ("erronious in love") will be its tragic heroine—"chief subject of this discourse" (205)—(as the narrator of *Arcadia* asserts his whole "matter is intended" to Philoclea's "memory" [143]), and that she will, as fictive designer, pare down the embellishments of Plangus ("complainer"), who told his story "with more tears and exclamations than I list to spend about it" (205). The reader now travels through a tragic story of love with this "twinned" pair of princesses, one the narrator, the other the subject and protagonist, experiencing self-loss in passionate love.

Philoclea tells a tale of Cupid's revenge in which the Princess of Lycia, Erona, at nineteen—Philoclea's age—seeing her country "so much devoted to Cupid as that in every place his naked pictures and images were superstitiously adored" (205), suddenly objects to his

Piero della Francesca's *Blinded Cupid* is the adolescent version with formidable weaponry. (S. Francesco at Arezzo.)

worship. Why she reacts so violently (and sacrilegiously) to the icon of love as a naked boy, Philoclea cannot tell us for sure. She asserts that Erona "either moved thereunto by the esteeming that could be no godhead which could breed wickedness, or the shamefast consideration of such nakedness, procured so much of her father as utterly to pull down and deface all those statues and pictures" (205). Philoclea leads us into entertaining Erona's attack on an icon of sexual love either as the product of concern for public morals and spiritual health or the result of an abstemious or underdeveloped sexuality that automatically reacts to the mysteries of human gender and procreation with over-curiosity and iconclastic violence.

Often we are confronted, I think, in reading literature of Sidney's period,[15] with the relative warmth of Elizabethan reaction to static images that pose iconological puzzles to an audience. Here, Erona's reaction to the statue of a boyish figure as god of love puzzles both Philoclea and her reader. Is this idol objectionable because it elicits homoerotic as well as heterosexual response (certainly one of Philoclea's obsessions)? Is Eros inappropriate for Erona and Philoclea and the reader because, though he seems to personify sexual love, he lacks, as we have seen, sexual maturity (like Erona, Philoclea, and the hypothetical identified reader)? Since his gender classification remains imperfect, does he symbolize a dangerous mix like Zelmane "herself"? Furthermore, if he is a sacred entity, up to godlike mischief, might he use mortals as victims of his boyish sadism, thus confirming Plangus's own three-fold fear about icons of the makeup of the universe—that we are punished by capricious gods with "earthy" mortality, played with as balls to the stars, or prematurely "staged" in life as fools?

In Philoclea's narrative, Erona's destruction of Cupid's images leads, at least in the popular mind, to her violent downfall: "which how terribly he [Cupid] punished (for to that the Lycians impute it) quickly after appeared" (205). As in the ambiguity concerning Erona's motives for iconoclasm, we are forced to find our way to a satisfactory conclusion by recognizing our own slipping sense of identity—to include gender as well as sense of place in society—in passionate love. But is Eros, therefore, a deity or a natural confusion in our own psyches that we externalize in icons? At the height of her narrative, Philoclea formulates this puzzle when love has caused far more violence than destruction of sacred images. She asks in apostrophe whether: "Cupid be a god, or that the tyranny of our own thoughts seem as a god unto us" (207). Our narrator jars us by an aside that reflects Philoclea's own present predicament as well as Erona's within the narrative.

Philoclea's story of a daughter's rebellion against her father in a matter of love culminates in the transformation of love into acts of violence when the Armenian King Tiridates ("to cut in half") cuts "poems" into enemy subjects, that is, terrorism for love. The latent violence and self-violence of Petrarchan conceits is made literal. When her father dies of a broken heart, as she is arranging for her own marriage to Antiphilus ("against love"), Tiridates—"who desired her more than the joys of heaven" (205)—invades her kingdom in an act of war "made upon her, only for her person, towards whom, for her ruin, love had kindled his cruel hart" (206).

That love might inspire cruelty, certainly a mythographic convention suggested by Cupid's hardware, gains resonance when we find love's worshipper, Tiridates, transforming love's violence into fact.

Tiridates, according to Philoclea, was

> indeed[16] cruel and tyrannous; for being far too strong in the field, he spared not man, woman, and child, but (as though there could be found no foil to set forth the extremity of his love but extremity of hatred) wrote as it were the sonnets of his love in the blood, and tuned them in the cries, of her subjects. (206)

Philoclea's image of composing love poems in blood reflects her obsession with the dangers of passion—Tiridates and Cupid exert a single erotic tyranny—even when she is describing political events. She makes clear that frustrated love generates the worst sort of violence, one she discovers in her own heart. The notion of tuning sonnets "in the cries of her subjects" suggests, furthermore, as we have seen, the myth of the tyrant Phalaris of Agrigento's melodious roasting alive his sacrifice, this time from the point of view of the sadistic pleasure of the "inspired" unrequited lover. Our image of Cupid or Love or Eros as an active "kindler of cruel harts" confirms the notion of the naked and blinded boy as a "breeder of wickedness" and tyrant that Erona suspected.

After several intrigues, and Tiridates's violent death, Philoclea elegantly requests a pause in her narrative that demonstrates her natural bias as well as her art:

> "But now methinks, as I have read some poets, who when they intend to tell some horrible matter they bid men shun the hearing of it, so, if I do not desire you to stop your ears from me, yet may I well desire a breathing-time before I am to tell the execrable treason of Antiphilus that brought her to this misery; and withal wish you all, that from all mankind indeed you stop your ears. Oh most happy were we, if we did set our

The "Unflattering Glass" 163

loves one upon another!"—and as she spake that word, her cheeks in red letters writ more than her tongue did speak. (209–10)

Philoclea directly compares herself to the manipulating poet, here a creator of fictions where infidelity in love constitutes a greater crime than the savage acts of violence that have dominated her story. Philoclea has represented true love as fact, but then an aspect of reality that easily transforms passion's care into unspeakable grief, violence, and torture, the Petrarchan or tragic fact. Cupid is all psychic arrows and gaffs. Considering her own erotic torture, the written word of Philoclea's blush tells all.

Miso ("hate") intervenes to thwart Philoclea's attempt to have Pamela continue the story of Erona and delivers, in a cynical story of conflict of young women with their fathers over marriage, an Ovidian allegorical image of love to replace the Petrarchan Eros. Though her tale is broad comedy and not complimentary to its narrator, we suffer unflattering images of ourselves as we travel with her, because her view of human nature in love is both derogatory and recognizable.

Miso narrates autobiography in earthy style—thus, less in control of nature and art—beginning with self-praise and denigration of her husband: "and if my father had not played the hasty fool (it is no lie I tell you) I might have had another-gaines husband than Dametas. But let that pass, God amend him" (210). In an elaborate parody of Socrates's recounting, in the *Symposium,* Diotima's allegorical wisdom on the nature of love, Miso, at this odd banquet of ladies, delivers an icon of Cupid, an old woman gave her, that reduces the concept of true love into extramarital desire and pan-possessive urge, the essential Ovidian theme.

Because of her bias, Miso specifically rejects the Olympian icon of the blinded and naked pubescent boy and his arrows to the amazed company of Zelmane, Philoclea, and Pamela, now augmented by her daugher, Mopsa: "You are full of your tittle-tattling of Cupid: here is Cupid, and there is Cupid. I will tell you now what a good old woman told me, what an old wise man told her, what a great learned clerk told him, and gave it him in writing; and here I have it in my prayer-book" (210). Miso parodies not only Plato's triple framing of the *Symposium,* but also his religion of *eros,* in Miso's guarding her version of love's secrets in a "prayer-book," and "conferring"—no doubt, sexually—with her priest.

In Miso's allegorical image of love,

there was painted a foul fiend, I trow, for he had a pair of horns like a bull, his feet cloven, as many eyes upon his body as my grey mare hath dapples, and for all the world so placed. This monster sat like a hangman upon a pair of gallows. In his right hand he was painted holding a crown of laurel, in his left hand a purse of money; and out of his mouth hung a lace, of two fair pictures of a man and a woman; and such a countenance he showed, as if he would persuade folks by those allurements to come thither and be hanged. (211)

This icon, glossed by the lengthy poem she adds as an emblem, pictures "Love" as not "a naked god, young, blind, with arrows two" (212) but horned like a cuckold, with a thousand eyes, some alert like a jealous lover's, others lasciviously "winking wily shifts." Love is hooved like the devil, thus sinful, but takes uncertain steps like a goat and is as lustful as a goat from the bestiaries. He is armed with poetic flattery and money for bribery in order to lead his worshippers to suicide or execution. In the horrible case of such a painful, embarrassing, and costly god in the universe, one should get one's sex where one can, and, by all means, keep it casual.

As Miso narrates, her mother tells her: "this same is even love; therefore do what thou list with all those fellows, one after another, and it recks not much what they do to thee, so it be in secret. But, upon my charge, never love none of them" (211). Such a comic eulogy of free love, which she elaborates fictively in terms of her own promiscuous life—with a parodic glance at courtly secrecy—of course, reflects back on our narrator and her audience, but also ourselves in our emotional loss of identity in the grips of desire. Miso may lack Philoclea's wavering overview, and she depends on inelegant narrative devices such as affirmation ("it is no lie I tell you" [210]) and other long-winded maneuvers, but her version of sexual desire, while limiting and hateful, remains consistent and appealing to our "infected will." Though she loses herself in its presentation, she passes on to us, in our travels, its unflattering truth. A comically hideous monster ultimately beckoning us to suicide symbolizes the universal urge to promiscuity as an expression of pan-sexual imperialism without relationship. For to love in truth would destroy us all.

When the female audience has finished making "sport at the description and story of Cupid" (213), our third female narrator, Miso's daughter, Mopsa, wins a straw-vote, and proceeds to get so wrapped up in her ragged yarn that Philoclea feels she must cut her off and bribe her with her would-be future wedding gown to remain quiet. As when Chaucer's persona in the *Canterbury Tales* is cut off by the host in mid-romance, however, Sidney's authorial mask has led his audience through a medicinal journey, albeit puerile and partial.[17] Mopsa delivers her romance in mechanical style, again presenting a father's unhappy involvement in a daughter's love-life, but this time in an account whose central image is not provocation and violence, nor psychic lust, but mere eating, whose icon of Cupid, if we can be sure we have one, turns out to be a nut.

In a parody of love in the romances:

> "In time past," said she, "there was a king (the mightiest man in all his country), that had by his wife the fairest daughter that ever did eat pap. Now this king did keep a great house, that everybody might come and take their meat freely. So, one day, as his daughter was sitting in her window playing upon a harp, as sweet as any rose, and combing her head with a comb all of precious stones, there came in a knight into the court upon a goodly horse—one, hair of gold; and the other, of silver. And so, the knight, casting up his eyes to the window, did fall into such love with her that he grew not worth the bread he eat." (214)

Consuming "pap," "meat," and "bread" dominates the imaginative world of this third love poet in such a way as to fashion a notion of love as an appetitie parallel or inferior to hunger for food.

Our nameless heroine elopes with her Knight and thus she too escapes her father: "And so, in May, when all true hearts rejoice, they stale out of the castle, without staying so much as for their breakfast" (214). Mopsa's parataxis underscores her alimentary obsession, but her tale of love also conveys to us a new iconographic truth. As we experience our heroine's vicissitudes of love, we enjoy a parody of narrative formulae, while engraving on the tablet of our memory a disturbing image, quite apt, in its reductionist way, of love as a necessary physical appetite. In an elaborate parody of Apuleius's elegiac tale of Cupid and Psyche, Miso's nameless heroine loses her lover out of curiosity to hear his name, and he is replaced by what promises to be an endless sequence of mysterious nuts which must not be opened, until she is rudely cut off by Princess Philoclea. Carrying one nut, her heroine

> "went, and she went, and never rested the evening where she went in the morning, till she came to a second aunt; and she gave her another nut."
>
> "Now good Mopsa," said the sweet Philoclea, "I pray thee, at my request, keep this tale till my marriage-day, and I promise thee that the best gown I wear that day shall be thine." (214)

What has happened? The reader has been sent through three versions of loss of identity in love by Philoclea, Miso, and Mopsa—in tragedy, epyllion, and romance—which present three generic definitions of love: first, the emotive account of the Petrarchan violence of psychic passion delivered by Philoclea's conscious art; second, Miso's cynical account of her own love as Ovidian lust and pride of possession leading to the gallows, delivered with vainglory; third, Mopsa's implication of the connection of love and hunger for food in her uncontrolled narrative of what promises to be an endless series of similar events. Pamela takes up Erona's tale and is suitably interrupted by her father to complete the cycle in Zelmane's bower. To this reader, Sidney demonstrates overview and control of his shifting personae most notably in their bias that leads to shaky control of genres.

I find no loss of direction in the generic variety of these successive narratives, rather a picture of tales whose versions of love are determined by their genres and their biased speakers, and an unruly feminine audience that provides a comic version of the Countess of Pembroke's coterie at Wilton or Penshurst in Zelmane's "little arbour only reserved for her" (198). Serious issues in these tales have not been reduced to the absurd for us but have been invigorated by humor, and passed on by our identification with female narrators and heroines delivered to a female audience.

As in "Zelmane's" melodramatic tale of the original Zelmane, or the sequence of picaresque reports and encounters with Dido and Pamphilus, the female reader loses her identity in empathy with central heroines experiencing self-loss. The women of the narrative, within and without, have lost a handle on themselves in relation to love, and the reader has travelled with them even to considering the puzzling icons of love that, like Mopsa's magical nut, remain uncracked kernels of truth we should carry with us in our own travels in the domain of eros. As in Greville's theory of the unflattering glass of fiction, we have seen a little more of our unsteady selves than we might want.

10
The Irony of the *Eiron* and *Alazon*

In *Directions for Speech and Style* (1599?), John Hoskins warns us how to be wary of the voices and masks of the *New Arcadia*'s fallen characters and implied characters—to include the narrator—and of the work's parodic design. Thus he finds means to return continually to discussion and examples of a single "figure of thought," irony. On separate occasions, in his discussion of "catachresis," "intimation," "ironia" itself, "diminution," and "sententia," he examines aspects of irony, from sarcasm, to understatement "which exceedeth speech in silence,"[1] in the narration, description, direct, and indirect discourse of the revised *Arcadia*. In the latter discussion, Hoskins implies that effectively complex use of language—as found in Sidney's hypotactic periods and antithetical juxtaposition—requires such a form because it conveys a sense of a speaker's, narrator's, or, indeed, author's overview.

Hoskins's discussion asks us to read Sidney's *Arcadia* on three levels. First we must seek out the author's own ironic personality as creator of the fiction. Secondly we must seek to understand Sidney's persona, his Chaucerian narrator, who criticizes the characters' own thoughts and words by puzzling over their motivation and by simplifying their action and thoughts by oblique indirect discourse. Thirdly, we must gauge the characters themselves in their distortion, selection, and imaginative recreation of events as they are tinged sometimes with *eironeia*, always with *alazoneia*, accidental dissimulation or boasting. In each case, Sidney requires us to respond to complex language in terms of a concept of natural characterization of personae who create comic narrative by intention or accident.

Parodic Design

Although Tillyard, Danby, Kimbrough, Hamilton, Greenblatt, and Lindheim have made significant contributions to its criticism, by far the most compelling account of book 3 of the revised *Arcadia* belongs to Richard McCoy. As usual, in his discussion of the sequence of hand-to-hand combat and elsewhere, McCoy maintains his argument that Sidney blurs his "focus" (174) and "fails" in his witty ambiguity in such a way that it makes it impossible for him to finish. In response, I would like to show in several brief cases from book 3 how Sidney's parodic forms serve to "medicine" our idealism concerning war, love, and poetry—with precision and control.

Critics often take up Sidney's book 3 positively or negatively in its most serious moments in part because it contains Sidney's final and arguably most ambitious attempts at prose fiction, and because its puzzling ending in mid-sentence supposedly demonstrates authorial strain, uncertainty, or fatigue. We have attempts at coerced lovemaking, tragic duels, near-suicides, atrocities, and speeches and prayers that show life's underbelly in dismal light, but we are also surprised to see all this grave matter suddenly placed under an ironic floodlamp.

Parodic forms throughout *Arcadia* present the reader with comic versions of tragic matter that force us to look at a situation that has just been blanketed by the darkness of tragedy now bathed in Apollonian, ironic light, most notably, perhaps, in the "combat of cowards," which, according to McCoy, relieves "the grim pathos of the situation" (179) of two lovers, Argalus and Parthenia, in fatal combat with Amphialus.

The hand-to-hand combat of Amphialus and the lovers, Argalus and Parthenia, enjoys the elevation of high tragedy, capped by an elaborate funeral. It is perhaps the most serious moment of book 3. The reader is startled by an image of the last moments of a Hector-figure Argalus, when, in his duel with the Achilles-figure Amphialus, he receives his death's blow, "and then, each thing beginning to turn round in the dance of death before his eyes, his sight both dazzled and dimmed; till, thinking to sit down, he fell in a sound" (377). Stunned by the death of this protagonist and its lamentation "with all the funeral pomp of military discipline" (379), however, we witness a comic non-duel between Clinias and the goatherd Dametas that parodies that *agon* and ceremony.

Greenblatt, though he rarely allows him full control of his materials, as we have seen, argues that Sidney creates a "mixed mode" in *Arcadia* in which irony often subsumes pathos, and suffering moves to pleasure, because we are presented with what is "tragic in possiblity but not in fact."[2] Argalus's death, however, in this case, is fact; the comedy of the duel of Clinias and Dametas serves, I argue, to undercut by ironic or parodic design the very concept of honor and revenge of lovers that motivates our tragic protagonists. Romantic versions of Hector and Andromache—Argalus and Parthenia, (notably without offspring), separately idealize the honor of combat and self-annihilating Petrarchan love. Both receive deaths that reflect their delusion, most notably in the grisly blason of Parthenia (379), which McCoy makes much of as an example of the failure of wit (179ff). The parodic picture of Dametas as tired husband and coward does not "relieve" the grimness of the romantic duels so much as provide a chastening criticism of idealistic attitudes, as Falstaff, for example, criticizes Hotspur's ideal of grinning honor in *Henry IV.*

Miso's husband, Dametas, no uxorious man, attends the king in battle, "whether to be present with him, or absent from Miso" (379), his wife. He parodies the vainglorious heraldry of the challengers to Amphialus by ringing his device (containing "a great army of pen and inkhorns, and books" (381) for "historifying" his deeds) with the words to his absent wife, "Miso, mine own pigsney, thou shalt hear news of Dametas" (381).

The "combat of cowards" (385) begins, with written and spoken challenges and insults and, of course, out of fear of honorable death, paralysis in hand-to-hand combat. More than comic relief, this episode paints a version of the dangers of maintaining one's honor in war, especially in the cause of love. In so doing, Sidney's distant authorial persona criticizes both honor and love. Honor is seen not as a proper ideal, but as a savage principle that forces one to reciprocate, even escalate, violence quite will-lessly in deadly rivalry. Love, of the Petrarchan type, is seen as a proper occasion for suicidal assaults.

The versions and perversions of love and the near rape of book 3 culminate, furthermore, in the fragment we have, not so much with a failure of autonomy, as McCoy argues, but with Zoilus, the boasting soldier, offering his precious body to Pyrocles in Amazon disguise. *Miles gloriosus* seeks to seduce or, indeed, assault a transvestite who can take care of "herself." By one more persona of the busy lover, Sidney parodies all the purported heroism of doing and suffering of this book. Cupid has the last laugh.

We read, near the end of our incomplete book, "for Zoilus smacking his lips as for the prologue of a kiss, and something advancing himself, 'Darling!' said he, 'Let thy heart be fully of joy! And let thy fair eyes be of counsel with it, for this day thou shalt have Zoilus, whom many have longed for—' (460)." Coquettishly—suitable to her provocative attire—Zelmane halts Zoilus's pompous advances with the warning that "she" will "never be apt to bear children" (460). The parody runs deep because Zelmane is not creating a heroic sarcasm, although, as an Amazon, she will soon offer to duel Zoilus. She is, as Thelma Greenfield shows,[3] practicing her womanhood. Therefore we hear a parody of Philoclea's and Pamela's tribulations, but in a serious jest that suggests that we know neither ourselves nor others in love relationships, and we can easily be fooled by our own self-glorification in sexual conquest (Zoilus), or by our identification with a lover (Pyrocles's female disguise with the name of his former lover, Zelmane). Sidney's noting once again the impossibility of a male bearing actual children provides a somber reflection of all the failed erotic and generative enterprises through the work, yet the moment is comic.

No fact about book 3 has received so much critical attention as its abrupt ending in mid-sentence. Because his theme is failure, McCoy even compares its irresolution to Sidney's soldier's death (214), no doubt anathema to the old historians. Whatever motivated Sidney to halt his revision, however, his parody of authorship of grand designs that opens the book reflects consciousness of the possibility of irresolution.

Recalling the authorial invention for the ladies of the *Arcadia* itself, as well as the difficulty of composition that may have led to its curtailment,[4] Sidney pictures an author's struggle to write for the female reader, and that audience's response. In the opening scene, Musidorus, distraught with Pamela's rejection of his rude embrace—a crude move that again reflects his disguise as an apprentice goatherd—attempts to compose a poem that gives voice to his grief and love. "Banished her presence," this authorial persona seeks

> some means by writing to show his sorrow and testify his repentance; therefore, getting him the necessary instruments of writing, he thought best to counterfeit his hand (fearing that, as already she knew his, she would cast it away as soon as she saw it), and to put it in verse (hoping that would draw her on to read the more), choosing the elegiac as fittest for mourning. But pen did never more quakingly perform his office, never was paper more double moistened with ink and tears, never words more slowly married together, and never the muses more tired than now with changes and rechanges of his devices—fearing how to end before he had resolved how to begin, mistrusting each word, condemning each sentence. (310)

Comically, Sidney comments by parody on his own persona Musidorus's agony of composing up to an idolized audience, the kind our narrator appeals to in the *Old* and *New Arcadia*. Altering "his hand," while it proves a failure, suggests fiction's necessary disguise of life by means of the ruse of impersonation, and the pain predicts lack of completion. Of course, Sidney again paints a self-image, both foolish and pedantic in love, in Musidorus's combining naivety in love with sophisticated choices of metrical forms for specific generic effect, such as the "elegiac"—when *Arcadia* "mixes modes"—but his authorial persona also speaks to us directly of difficulties, emotional and other, in the creation of effective poetry for his audience at Wilton.

At this moment in the narrative of so many serious, even tragic, communications and miscommunications, we glimpse the process of reception of the artifact by an intelligent but unidealized, curious, intuitive, and emotive female reader in Pamela:

> But when she saw the letter her heart gave her from whence it came; and therefore clapping it to again, she went away from it as if it had been a contagious garment of an infected person, and yet was not long away but that she wished she had read it, though she were loath to read it.
> "Shall I," said she, "second his boldness so far as to read his presumptuous letters? And yet," said she, "he sees me not, to grow the bolder thereby. And how can I tell whether they be presumptuous? The paper came from him, and therefore not worthy to be received—and yet the paper," she thought, was not guilty. At last, she concluded, it were not much amiss to look it over, that she might out of his words pick some further quarrel against him. Then she opened it; and threw it away; and took it up again; till, ere she were aware, her eyes would needs read it, containing this matter. (310–11)

In the center of all this comic casuistry and equivocation lies the image of taking up the clothing of a person with a "contagious" disease. Indeed good fiction, an apt parallel to love letters from guilty suitors, serves the function of causing one to catch a healthful sickness, but only a master of irony can keep us in the mood for such salutary dis-ease.

Narrative *Eironeia*

Hoskins states that, while Aristotle's ten books of the *Ethics* and first two books of the *Rhetoric* were important to Sidney in his development of "voices" in the *Arcadia*, "lately I think also that he had much help out of *Theophrasti Imagines*."[5] Theophrastus's relevance to Sidney hinges, I believe, on two of his "possessed" or "humorous" personalities: the *eiron* (dissimulater) and the *alazon* (boaster), the first and last characters of his edition.[6] Sidney's narrator, ironically comments on his characters' actions and words. His relationship to the reader is one of pretended ignorance. Like the *eiron,* he affects ambiguity or doubtfulness about what he sees or hears. He may propose, as we have seen before, apparently opposite and irreconcilable interpretations of the behavior of his characters; and he seems obsessed.

When, for example, Pyrocles's amorous mind is wandering during Musidorus's first set of Catonian lectures, we read that "he [Pyrocles] no more attentively marked his friend's discourse than the child that hath leave to play marks the last part of his lesson, or the diligent pilot in a dangerous tempest doth attend the unskilful words of a passenger" (49). Both similes provide examples of disregard, but the causes seem diametrically opposed in seriousness. The reader must picture Pyrocles either as a boy anxious to exercise during the concluding lecture of a schoolmaster (Musidorus), or as a pilot in a storm being queried by an inept passenger (again Musidorus). We feel we must decide whether Pyrocles's love, which causes his inattention, is child's play or something as serious as death risked at sea, a recurring event in Sidney's work.

Is Musidorus being wise or merely inept or inexperienced? Although the reader may be puzzled by the narrator's apparent ambivalence, the effect is not ultimately ambiguous. We understand finally that Pyrocles's love, like all passionate love, is juvenile in its egoism, and absolutely vital to existence, a matter of life and death for that ego and for society itself. Again, by this irony, we recognize in Musidorus both the wise moral philosopher and the novice, for shortly he discovers himself drowning in the storm of passionate love himself. Our puzzlement at the "either-or" construction of the persona of the narrator yields to a synthesis that combines both implications. As we become familiar with the voice of the contradictory narrator, we come to expect his fine antithetical distinctions to dissolve, but for a purpose.

The reader also experiences initial puzzlement in passages of what I call oblique indirect discourse, a technique that helped perfect the English novel. The narrator reproduces the thoughts of a protagonist with oblique parody as well as alteration, so that the reader receives the thought but also ironic comment upon the quality of that thought. In the scene we have been discussing, for instance, we move for a moment into the mind of Musidorus by means of indirect discourse. In reaction to his friend's praising the landscape in Arcadia, we read that "when he found Pyrocles leave that and fall into such an affected praising of the place, he left it likewise" (52). We pause at the word "affected," wondering for a moment whether it serves to convey the narrator's opinion or Musidorus's. The adjective explains Musidorus's annoyance with what he believes to be his friend's "affectation" or "foible" in overpraising Arcadian landscape, and it serves to explain the narrator's attitude toward the speech. The speech is "affected," a "pretence" because it is part of Pyrocles's subterfuge: his attempt to disguise the real cause of his delight in Arcadia, his passionate love for Philoclea. The narrator's attitude to the reader is that of a dissembler, but the reader quickly realizes this and pushes by his remarks to the unambiguous truths that he only implies, never affirms.

A parallel to the narrator's use of oblique indirect discourse lies in his use of a menu of names for his leading characters. This scene opens with Daiphantus and Palladius in the woods together—but as their intimate debate develops, the reader notes that their original names, Pyrocles and Musidorus, take precedence. Later, when Pyrocles Daiphantus also becomes transformed into Zelmane the Amazon, the narrator will allow him to become "she" for the most part, in order to point up to the reader the absurdity of his elaborate disguise as well as incongruities of circumstance and blurred gender distinction on his part, as we have seen.

A broadly comic example of "oblique name-changing" occurs when Pyrocles/Daiphantus/Zelmane chases down a lion that is in turn chasing down Philoclea. He simply knocks the lion ("him") with a blow to the spine that is so violent "with force of affection . . . that she opened all his body" (112). The narrator's persona uses "she" here to remind us of the incongruity of Pyrocles's female attire as he opens up the lion only to be mildly scratched in return. It also recalls the force of his apparently "strange" affection for Philoclea as long as he remains in female attire. And it suggests a concept of invincible femininity, something "she" reiterates for us.

Dramatic *Alazoneia*

The final character in Sidney's version of the *Characters* is the *alazon*. *Alazoneia* or "Pretentiousness, of course, will seem to be a laying claim to advantages a man does not possess."[7] Like the *eiron*, the *alazon* takes many forms in Sidney's *Arcadia*. Every character, I argue, in the romance exaggerates his or her importance at one point or another. Just as Musidorus (in his debates with Pyrocles) boasts of his moral wisdom, or Philanax, (in his abrupt letter to the king) brags of his "humble service" (24), Strephon and Claius boast of rising above their fellows in Platonic contemplation of the ideal, and are brought back to earth in a variety of ways.

We see moments of pretension in Pamela, Philoclea, Kalender, Gynecia, Amphialus, and all others. In the context of Sidney's characterization, Hoskins states that while Aristotle's *Ethics* teaches the "perfect expressing of all qualities," Machiavelli has helpfully pointed out that "perfect virtue and perfect vice are not seen in our times."[8] Hoskins assumes that the characters of *Arcadia* are "men of our time." They are, in the phrase he borrows from *Discorsi* 1.26, "humorous and spurting" because of the effects of *amour propre*.

Critics often single out Evarchus, Pyrocles's father and king of Madecon—whose name suggests "good rule"—as an example of Sidney's idealization of character,[9] and exemption to this ironic procedure, but Evarchus clearly loses himself in exaltation of a sense of his own justice in his trial of Gynecia, Pyrocles, and Musidorus. Sidney makes Evarchus not only feel certain that he can understand and pass on eternal principles of law. He also lives with a concept of social order that, like Socrates's scheme in Plato's *Republic*, impossibly "banishes" *eros* and all but high-minded civic passion.

In the grand recognition scene that makes up the bulk of the "Last Book or Act" of Sidney's *Old Arcadia*, Evarchus initially cuts the figure of unwilling but necessarily harsh judge. Although melancholic concern for his lost son and nephew lead him into visiting Arcadia in the first place, he abruptly condemns the supposed widow of his old friend to burial alive, his son to being thrown off a high tower, and his nephew to beheading, for various passionate acts that remain undiscovered by due process of law. In other words, Evarchus's rigid Platonic concept of equity leads him to ignore the important emotive aspects of a complex human situation that requires full disclosure and compassion.

Evarchus's attempt to be just is initially undercut by his nephew's Musidorus's, humble remark that all "our doing in the extremest interpretation is but a human error" (402.30), that is, both a wandering, as Evarchus has casually arrived in Arcadia, and a fallacy. But we are so caught up in Evarchus's precision in his sentencing that we only gradually discover his double error: his oversight and vainglory. We must retreat in the text, as so often in Sidney, to see how Evarchus wanders.

Evarchus becomes a spectacle when he reconfirms his death sentence over his son Pyrocles's objection that he seeks "too precise a course of justice" (414.15) by emphasizing his immortal incapacity for error in his own conceptualizing of the law: "never, never, let sacred rightfulness fall. It is immortal, and immortality ought to be preserved. If rightly I have judged, then rightly have I judged mine own children, unless the name of a child should have force to change the never-changing justice" (411.24). Immortality will, by definition, be preserved. To remind us of what is missing, at the end of this speech, Evarchus's passionate rigor causes tears to "drop down his long white beard, which moved . . . all the assembly dolefully to record that pitiful spectacle" (412.10). Compassion is missing.

As when Shakespeare stages a similar circumstance in the trial scene of *The Merchant of Venice*, we, in the audience, are made to realize—in our grief for Evarchus the stern judge—that only mercy is immortal. This grand spectacle belies Evarchus's Platonic view of justice, and Sidney, by his "web" and "figured story," has Basilius rise from the dead to make his point. Miraculously, Evarchus is "thwarted" in his "immortal" sacrifice and self-sacrifice to his ideal, by the strange event of Basilius's return from the dead, which instantly converts *Arcadia*'s near tragedy into comedy, or rather, tragicomedy. What proves not to be dead—Basilius stirring on his bier—comically overturns Evarchus's "mortal judgements" (416.34).

Sidney, in gently criticizing Evarchus's Platonic *alazoneia*, lends him an eloquent attack on all forms of love that show signs of human passion, the kind that produces all the congregation of "children" before him as well as their misbehavior. Going backward in his summation, as we must, we hear again Evarchus's magniloquent dismissal of lower forms of love, rife with echoes of Plato's *Symposium* and *Republic*, maintaining an impossible human ideal: "That sweet and heavenly uniting of the minds, which properly is called love, hath no other knot but virtue; and therefore if it be a right love, it can never slide into any action that is not virtuous" (407.2). Surely this rhetoric at the close of *Old Arcadia* is as glorious as that of Strephon and Claius, which opens the *New,* but in both cases, Sidney reminds his idealistic personae and his readers that we must live in "passionate error" through the actual world, the human one with its necessary yoking of desire and restraint, as well as through the entire labyrinth of the two *Arcadia*'s. This huge trial scene, filled with judicial fallacy and ill-humored participants, reminds us as it might have Sidney's young lawyer friend Hoskins, that "perfect virtue or perfect vice is not seen in our time." Nor any time. Sidney's ironic design, his Chaucerian narrator, and his boasting, though glorious, personae make this lesson crystal clear.

11
Sidney's Self-Effacement

In the letter of dedication of *Arcadia* to his sister Mary,¹ the Countess of Pembroke, Sidney asks us to look on his work as a version of himself. He develops an image of his romance first as offspring, then as child, then as monstrous brainchild, a son produced by means of asexual reproduction. And though he "spurns" the child, it is his child, and it resembles its sole parent. In a characteristic mood of self-deprecation—"a young head not so well stayed"—and of disparagement of his romance—an "idle work," full of "errors," "done in loose sheets of paper"—Sidney suggests that *Arcadia* is spun out of his innards like "the spider's web" though fit to be "swept away." It is his "child" whom he might "cast out in some desert of forgetfulness" like "the cruel fathers among the Greeks," thus invoking again the romantic and tragic theme of the exposed baby.

In a hopeful moment, the author feels that though his work is deformed, in bestowing it on his sister "for the father's sake, it will be pardoned, perchance made much of." Then he speaks of the difficulties of labor and of the delivery of the mutant prodigy from his impregnated brain, which, "having many many fancies begotten in it, if it had not been in some way delivered, would have grown a monster, and more sorry might I be that they came in than that they gat out" (3.19). Sidney alludes to the delivery in Greek myth, of Athena from the head of Zeus and the unnatural births of Dionysus and Hercules. But in this case the child is not a real or potential immortal, but an offender that needs the "livery" of the Countess of Pembroke's name as his "chief protection."

Sidney's characterization of the *Arcadia* as a brainchild urgently delivered—as well as the work's adoption by his sister—asks us, as always, in Sidney, to look for a resemblance to the author in the work. For example, when we hear, in the opening sonnet of *Astrophil and Stella* that Astrophil is "great with child to speake," we know we are embarking on a personal narrative of some sort. We are supposedly reading a first-person account that will convey some urgent autobiographical matter, which is conceived, and delivered, so to speak, into the world, like a son. Clear-cut autobiographical elements internal to the tales of *Arcadia* beckon the reader to locate the author's likeness in the work. Parthenia's disfigurement and miraculous recovery from poison smeared on her face[2] remind us of his mother's permanent scars from smallpox, caught attending on the queen, and Sidney's hopes for a miraculous recovery of her looks that could return her to the world's regard and the queen's own favor as a lady-in-waiting.

The sarcastic persona of the courtier tired of courtly convention of the sonnet to Mopsa, furthermore, reminds us of the "busy loving courtier" of *Astrophil and Stella*. As the melancholic shepherd Philisides, in the eclogue opening, "As I my little flocke on Ister Banke," Sidney adopts a persona who refers openly to one of his mentors, Hubert Languet.[3] Some of the heraldry reminds us of Sidney's own inventions for himself, and the sardonic narration of the *"painted muster of an eleven conquered beauties"* and the "Lovers' Tilt"[4] calls our attention to Sidney's own role in the court as a fellow-creator of entertainments for the Queen's festive occasions—thus it is not surprising that the description of a tilt is the main authorial narration of book 1 of the *1590 Arcadia*. But these specific references to facts, sometimes boldly autobiographical, merely beckon us to search for a purposely elusive and self-ironic biographical Philip Sidney.

When we focus on those moments in the text that seem most likely to approximate the author's voice, above all, in the sonnet to Mopsa—the *New Arcadia's* first poem—or in the narration of the "Lovers' Tilt," we find that Sidney disappears behind a mask, and leaves us with puzzle and paradox. I take up these two cases of self-irony because they demonstrate Sidney's self-effacement in his dual career of poet and courtier-propagandist, positions not altogether distinguishable given the notion of political love poetry Elizabeth promoted. What we gain is a mirthful view of the vanity of human wishes in poetry and courtly entertainment. Sidney's mask is a remote one that effaces self and pictures the poet not as a prophet or a bold imitator of nature but one who reconstitutes conventional forms to produce novelty.

The opening poem of the 1590 *Arcadia*, the jesting sonnet in praise of Mopsa's parts, is a tactic in a larger authorial strategy in its introduction to the reader of problems created by the king's self-transformation into a shepherd and the pastoralization of the court. I might call this second major episode in the 1590 *Arcadia* "Musidorus's encounter with garrulity." Throughout the passage, we observe the action through Musidorus's—alias Palladius's—eyes. The talkative Kalender is a humorous man, inquisitive—"curious" and "curiosity" in their various meanings become key words in the passage—and generous with everything he has, from his home and company to state secrets contained in Philanax's letter, and slander and libel.

The reader—by way of Musidorus's observation—comes to realize that Kalander's leading opinion, that his nation is in grave danger, is founded more upon hatred for Dametas and admiration for Dametas's "charge," the princess Pamela—a contagious admiration for Musidorus—than any understanding of the political vacuum created by Basilius's transformation into a shepherd. As readers, we are taught that by devaluing rank and position in the kingdom, Basilius has rendered impotent the aristocracy of which Kalander is a leading member, but Kalander does not know that problem.

The need for a strong aristocracy is a reasonable cause in the context of book 1, as we see in the quasi-authorial beast fable of Philisides in the first eclogues. However, Kalander seems to have missed the point in his obsession with Dametas's "doltish" and "loutish" qualities (17), qualities which rub off for him onto his daughter Mopsa, whose appearance and manner are portrayed as opposite in quality to the "majesty in Pamela" (17). In the tone of the poem to Mopsa, we discover a more profoundly ironic voice than that of Astrophil, a thoroughly comic Sidneian persona, creating an anatomy of poetic failure.

In the *1590 Arcadia*, Kalander says the author of the poem is "a pleasant fellow of my acquaintance" (18), yet in the *Old Arcadia* he was described as "*Alethes* an honest man of that time."⁵ This alteration of the poet's name and quality serves to declare openly that the poem is ironic. This uncharacteristic warning of Sidney's strategy may result from the failure of readers of the manuscripts of *Old Arcadia* to take full account of the poem's "pleasantness." Perhaps Alethes ἀληθής in its connotation of "truthful," and the authorial emphasis on honesty was found to be an impediment to readers. Was it a sarcasm—meant to apply to the Sidney persona as poetic "liar"—that readers missed? The only other fact about the song to Mopsa that we are given in advance is that Kalander has "so often" had it sung that he has memorized it. That the poem is on the face of it a bad poem may serve to impugn Kalander's taste. Clearly he loves it for its libelous version of Mopsa's image.

Sidney's new placement of this sonnet at the opening of the 1590 *Arcadia* emphasizes its comic investigation of the nature of poetry and the "title of a poet" that Sidney has "slipped into." It is a version of the body catalogue or "blason," that most ancient form of lyric poetry found in the "Song of Solomon" and in the versions of ancient

Egyptian poetry then in vogue. It is also the first kind of poetry in which we observe a child reacting to with his satiric versions of the strained conventions of love lyric: "your ears are flowers, cauliflowers / Your eyes are pools, cesspools," and so forth. Thus the poem takes on the form of ur-poetry whether, historically, you seek the earliest poetry or, psychologically, you seek the kind of poetry the child first comprehends and criticizes for its absurd—at least for the pre-sexual mind—idealization of the love-object. The religious praise of Isis's precious parts—an icon of precious metals and stones—and the child's sneer at unearthly exaggeration of the beauty of the beloved's body have in common their originality, their quintessential origins.[6] Nancy Vickers and others have emphasized the dismemberment suggested by such a catalogue as well as the negotiable commercial value of the vehicles attached by simile to the individual parts. Such latent violence and capitalizing is, in the largest sense, always present in such drinking-song procedure—most explicit in Spenser's Sonnet 15, calling on "tradefull Merchants" to share the mistress's riches—but the blazon of male or female parts primarily establishes a religious icon by description and idealization. And love poets, male and female, universally avail themselves of this rhetorical tool.

Thanks to Sidney's ironic delivery, the reader may be well into the work before he makes sense of the poetic persona's intention.

> What length of verse can serve brave Mopsa's good to show,
> Whose virtues strange, and beauties such, as no man them may know?
> Thus shrewdly burdened then, how can my muse escape?
> The gods must help, and precious things must serve to show her shape:
> Like great god Saturn, fair, and like fair Venus, chaste.[7]

In spite of several oddities, the poem seems at first just another Petrarchan sonnet of idealization of a lady's parts, like, for example, Sonnet 15 of Sidney's fellow-poet Spenser's *Amoretti*, where his Elizabeth's—and by extension our Elizabeth's—eyes, lips, forehead, hair, and hands are compared to precious gems and minerals in succession.

Perhaps a reversal occurs for the reader in the third line when the poetic praiser describes himself as "shrewdly burdened," suggesting both "heavily burdened" and "burdened with a shrew," possibilities that serve to articulate the poet's feeling of encumberment. Perhaps the reader makes new sense of the tone of the piece only when Mopsa takes on the aspect of gloomy Saturn, or when her chastity becomes that of adulterous Venus in the fifth line—though our "pleasant fellow" suggests a notion of the two versions of Venus—Uranos and

Pandemos—in the *Symposium*. As in our reading of Claius's praise of Urania's parts, once we have located the author's ironic design—here in an open jest—we must go back and reinterpret the poem and, above all, its form, from the first line.

"What length of verse can serve Mopsa's good to show?" is a typical example of Sidney's use of irony to entrap the reader. Extra words are the essential tool of the ironist, because they warn us of complex meaning, and the poet must ask us to question our first response to his words. Of course, any kind of language can be used to ironic effect. The reader merely has to be warned that the obvious meaning is not the entire intended one. But Sidney provides the reader with warnings by means of a special form of circumlocution here.

Sidney could have had his persona of the pleasant poet deliver the content of this first line in a number of briefer ways. And it is self-conscious on the "poet's" part—like Musidorus at the beginning of book 3—to ask what verse is suitable for Mopsa's praise. Such conventional aporia would suit a much longer poem than a sonnet. Here he manages to fill an improbably high number of beats (12) for the line of a sonnet with syllables of the longest duration, and therefore he is, in a sense speaking of a laborious, time-consuming task and doing it simultaneously. Single syllable words for example (ten out of eleven words) simply take more time to pronounce than syllables of multisyllabic words.

In this context, one may recall Sidney's comments on the duration of syllables, not in the experiments in Greek and Latin meter, but, for example, in Strephon's remark in the opening of the *1590 Arcadia*, "alas, that the word *last* should so long last!" (3). The word "last" takes a relatively long time to pronounce with its three consonants ("l," "s," "t"), but not as long, for example, as the five consonantal sounds ("l," "n," "g," "th") of "length," the second word of this line. Here Sidney creates the impression of an interminable line to warn the reader of the difficulty, tedium, even impossibility, involved in praising "brave Mopsa."

The epithet "brave" also gives us pause, since it cannot refer to her peasant's clothing or her active courage. The choice of modifier, however, does not turn ironically on the lady, but on our ironic persona of a poet who could not think of a more apt term. The lady might well be bravely clothed or indeed virtuously brave like the Pamela of Kalander's remarks immediately prior to his presentation of the poem. There his praise of Pamela's aggressive style and beauty and "high thoughts" seems to be preparing Musidorus for love. Here the choice reflects the incompetence of the poet himself, the Sidney persona who produced it, and reminds us that in his court life Sidney "slipped" into the title of poetic praiser of ladies for the ostensible purpose of seduction.

This poem is a criticism of a bad poetic and of poetic incompetence. The irony is not the sarcasm of the iconoclast who simply reverses the terms of a convention. It is not a version of the traditional schoolboy reaction to Petrarchanism because the maker of the poem itself is ironically portrayed as fighting a losing battle with poetic technique. Thus, throughout, we see the poet making comically poor choices, formally speaking, employing all the stiffness of alliterative formulae and archaism that Sidney condemned in English poetry in his *Defence of Poetry*. The first line is choppy and disjoined by the breaking up of the verb "serve to show" seemingly in order to place the rhyme word "show" at the end.

This awkward maneuver serves no better purpose than to set up a rhyme with the "know" of the formulaic filler "as no man then may know," of the following line. This verbal incompetence parallels the pleasant poet's formal incompetence in choosing to construct his fourteen-line Petrarchan edifice out of couplets in poulter's measure. Choosing this verse form for the elegant sonnet is on one level ironically foolish, giving the poem a mechanical movement through seven long couplets that may remind his readers of the days of Gascoigne.

Structurally the fourth line is normally a central one in the Elizabethan sonnet, summing up the conceit of the first quatrain. Here the poet exposes his mechanical procedure of looking up his metaphors in books, in primers of mythography and precious and semiprecious gems and metals. We picture the imitative or conventional poet in a crisis of metaphorical need reaching up for his dusty manuals in order to find apt comparisons, and he announces this fact: "The gods must help, and precious things must serve to show her shape." This line closes with an ironic reversion to an alliterative pattern recalling Sidney's complaint about English poets who compose "as if they were bound to follow the method of a dictionary" (117).

> As smooth as Pan; as Juno, mild; like goddess Iris, fast;
> With Cupid she foresees, and goes god Vulcan's pace,
> And for a taste of all these gifts, she steals god Momus' grace;
> Her forehead, jacinth-like; her cheeks of opal hue;
> Her twinkling eyes, bedecked with pearl; her lips, as sapphire, blue;
> Her hair like crapal stone; her mouth, O, heavenly wide;
> Her skin like burnished gold; her hands like silver ore untried.

The poet in his imaginative quandary proceeds to get the gods, gems, and metals all wrong. Beyond "Saturn fair" and "Venus chaste," we now have comparisons of Mopsa's physical and spiritual qualities with those of the shaggy Pan and of "Juno mild"—no doubt the savage principle, the *saevissima Juno* of Virgil's *Aeneid*—and of a securely placed goddess of the rainbow, "Iris fast."

Ironic incompetence in interpreting mythography and metallurgy is parodically capped by the formal monotony of setting five similes in a row, by means of three "like's" and two "as's," with what turns out to be a parody of poetry itself. In line six the poet again "accidentally" touches on a Neoplatonic commonplace by suggesting that "with Cupid she foresees," but he is apparently referring to a blind Cupid. Mopsa's walk is compared with that of the club-footed god, Vulcan. What the poem has done so far is assault the reader's expectation of finery with a picture of poetic incompetence.

Of course, mistaking significances of gods and "precious things" enables the "pleasant fellow" to make fun of Mopsa. And it is broad comedy, in Kalander's precious slander, to picture Mopsa glowering, promiscuous, hairy, ferocious, wavering, blinded, bandy-legged, and finally (in a comparison to Momus), rude, or, by means of the comparisons with jewels and metals, with a reddish forehead, rainbow cheeks, leaking eyes, blue lips, tangled (?) hair, wide mouth, bronze skin, and black hands. Sidney's humor is thoroughly Elizabethan in it earthiness, as we see in the closing couplet which contains no summation, merely at indirect observation about Mopsa's private parts:

> As for her parts unknown, which hidden sure are best,
> Happy be they which well believe, and never seek the rest.

Here we seem to have, impossibly, a bathetic response to Spenser's famous blazon produced sixteen or eighteen years later. Spenser in the religiously erotic mode turns us away from his mistress' body in his final couplet to a "Platonic" contemplation of her mental powers and spirit:

> But that which fairest is, but few behold,
> Her mind adornd with vertues manifold.[8]

Sidney allows his poem to die in contemplation of Mopsa's genitals evoked by euphemism and innuendo in sing-song. More than a joke directed at an image of Mopsa, however, the poem is a serious jest at the expense of the sonnet and its maker, the structure of the sonnet depending on a final line of pure filler. "Happy be they which well believe, and never seek the rest" reminds us of the verbiage at the other key structural moments of the poem, "as no man then may know" (line 2), "Must serve to show her shape" (line 4), and to culminate the comparisons to the gods, "And for a taste of all these gifts" (line 8). This nonsense jingle in fourteener causes us to ask— "believe what?" "what have we been given to believe?"—only to discover that this line represents another default of imagination on our poetic persona's part.

In the opening poem of the 1590 *Arcadia*, Sidney's "pleasant" mask speaks to the reader indirectly about bad, convention-bound poetry, the kind that he attacks in his *Defence of Poetry*. But Sidney himself was a convention-bound court poet. Not only is this type of sonnet passionless ("so coldly they apply fiery speeches, as men that had rather read lovers' writings . . . than that in truth they feel those passions" (117)), but it contains verses without "poetical sinews in them" (112). Sidney has produced a poem that fulfills his rhetor's worst fears about English poems whose "one verse did but beget another, without ordering at the first what should be the last; which becomes a confused mass of words, with a tingling sound of rhyme, barely accompanied with reason" (112). Thus Sidney not only presents a hyperbolically negative image of Mopsa, but also a self-ironic picture of the versifier as overreacher, with rhyme and without reason.

Like the opening sonnet of *Astrophil and Stella*—which it resembles in several ways—this poem presents us with a paradox. Poets must write "by the book," and according to the conventions, but they will not write well if they do. When the Muse of Sonnet 1 tells Astrophil to look into his "heart and write" (1.14), she is giving an impossible command. There are no words in the heart. Poets live by conventional formulations and imitations of imitations, gotten from books, such as the concept of Muse itself, as we have seen, and from conventions of "others' leaves," all found in this seemingly anticonventional poem. Plainness is, in fact, a convention itself, as Sidney often points out. Conceited poems require conceits. Sidney resurrects a central epistemological argument that language is fallen and conventions which we must depend upon to view the world are imperfect, and tend to blind us to the reality of our situation. Like the roles we play, our language of the moment is ultimately a tool for approximation as well as a disguise. Yet it is our one essential means to making sense of the world.

This self-deprecating voice of the poet frustrated in his attempts at icastic imitation is the familiar voice of Sidney's sonneteering persona on the verge of rhapsody but withdrawing in distrust of its exaggeration of a truth. Thus we return to the paradoxical image of the poet as imitator of nature yet prophet, in this ironic moment, who "shapes dreams." As readers, we were invited to seek out the actual Sidney, the comically cruel sonneteer, but we are given another version of Sidney's self-irony. The biographical image we sought out proved to be a mask; Sidney himself remained at least one remove, a critic of poets and of poetic activity. Creation of conventional love poetry—as well as of neo-chivalric festivities—comprised, in a sense, his real profession. Yet the closer we come to his courtly persona and his comments on these activities the more profoundly ironic—even paradoxical—he becomes. Let us now turn to Sidney's version of the work of the courtly propagandist.

In a work made up of a web of tales within tales, a central moment of authorial narration in book 1 is contained in the two chapters describing the "muster" of eleven portraits and the "Lovers' Tilt" that Basilius provides largely to entertain his beloved Zelmane (Pyrocles in disguise). Not surprisingly, Sidney's own authorial persona delivers this passage. For one, he presents the kind of tilt, on a smaller scale perhaps, that Sidney helped devise for the queen's ceremonial occasions. Here Sidney provides a scenario for the court of Basilius similar to the ones he had already composed, and he can comment again gently on the sentimental refeudalization of the queen's court and on his own courtly activities from this posture.

Sidney's best-known work in the actual court of Elizabeth was the tournament of the "Fortress of Perfect Beauty," described by Henry Goldwell in *A Briefe Declaration of the Shews* (1581),[9] which took place on Whit Monday and the Tuesday following in 1581. This tournament, provided for, among many others, high and low, the French commissioners, was another characteristic pageant in glorification of the Virgin Queen. Elaborately equipped, Sidney and the other three "Foster Children of Desire," the Earl of Arundel, Lord Windsor, and Greville, make an assault on the queen's fortress of beauty. The armory includes the sonnet, probably Sidney's, beginning,

> Yeelde yeelde, O yeelde, you that this Forte do holde,
> which seated is in spotlesse honor's field[10]

which is answered in kind,

> Allarme allarme, here will no yeelding be,
> such marble eares, no cunning wordes can charme.

After staged assaults and rebuffs—a gentle hint to the French ambassadors that the Duc d'Alençon will be refused—the message that the foster children "be slaves to this Fortress forever" is delivered by a pretty boy "clothed in ash-coloured garments in token of humble submission," who then proceeds to fall "down prostrate on his face"[11] before the queen to conclude the pageant.

Like the sonnet to Mopsa, however, the "Lovers' Tilt" in the 1590 *Arcadia* presents the reader with an ambiguous version of anticonvention, a parody of the tournament of the "Fortress of Perfect Beauty." Again, however, Sidney's uncertain Chaucerian persona not only exposes the sham and the tendency to ill-humor and envy in courtly activity; he shows us that the conventions, the rules of the game, may be arbitrary, even silly, but they give society form; without them, undifferentiation would descend like night on us all. Hierarchy or some set of rules must be set by fallible referees. Without such forms, we would be savages engaged in the mutual destruction that the tournament symbolizes and domesticates.

The narrator first functions to bring the reader to an understanding of an actual tilt, the kind that Sidney devised for the queen. Then he caps his descriptions of the gay festivity and gaudy trappings of the affair with muted reservations about the humor of the participants and even mood of the ladies who play the game in earnest, all of whom behave like angry children. Words describing "rage," "anger," and "choler" ring throughout the passage. Nestor departs "remedilessly chafing at his rebuke" (98); Gynecia's "champion went away as much discomforted as discomfited" (99). Lalus the shepherd boy is furious that he does not have the means to challenge Phalantus and returns to the crowd "even weeping-ripe" (100).

Phebilis, furthermore, wants to pull his sword on the victorious jouster after fairly losing, and, last but not least, on her champion's fall, "a pretty blush in Philoclea's cheeks bewray a modest discontentment" (101). Clitophon is "so angry" (101) at the judge's impartial ruling that he snubs "his prince and uncle" (101). Pyrocles and Musidorus, finally, in disguise, squabble and destroy property in vandalistic rage, and the original challenger and his lady trade insults and determine to break up forever. Thus Sidney presents a picture of men and women behaving according to the non-law of savagery as well as all precedents of poor sportsmanship. When the players actual identities are lost, as in this tilt, a breakdown of rank and order follows. Thus the king is insulted, and the "sticklers' authority" must be invoked. Arbitrary rules must be reinstituted, or disaster will follow.

The ironic voice of Sidney's narrator once again proceeds to undercut—to implode—what we expect to be an idealistic description of an ideal, in this case, of martial heroism and ladylike modest virtue. In the challenge of the lovely shepherd boy, Lalus, in fact, we find an anticonventional version of the pretty boy who read the sonnets or delivered the surrender of the "Foster Children of Desire" in the tournament of the "Fortress of Perfect Beauty" and then prostrated himself before the Virgin Queen.

The narrative of his adolescent persona's action remains noncommital in description, dividing perhaps where divisions do not hold. He says, for example, that the boy's complexion is brown "(whether by nature or by the sun's familiarity)" (99), but we know or guess that both are to a certain extent true. The semi-allegorical Lady Nature is then invoked in the description of his well proportioned body as a goddess who "doth not, like men, who slubber up matters of mean account" (99). Thus, he at once comments ironically on administrative inefficiency and praises the boy's physique.[12] The boy is beautiful, but he has no place in this game.

Lalus's mock-heroic appearance is subtly seen as the product of a naive yet pretty anger at circumstances, even the rules of the game. He comes up to lay his challenge before the king "with a look full of amiable fierceness (as in whom choler could not take away the sweetness)" (99). Of course, he is a human oxymoron, a displaced individual as were Strephon and Claius challenging the "great clerks" on the beach, even as Basilius is as a shepherdish king. He has lost a sense of his own identity in his desire to be Urania's champion in this ceremonial joust. And his anger at Artesia's supposed presumption consumes him.

Furthermore, Lalus mistakes game for reality. Because Artesia is in possession of Urania's picture, he angrily charges that men will say Urania "is not so fair as yonder gay woman" (99). Like Claius, he is here bound rhetorically by his shepherdish world in his further insulting of Artesia who is, as he says, no "more match to Urania than a goat is to a fine lamb, or than the dog that keeps our flock at home is like your white greyhound that pulled down the stag last day" (99). Sidney, in recreating a naturalistic speech rhythm in the homely simile of the shepherd boy, brings our attention to the artificiality of the occasion.

Anger causes the boy to run on anticlimactically, now at the climax of the tilt. When Lalus offers to break all formal strictures by taking Phalantus on with his shepherd's staff, he is reminded by the referee, Basilius, to be content with the rules of the game. And though he storms off in a rage—a typical example of the sportsmanship of the participants "praying heartily for everybody that ran against Phalantus" (100)—he has learned a fundamental lesson about preserving his own identity, and respecting arbitrary rules, including those of rank.

By means of this parodic version of the boy messenger of the tournament of the "Fortress of Perfect Beauty"—here hoping to be accepted as a warrior—we again glimpse a persona of the "self-effacing" Sidney—the sometime adolescent shepherd knight—viewing, paradoxically, what he was made to take in earnest in his own life: the court, its pomp, and especially its rank. He creates an anti-tilt, which investigates the comic side of courtly entertainment—the human side—emphasizing simultaneously the need to play by the rules, and the limitations of those rules, but the greater limitations of the players of the game in their characteristic rage.

Irony is not an end in itself for Sidney. Pure irony is, in fact, thoroughly suspect. In the first place, the ironist is wearing a mask; he or she is disguising himself or herself and denying his or her own identity. The ironist is committing what for Sidney was the fundamental social error: assuming for whatever purpose the identity of someone else. In borrowing the mask of the *eiron* in actual life, Sidney is exposing himself to the possibility of exchanging his identity of *eiron* to that of *alazon*, from conscious to unconscious denier of his identity, from amorous courtier, for example, to sham prophet. But whatever he was in the court—and he has made it difficult for us to know—as an artist, he generally chose to remain behind a mask. Only the serious jester is allowed to play that dangerous game.

Notes

Introduction

1. Autobiographical elements in Musidorus include the fact that, (1) while he was not a duke, like Musidorus, Sidney was, off and on, the heir to both the earls of Leicester and Warwick. (2) Like Musidorus, he was famous for adventures in travel to foreign parts. No doubt, for example, his witnessing elements of the Massacre of St. Bartholomew's Day from Walsingham's house in Paris, on 24 August 1572 when he was seventeen, helps inform Musidorus's dealing more directly with collective violence on two occasions in Arcadia. (3) In the first sonnet of his quasi-autobiographical *canzoniere*, his persona is given enlargement to speak truth by his muse; thus he is, in some sense, like Musidorus, a "gift of the muse." (4) In the sonnet sequence, like Musidorus, Astrophil steals a kiss from his sleeping beloved (song 2), and (5), at one point, like Musidorus, becomes a shepherd and sings in country style of his rejection of Stella (song 19) who treats him worse than he treats his dog. But this list is not exhaustive. In his autobiographical drama Sidney always made use of reference to details of his life, well-known especially among the "ladies" in his audience.

2. I use William Empson's substitute term for "pastoral" (*Some Versions of Pastoral* [London: Chatto and Windus, 1935]) advisedly, because Sidney does not idealize shepherds exactly, as we shall see in chapters 3 and 8. Shepherds and goatherds may sing, but they remain an underclass, and Basilius's decision to become a herder of animals marks a case of the "overclass" determining to become underclass.

3. *The Poems of Sir Philip Sidney,* ed. William Ringler (Oxford: Clarendon Press, 1962). By page number in text.

4. For example, of what became known as "apprentice's blue," C. Willett and Phillis Cunnington write, "A certain shade of blue was used for the dress of apprentices and servants, and gradually blue became the recognized colour for them." *Handbook of English Costume in the Sixteenth Century* (London: Faber & Faber, Ltd., 1954), p. 16, but other strictures existed. See below, p. 13, when courtiers were required to wear black. Other "color-coding" and controls of fabric and fur existed.

5. In real life, of course, a jester could be an entrepreneur. Witness Archibald ("Archy") Armstrong, fool to James I and Charles I, who after losing his motley in a feud with Archbishop Laud, settled down in his estates in Cumberland. See H. R. Trevor-Roper, *Archbishop Laud: 1573–1645* (London: Macmillan, 1940), pp. 364-65, 411, and the *DNB* for mythic and other elaboration of this feud.

6. *The Countess of Pembroke's Arcadia,* (*The Old Arcadia*), ed. Jean Robertson (Oxford: Clarendon Press, 1973). Cited by page number in the text.

7. See the preface to *Essential Articles for the Study of Sir Philip Sidney* (Hamden, Conn.: Archon, 1986), pp. xiii-xvii, where "others" are cited.

8. Quoted from *The Miscellaneous Prose of Sir Philip Sidney,* ed. Katherine Duncan-Jones and Jan Van Dorsten (Oxford: Clarendon Press, 1973), cited by page number in the text.

9. Barbara Bowen, *The Age of Bluff: Paradox and Ambiguity in Rabelais and Montaigne*, Illinois Studies in Language and Literature, 62 (Urbana: Univ. of Illinois Press, 1972), p. 6.

10. *Rhetoric*, III.xviii.7, found in Aristotle. *The "Art" of Rhetoric*, trans. John Henry Freese. The Loeb Edition (London: William Heinemann, 1926), p. 466.

11. *Illustrissimi & Generosissimi Viri/Philippi Sidnaei Angli.*" Malcolm William Wallace, *The Life of Sir Philip Sidney* (Cambridge: Cambridge Univ. Press, 1915), p. 174, quoted from Collins, *Memoirs*, p. 100.

12. See Greenblatt's *Sir Walter Ralegh: The Renaissance Man and His Roles* (New Haven: Yale Univ. Press, 1973). *Renaissance Self-Fashioning: From More to Shakespeare* (Chicago: Univ. of Chicago Press, 1980), but also Richard Helgerson, *The Elizabethan Prodigals* (Berkeley: Univ. of California Press, 1976); Louis Montrose, "Celebration and Insinuation: Sir Philip Sidney and the Motive of Elizabethan Courtship," *Renaissance Drama*, 18 (1977): 3–35; "'Eliza, Queene of Shepheardes,' and the Pastoral of Power," *ELR*, 10 (1980): 153–82; "Of Gentlemen and Shepherds: The Politics of Elizabethan Pastoral Form," *ELH*, 50 (1983): 415–59; "The Elizabethan Subject and the Spenserian Text," in Patricia Parker and David Quint, eds., *Literary Theory/ Renaissance Texts* (Baltimore: Johns Hopkins Univ. Press, 1986), pp. 303–40; "Renaissance Literary Studies and the Subject of History," *ELR*, 16 (1986): 5–12; Richard McCoy, *Sir Philip Sidney: Rebellion in Arcadia* (New Brunswick: Rutgers Univ. Press, 1979); and Margaret Ferguson, *Trials of Desire: Renaissance Defences of Poetry* (New Haven: Yale Univ. Press, 1983).

13. *The Progresses and Public Processions of Queen Elizabeth*, 3 vols. (London: T. Nichols and Son, 1823), vol. 2, p. 301. Although she supports the "rebel" theory, Maureen Quilligan calls the gift "witty, apologetic, and insistent on their differences." "Sidney and His Queen," in *The Historical Renaissance: New Essays on Tudor and Stuart Literature and Culture*, ed. Heather Dubrow and Richard Strier (Chicago: Univ. of Chicago Press, 1988): 171–96, p. 180.

14. Wallace, *The Life of Sir Philip Sidney*, p. 260.

15. *The Elizabethan World Picture* (New York: Vintage, 1966). Walzer's discussions are contained in *The Revolution of the Saints: A Study of the Origins of Radical Politics* (Cambridge: Harvard Univ. Press, 1965), esp. pp. 67, 88, 116, 241, and in a parallel discussion of Coriolanus as radical aristocrat in *Obligations: Essays on Disobedience, War, and Citizenship* (Cambridge: Harvard Univ. Press, 1970), p. 200

16. My translation of "*atque insolita hilaritate enituerunt*" in Clarence H. Miller, ed., *Moriae Encomium id Est Stvltitiae Lavs* (1979), *Opera Omnia*, 16 vols. (Amsterdam: North-Holland Publishing Company, 1969–83), p. 70, 1. 9.

17. The patchwork symbolizes variety of personae but also poverty. Motley is meaner, as I have suggested, than hand-me-down clothing: Mere patches of the same. Even though the court jester's outfit was normally opulent, it symbolized no economic interest in his or her society that might cloud one's analysis of social and personal ills.

18. "Back to the Future: A Review-Article on the New Historicism, Deconstruction, and Nineteenth-Century Fiction. *TSLL*, 30 (1988): 120–49, p. 132.

19. McCoy, *Rebellion in Arcadia*, p. x.

20. Ibid.

21. Ferguson, *Trials of Desire*, p. 138.

22. See chapter 2, fn. 11. The term is found in Nancy Lindheim, *The Structures of Sidney's Arcadia* (Toronto: Univ. of Toronto Press, 1982). p. 58.

23. Stanley Fish, *Surprised by Sin: The Reader in Paradise Lost* (New York: St. Martin's Press, 1967); Paul Alpers, *The Poetry of the Faerie Queene* (Princeton:

Princeton Univ. Press, 1967); and Stephen Booth, *Shakespeare's Sonnets* (New Haven: Yale Univ. Press, 1977).

24. See *Renaissance Self-Fashioning*, p. 2. I quote from *The Works of Edmund Spenser: A Varioum Edition*, ed. Edwin Greenlaw, et al., 10 vols. (Baltimore: Johns Hopkins Univ. Press, 1932–57), vol. 6 (1938), p. 109, cited by book, canto, stanza, and line in the text.

Chapter 1. A Dazzling Mirage

1. *The Monty Python Show.*
2. Sir Philip Sidney, *The Countess of Pembroke's Arcadia* (*The Old Arcadia*).
3. Alexander C. Judson, *Sidney's Appearance: A Study in Elizabethan Portraiture*, Indiana University Publications in the Humanities Series, 51 (Bloomington: Indiana Univ. Press, 1958).
4. Frances A. Yates, *Giordano Bruno and the Hermetic Tradition* (Chicago: Univ. of Chicago Press, 1964), esp. chapter 13, "Giordano Bruno in England"; John Buxton, *Sir Philip Sidney and the English Renaissance* (London: Macmillan, 1954); Jan Van Dorsten, *Poets, Patrons, and Professors: Sir Philip Sidney and the Leiden Humanists* (Leiden: Sir Thomas Brown Institute, 1962) and "Literary Patronage in Elizabethan England: The Early Phase," chapter 7 of *Patronage in the Renaissance*, ed. Guy Fitch Lytle and Stephen Orgel (Princeton: Princeton Univ. Press, 1981): 191–206, esp. pp. 200–206; Richard Lanham, "Sidney: The Ornament of His Age," *Southern Review: Australian Review of Literary Studies*, 2 (1967), 319–40; McCoy, *Rebellion in Arcadia*, p. 9, says, "His death capped a career of noble failure." Also see Helgerson, *The Elizabethan Prodigals.*
5. Tillyard, *The Elizabethan World Picture*, p. 45.
6. Lanham, "The Ornament of His Age," p. 335.
7. Thomas Moffet, *Nobilis, or A View of the Life and Death of a Sidney and Lessus Lugubris*, ed. Virgil B. Heltzel and Hoyt H. Hudson (San Marino: Huntington 1940).
8. Wallace, *The Life of Sir Philip Sidney*, pp. 396–7. Shrewsbury school has a statue of Sidney, but it is dedicated to its World War I dead.
9. Lanham, "The Ornament of His Age," p. 323.
10. John Philip (Phillips), *Life and Death of Sir Philip Sidney* (London: Robert Waldegrave, 1587), no pagination.
11. Wallace, *The Life of Sir Philip Sidney*, pp. 177–9; 287. Sidney was so courteous in discussions with Campion that the Jesuit suspected Sidney had Catholic leanings.
12. Frances A. Yates, "Elizabethan Chivalry: The Romance of the Accession Day Tilts," *Journal of the Warburg and Courtauld Institutes*, 20 (1957), 4–25; and "Queen Elizabeth as Astraea," *Journal of the Warburg and Courtauld Institutes*, 10 (1947), 27–82. Now edited and collected in *Astraea: The Imperial Theme in the Sixteenth Century* (London: Routledge & Paul, 1975).
13. Yates, "Elizabethan Chivalry," p. 22; *Astraea*, p. 108.
14. Ibid., p. 15; *Astraea*, p. 101.
15. See Norman Council's discussion of the progress of Elizabeth's image from earthly to unearthly beauty in "'O Dea Certe': The Allegory of *The Fortress of Perfect Beauty*," *The Huntington Library Quarterly*, 39 (1976), 329–42. John H. King provides an interesting survey of the queen's images, with bibliography, in Queen Elizabeth I; Representations of the Virgin Queen," *Renaissance Quarterly* 43 (1990), 30–74.

16. Francis Bacon, *The Works of Francis Bacon*, ed. James Spedding (London: Longmans, 1878), 14 vols., vol. 7, p. 157.
17. Stephen Orgel, "Sidney's Experiment in Pastoral: *The Lady of May*," *Journal of the Warburg and Courtauld Institutes*, 26 (1963): 198–203.
18. *The Poems of Sir Philip Sidney*, p. 4.
19. The incident is found in Wallace, pp. 213–16, but its "best account," as McCoy points out, *Rebellion in Arcadia*, p. 2, is found in Sir Fulke Greville, *The Life of the Renowned Sir Philip Sidney*, intro. Nowell Smith (Oxford: Clarendon, 1907), pp. 67–8. More recently it appears in *The Prose works of Fulke Greville, Lord Brooke*, ed. John Gouws (Oxford; Clarendon Press, 1986), pp. 38–41.

Maureen Quilligan, "Sidney and His Queen," pp. 171–76, discusses the "one-up-man-ship" of the affair in the terms of Pierre Bourdieu, *Outline of a Theory of Practice*, trans. Richard Nice (Cambridge: Cambridge Univ. Press, 1977).
20. Bacon, vol. 6, p. 302; *In Felicem Memoriam Elizabethae Regina Angliae*, 1608, "ultra sortem aetatis," "nil prorsus majestati ejus officerent."
21. Joseph Levine, ed., *Great Lives Observed: Elizabeth I* (Englewood, N.J.: Prentice-Hall, 1969), p. 5.
22. *The Prose Works of Sir Philip Sidney*, ed. Albert Feuillerat, 4 vols. (Cambridge: Cambridge Univ. Press, 1912), vol. 3, p. 167.
23. George Peele, *Polyhymnia* (London: Richard Ihoner ?, 1590), no pagination, leaf 6.
24. See the discussion of Sidney's will in *Miscellaneous Prose*, pp. 143–6. His bequest of the sword is found on p. 152.
25. Bacon, vol. 10, p. 147.
26. Ibid., vol. 6, p. 29. In *The History of Henry VII*.
27. Neville Williams notes this fact in *Elizabeth, Queen of England* (London: Weidenfeld & Nicholson, 1967), p. 293. He goes on to suggest that the extravagant funeral arrangements had another propagandistic aim, to draw attention away from military failures on the continent. See also Ronald Strickland's fascinating account of the accounts in "Pageantry and Poetry as Discourse: The Production of Subjectivity in Sir Philip Sidney's Funeral," *ELH*, 57 (1990): 19–36.
28. Berta Siebeck, *Das Bild Sir Philip Sidneys In Der Englischen Renaissance* (Weimar: Hermann Bohlaus, 1939), p. 72, "Vielleicht sah Elizabeth das Interesse des Volkes nicht ungern von der peinlichen Erinnerung und die Hinrichtung abgelenkt auf ein unverfänglicheres Schauspiel."
29. Michel Poirier, *Sir Philip Sidney: Le Chevalier Poete Elizabethian* (Lille: Univ. de Lille, 1948), p. 269, "C'est peut-être pour détourner l'attention du peuple d'un régicide qui risquait d'ébranler son propre loyalisme que le gouvernement anglais decida d'entourer cette inhumation d'un tel éclat."
30. Greville, *Prose Works*, pp. 72–96.
31. Stephen Greenblatt, *Sir Walter Ralegh: The Renaissance Man and His Roles* (New Haven: Yale Univ. Press, 1973), pp. 1-21.
32. Ibid., p. 16.
33. *The Countess of Pembroke's Arcadia (The Old Arcadia)*, p. 3.
34. See Kenneth Myrick, *Sir Philip Sidney as a Literary Craftsman*, 2nd edition, orig. 1935 (Lincoln: Univ. of Nebraska Press, 1965), pp. 3–45.
35. Thomas Moffet, *Nobilis, or a View of the Life and Death of a Sidney and Lessus Lugubris,* ed. Virgil B. Heltzel and Hoyt H. Hudson (San Marino: Huntington, 1940), pp. 6, 70.
36. William Camden, *Remaines Concerning Britaine, Fift Impression* (London: T. Harper for J. Waterson, 1636), p. 357. Katherine Duncan-Jones makes this connec-

tion in "Sidney's Personal Imprese," *Journal of the Warburg and Courtauld Institutes*, 33 (1970): 123. The reference to the device "SPERO" is found in George Whetstone, *Sir Philip Sidney* (1587), sig. B3, as Duncan-Jones points out.

37. Greville, *Prose Works*, p. 79.
38. Ibid., p. 82.
39. Ibid.
40. Some of Sidney's name-changing may be a reflection of the irony of having been named for a man, in this period of international strife, who was emerging as England's chief enemy, his godfather, Philip II of Spain. Elizabeth emphasized the identity of the two names by calling Sidney "'her Philip,' in opposition to Philip II, of Spain." Sir Robert Naunton *Fragmenta Regalia, 1641*, in *The Harleian Miscellany* (London: John White, 1809), p. 93 fn.
41. *The Countess of Pembroke's Arcadia (The New Arcadia)*, ed. Victor Skretkowicz (Oxford: Clarendon Press, 1987), p. 255.
42. Duncan-Jones, "Sidney's Personal Imprese," p. 323.
43. "Nullus in egregio reperitur corpore naevus," in D. Coulman, "Spotted to Be Known," *Journal of the Warburg and Courtauld Institutes*, 20 (1957), 179–80.
44. *Miscellaneous Prose*, p. 169, discussed on p. 164. See also Duncan-Jones further discussion of Gifford in "Sidney, Stella and Lady Rich," in *Sir Philip Sidney: 1586 and the Creation of a Legend*, ed. Jan Van Dorsten, Dominic Baker Smith, and Arthur Kinney (Leiden: Leiden Univ. Press, 1986), pp. 170–92.
45. *The New Arcadia*, p. 478.
46. *The New Arcadia*, p. 256.
47. C. S. Lewis, *English Literature in the Sixteenth Century Excluding Drama* (Oxford: Clarendon, 1954), p. 325.
48. Ringler (quoted in McCoy, p. 69) points out that "Sidney went out of his way to identify himself as Astrophil and Stella as Lady Rich." *The Poems of Sir Philip Sidney*, p. xliv.
49. Moffet, p. 135, note to p. 92.
50. Moffet, p. 91.
51. Wallace, *The Life*, pp. 237, 245; and Bertram Dobell, "New Light Upon Sir Philip Sidney's 'Arcadia,'" *Quarterly Review*, 420 (1909): 100.
52. John Aubrey, *Aubrey's Brief Lives*, ed. Oliver Lawson Dick (Ann Arbor: Univ. of Michigan Press, 1962), p. 280.
53. *Brief Lives and Other Selected Writings by John Aubrey*, ed. Anthony Powell (New York: Charles Scribner's Sons, 1949), p. 36.
54. Lewis, *English Literature in the Sixteenth Century*, p. 324.
55. William Hazlitt, *The Collected Works of William Hazlitt*, ed. A. R. Waller and Arnold Glover (London: J. M. Dent, 1902), 12 vols., vol. 6, p. 318. The fn. corrects the citation from *Troilus and Cressida*, III, 3 to "receives and renders."
56. Lewis, *English Literature in the Sixteenth Century*, p. 324.

Chapter 2. Charted Problems

1. In the stylistic camp, see: Abraham Fraunce, *The Arcadian Rhetorike*, ed. Ethel Seaton (Oxford: Luttrell Society, 1950); Hoyt H. Hudson, ed., *Directions for Speech and Style by John Hoskins* (Princeton: Princeton Univ. Press, 1935); P. P. Howe (after the edition of A. R. Waller and Arnold Glover), *Lectures on the Age of Elizabeth* in *The Complete Works of William Hazlitt in Twenty-One Volumes: Centenary Edition* (London: J. M. Dent, 1931), vol. 6, pp. 318–26; J. J. Jusserand,

The English Novel in the Time of Shakespeare (London: Unwin, 1890; repr. New York: AMS Press, 1965); Mario Praz, "Sidney's Original *Arcadia*," *London Mercury*, 15 (1926–27): 507-14.

In the school of content, see: Greville, *Prose Works;* E. V. Lucas, ed., "Some Sonnets of Sir Philip Sydney" in *The Works of Charles and Mary Lamb* (London: Methuen, 1904), 7 vols., vol. 2, pp. 213–20; S. L. Wolff, *The Greek Romances in Elizabethan Prose Fiction* (New York: 1912); Edwin A. Greenlaw, "Sidney's *Arcadia* as an Example of Elizabethan Allegory," in *Kittredge Anniversary Papers* (Boston: Ginn, 1913; repr. New York: Russell & Russell, 1967).

2. *The Works of Charles and Mary Lamb*, vol. 2, p. 218.
3. *The Old Arcadia*, p. 3; *Paradise Lost*, 7.31.
4. *The New Arcadia*, by page number in the text.
5. Hazlitt, vol. 6, p. 324.
6. Lamb, vol. 1, pp. 218–19.
7. Ibid., p. 218.
8. Hazlitt, p. 325.
9. Lamb, vol, 1, p. 53 in "Characters of Dramatic Writers," under "Francis Beaumont—John Fletcher."
10. E. M. W. Tillyard, *The English Epic and Its Background* (New York: Oxford Univ. Press, 1954); and Lewis, *English Literature in the Sixteenth Century.*
11. David Kalstone (*Sidney's Poetry: Contexts and Interpretations* [New York: Norton, 1965]) sees an elemental debate in the form and content of *Lady of May* and *Arcadia* between antithetical demands of the active life and pastoral love, but while Sidney maintains tension and balance between "the demands of the heroic life and the inroads of passion" (p. 20), resolution is lacking. Unlike in Sannazaro or Spenser, "confusions and bafflements multiply rather than disappear when heroes enter the pastoral world" (59), a disorder reflected in the undermining of "rigid rhetorical positions" (48). Neil Rudenstine (*Sidney's Poetic Development* [Cambridge: Harvard Univ. Press, 1967]) locates the central antithetical design in *Arcadia* in Sidney's "vacillations between court and country" (16). Thus the basic debate in Sidney's romance concerns the relative virtue of the life of action as opposed to the life of contemplation, especially as it relates to the central theme of the autonomous power of love.

Since the debate between the court and country, according to these critics, can never be resolved in relation to love, Sidney has recourse to a kind of "toneless" rhetoric (60, 64, 75), which sets up oppositions but does not resolve them. His fondness for *anadiplosis*—the repetition of words in the end and beginning of successive syntactical units—as in "Why those that die, men say they do depart / Depart, a word so gentle to my minde" (127)—leads him to set up oppositions but also "emphasized . . . the autonomous inevitable movement of omnipotent desire" (72). Thus, non-resolution, for this critic, is "resolved," inadequately, of course, in desire. Rudenstine relates Sidney's rhetorical configurations to unresolved thematic problems he discovers at the core of the work. His poetry in *Astrophil and Stella* is marked by "its courtly qualities, its playful wit and delight in ornament, its Petrarchan ceremoniousness and its concern for chivalric and heroic values" (172). Ceremony suggests style, chivalry ideal content.

Richard Lanham, on the other hand (*The Old Arcadia* in *Sidney's Arcadia* [New Haven: Yale Univ. Press, 1965]), sees the basic theme in *Old Arcadia* to be that of "an inward surrender of the proper dominance of reason over passion" (211). He sees the work as a series of rhetorical occasions where the essential debate between reason and passion can be set up but resolved perhaps only in comic irresolution (230, 253 fn.).

The very similarity of the theses and methods of Lanham and Rudenstine suggests the validity of the connection between the antithetical style and the antithetical content of the work. Their emphasis on style, however, gives the impression that *Arcadia* is made up of a series of rhetorical matches, debates which are ultimately unresolved, and, in a sense, ornamental to theme. Sidney's lack of resolution begins to resemble mere game or failure.

While Walter Davis ("Thematic Unity in the *New Arcadia*," *Studies in Philology* 57 [1960]: 123–143) does not specifically concern himself with the style of the *1590 Arcadia*, he does argue that the antithetical structure of book 2 is based on the opposition between "civil strife, usually a result of Passion's overpowering Reason" (131), and the "inner workings of passion in a character rather than its effect in deeds" (131). This opposition informs us in part why the first part is "told in a straightforward manner" and why the second is "more complexly interwoven" (131). Plot and episode are subtly related subordinate to an "overall unifying theme by means of the motif of *Reason* and *Passion*" (135), which produces among other things the "self-division" in the speeches, and the "conflict between the inner man and the outer man" (126).

Elsewhere (*A Map of Arcadia* in *Sidney's Arcadia* [New Haven: Yale Univ. Press, 1965]) Davis shows how at least the plot is structured around conventional oppositions, active and contemplative life (59), heroism and love (69), and, by way of John Danby's criticism (75), secular *virtus* and Christian patience. Like Lanham and Rudenstine, Davis also suggests that these oppositions are not resolved except perhaps in the denouement of the *Old Arcadia* until which "the control of reason over appetite is at best sporadic" (83).

In fact Danby (*Poets on Fortune's Hill* [London: Faber & Faber, 1952]), who originally proposed as thematically central the opposition of worldly heroism and Christian patience, is the only recent critic who feels such opposition is satisfactorily resolved, here in favor of suffering. That his argument is based largely on his reading of the incomplete book three of the *1590 Arcadia* may compromise his position, unless we accept Kimbrough's remark (*Sir Philip Sidney* [New York: Twayne, 1971]) that Sidney simply gave up "in disgust" (142). Book 3 ends in the middle of a sentence—"whereat ashamed, as having never done so much before in his life . . ."— that adumbrates a return to violent action in the work. Anaxius, discovering that he is capable of cowardice in his duel with Zelmane (Pyrocles), seems on the verge of a most violent overreaction. Doing seems about to overcome suffering. More recently, A. C. Hamilton (*Sir Philip Sidney: A Study of His Life and Works* [Cambridge: Cambridge Univ. Press, 1977]) simply determines that the work as a whole demands a divided response between its "delight" and its "instruction" (140–41) thus returning us to our old distinction between courtly style and heroic content.

12. Helgerson, *The Elizabethan Prodigals*.
13. McCoy, *Rebellion in Arcadia*.
14. (Oxford: Clarendon Press, 1965).
15. Helgerson, *The Elizabethan Prodigals*, p. 125.
16. Ibid., pp. 128, 155.
17. Ibid., p. 132.
18. Lindheim, *The Structures of Sidney's Arcadia*, p. 76.
19. Ibid., p. 28.
20. Ibid., p. 58.
21. Ronald Levao, *Renaissance Minds and Their Fictions: Cusanus, Sidney, Shakespeare* (Berkeley: Univ. of California Press, 1985), chapter 5, "Sidney's Feigned Apology," pp. 134–56. See also Dorothy Connell, *Sir Philip Sidney: The Maker's Mind* (Oxford: Clarendon, 1977).

22. David Norbrook, *Poetry and Politics in the English Renaissance* (London: Routledge & Kegan Paul, 1984), chapter 4, "Sidney and Political Pastoral," pp. 91–108.

23. Annabel Patterson, *Censorship and Interpretation: The Conditions of Writing and Reading in Early Modern Europe* (Madison: Univ. of Wisconsin Press, 1984), chapter 1, " 'Under . . . pretty tales': Intention in Sidney's *Arcadia*," pp. 24–43.

24. Ferguson, *Trials of Desire*, p. 229, fn. 22.

25. For Sidney's purported Calvinism, see Andrew Weiner, *Sir Philip Sidney and the Poetics of Protestantism* (Minneapolis: Univ. of Minnesota Press, 1978). For his Ciceronian didacticism, see William Craft, "The Shaping Picture of Love in Sidney's *New Arcadia*," *Studies in Philology*, 8 (1984): 395–418, and "Remaking the Heroic Self in the *New Arcadia*," *SEL*, 25 (1985): 45–67.

26. I am using the term in the sense of Stanley Fish's stylistic criticism, notably in *Surprised by Sin*. In this context, Robert E. Stillman says that Sidney "anticipated Fish's claims for meaning as an event," in *Sidney's Poetic Justice: The Old Arcadia, Its Eclogues, and Renaissance Pastoral Traditions* (Lewisburg: Bucknell Univ. Press, 1986), p. 235, fn. 56. As I suggest in the introduction, more than merely being "anticipated" by Sidney, the affective critics have in fact rediscovered the Renaissance mode.

27. Lindheim, *The Structures of Sidney's Arcadia*, p. 40.

28. I retain the reading "only, only" of one manuscript and of Ponsonby's *The Defence of Poesie* here.

29. We have here, of course, Sidney's notorious figures of repetition, *anadiplosis* ("only, only") and *antimetabole* ("conceit . . . matter . . . matter . . . conceit"), Rudenstine, *Sidney's Poetic Development*, pp. 66–69, but we also have "readable" affects.

Chapter 3. Sidney's Official Indirection

1. See ch. 1, fn. 12 and Connell, *The Maker's Mind*, pp. 56–58.

2. John Nichols, in *Progresses*, 2.94, locates the date of the quasi-masque in early May of 1578. While Duncan-Jones, (*Miscellaneous Prose*, p. 13) and Connell, (*The Maker's Mind*, p. 55) both pose 1578 or 1579, (though Connell [p. 83] favors 1579) I see no reason to doubt Nichols's placement in what is a densely described series of events and documents. As Duncan-Jones points out, the "light" (13) quality of the defense of Leicester in this piece would be unlikely in 1579 between Leicester's secret and public marriages to Essex's widow Lettice Knowles at Kenilworth and Wanstead. As Andrew Weiner has pointed out to me, the date is crucial. Here, in 1578, Leicester has just (March) been denied an army to take to the continent (after extended royal encouragement), and so he is, in a sense, making up to the Queen after that personal disappointment, but he is also reminding her of the Catholic insurgency, even on British soil, that motivated his request.

3. *Miscellaneous Prose* by page and line number in the text. Duncan-Jones has judiciously edited the text of Sidney's dramatic work looking at both the printed version in the 1598 *Arcadia*, pp. 570–76, and the Helmingham Hall manuscript. She has also modernized spelling and punctuation.

4. (London: Hutchinson, 1968), pp. 154–55.

5. Robert Kimbrough and Philip Murphy, "The Helmingham Hall Manuscript of Sidney's *The Lady of May*: A Commentary and Transcription," *Renaissance Drama*, New Series 1 (1968): 103–19. Hereafter "Kimbrough and Murphy."

6. *Miscellaneous Prose*. p. 79. From *A Defence of Poetry*. Hereafter by page number in the text.

7. Ringler, *The Poems*, pp. x–xii. On p. 362, he says that "topical allusion" or "hidden significance" in the play "perhaps," "concerns the chief point of national policy at issue in 1578–9, whether England should actively support the cause of continental Protestantism by giving military aid to the Netherlands." He adds that if the queen considered this implication, she rejected it "by giving judgement in favour of the peaceful Espilus." Ringler rejects William Gray's suggestion that Therion be connected with d'Alençon's marriage proposal on the grounds that Sidney gives Therion virtues that he does not give the duc d'Anjou in his *Letter written . . . to Queen Elizabeth, touching her marriage with Monsieur.* Thelma N. Greenfield (*The Eye of Judgment: Reading of the New Arcadia* [Lewisburg: Bucknell Univ. Press, 1982], p. 157) also suggests a reference to the Queen's marriage arrangements.

8. Ringler, *The Poems*, p. 361. "θεριον, wild beast."

9. Kimbrough and Murphy, pp. 103–7.

10. Montrose, "Celebration and Insinuation," pp. 3–35. For a similar view of Sidney's implicit "defiant feelings," see McCoy, *Rebellion in Arcadia*, p. 26.

11. "Impeding the Progress: Sidney's *The Lady of May*," *Iowa State Journal of Research*, 60 (1986): 395–405.

12. *The Elizabethan Prodigals*, pp. 131–2.

13. Penny Pickett, "Sidney's Use of *Phaedrus* in *The Lady of May*," *SEL*, 16 (1976): 33–50.

14. "Justice and the 'Good word' in Sidney's *The Lady of May*," *SEL*, 24 (1984): 23–28.

15. Pickett, "Sidney's Use of Phaedrus," p. 50.

16. "Sidney's Experiment in Pastoral, pp. 198–203.

17. Ibid., p. 199.

18. *Censorship and Interpretation*, p. 28.

19. Ringler in *The Poems*, suggests the professional actor under Leicester's aegis, Richard Tarlton, but Ringler is not working with the Helmingham Hall manuscript where the final oration is accompanied by the gift of an agate necklace. Sidney later adopts a schoolmasterly persona, both in his *Letter to Queen Elizabeth* and in his *Defence of Poetry.*

20. Lewis, *English Literature in the Sixteenth Century*, Book III, "Golden," esp. pp. 318–47.

21. Orgel was the first to note this anomaly, the subject of much debate more recently among the critics, in "Sidney's Experiment in Pastoral," p. 202. For further discussion, see my "The Exemplary Mirage: Fabrication of Sir Philip Sidney's Biographical Image and the Sidney Reader," *ELH*, 48 (1981): 1–16, p. 5.

22. *Miscellaneous Prose*, p. 19.

23. Stillman, "Justice and the 'Good Word,' " p. 32.

24. Variations on this character appear not only in *commedia dell'arte* but also in *le commedie rusticali* and other farce, such as *farse cavaiole*. See Marvin T. Herrick, "Italian Farce," *Italian Comedy in the Renaissance* (Urbana: Univ. of Illinois Press, 1960), pp. 26–59 (referred to by Kimbrough and Murphy, p. 104). See especially the discussion of the farce, *Della Oscola*, on p. 29.

25. Ringler, *The Poems*, p. 361, notes the possible influence on Rombus's speech of the Latinisms that creep into "An ynkehorne letter" found in Sidney's friend Thomas Wilson's *The Arte of Rhetorique.* See the facsimile, intro. Robert Hood Bowers (Gainesville, Fla.: Scholars' Facsimiles and Reprints, 1962), p. 184.

26. Montrose, incidentally, in "Celebration and Insinuation," pp. 14–15, connects this device with other "compliments to Tudor royalty," such as in "George Peele's courtly pastoral, *The Araygnement of Paris.*"

27. Stillman, "Justice and the 'Good Word,' " p. 33.

28. *OED*, 9, for "dig," "To spur (a horse) vigorously," seems appropriate.

29. Janel Mueller has suggested to me that Sidney takes an oblique look at Elizabeth's sometime Latin tutor, the author of *The Schoolmaster*, Roger Ascham, in Rombus. I agree that Ascham's work, especially in its aspect of Latin instructor's manual, is glanced at, and, as with Sidney's oblique look at George Gascoigne's court entertainment, which, in fact the Queen missed attending at Kenilworth in July of 1575, *The Princely Pleasures*, the earlier generation goes unmentioned and mildly satirized.

30. Virgil. *Complete Works*, trans. H. Rushton Fairclough, Loeb edition. 2 vols. (London: Heinemann, 1932). With Stillman, I see a geometric figure, a "rhombus" or "rhomboid" behind this name. Pickett, in "Sidney's Use of *Phaedrus*," p. 48, fn. also suggests Ramus which could very well be in keeping with Sidney's satire of all Rombus's distinctions and divisions. "Did Sidney both mock Ramus by the caricature Rombus and praise him by the imitation? I submit that he did." I have doubts, however, whether Sidney might spoof even the endless "distinctions and divisions" of an older friend who was murdered in the Massacre of St. Bartholomew's Day he witnessed from Francis Walsingham's house in Paris in 1572. I remain uncertain. "Rombus," like "Ramus," smacks of self-conscious Latin pseudonym. On Pierre de la Ramée's self-conscious alteration of his name, see *Arguments in Rhetoric Against Quintilian: Translation and text of Peter Ramus's Rhetorical Distinctions in Quintilianum (1549)*, trans. Carole Newlands, introduction by James J. Murphy (Dekalb: Northern Illinois Univ. Press, 1986), p. 1 and fn. 4, p. 47.

31. On contemporary recusancy in the kingdom, see Connell, p. 56.

32. See "British Virgil: Four Renaissance Disguises of the Laocoön Passage of Book 2 of the *Aeneid*," *SEL*, 22 (1982): 21–38, esp. p. 35

33. That Elizabeth's propagandists pictured her collapsing dangerous distinctions, as we will see in Sidney's picture of the operation of her eyes, is reflected in a separate iconographic tradition memorialized in the poem,

> Division kindled stryfe
> Blist Union quenchte the flame:
> Thence sprang our noble Phoenix deare,
> The pearlesse Prince of Fame.

delivered to her on 16 August 1578 at the gates of Norwich. In Nichols's description (*Progresses* 2.143), the poem follows what might be a puzzling error "on the right side was gorgeously set forth the redde rose, signifying the House of Yorke; on the left side the white rose, representing the House of Lancaster." Since the wrong roses are meant to be joined, is it possible that the mistake was intentional, thus entirely collapsing this dangerous distinction?

34. *Progresses* (1823), 2.214, fn. 1, " 'After so much mirth succeeded as much sorrow. The traines of her Majesty's carriage being many of them infected, left the plague behind them; which afterwards so increased and contynued, as it raged above a year and three quarters after: in which time 2335 English and 2482 alyan strangers died, from August 20, 1578, to Feb. 19, 1579. Among which were ten Aldermen.' Blomefield."

35. The connection of Elizabeth with the icon of the basilisk or cockatrice may help explain the presence of serpents in her state portraits as well as the often received gift jewelry in the form of a serpent, the most striking iconic present, along with butterflies, the squirrel (ermine?), and Sidney's famous whip. See Skretkowicz on the "Catoblepta," *New Arcadia*, p. 573, fn.

36. *Miscellaneous Prose*, p. 17.

37. On this odd reversal, see A. C. Hamilton, *Sir Philip Sidney: A Study of His Life and Works* (Cambridge: Cambridge Univ. Press, 1977), p. 21; and Connell, *The Maker's Mind*, pp. 54–57. Of course, Leicester was accused at one time or another of being a treacherous Papist, as he was of nearly every crime imaginable, from murdering his wife, Amy Robsart or Walter Devereux, First Earl of Essex, to planning to marry and murder the queen in order to ascend the throne. See, for example, *Leicester's Commonwealth*, or its offspring *Leicester's Ghost*. D. C. Peck, ed. *Leicester's Commonwealth: The Copy of a Letter Written by a Master of Art of Cambridge (1584) and Related Documents* (Athens Ohio: Ohio Univ. Press, 1985). And in a particularly attractive edition, produced for the Newberry Library, Thomas Rogers, *Leicester's Ghost*, ed. Franklin B. Williams, Jr., (Chicago: Univ. of Chicago Press, 1972).

38. See *In Felicem Memoriam Elizabethae Regina Angliae* (vol. 6, p. 302) and vol. 10, p. 147, in *The Works of Francis Bacon*, ed. James Spedding (London: Longmans, 1878). Also see "The Exemplary Mirage," pp. 5–7.

39. See Yates, *Astraea*, esp. pp. 101–108.

40. Stillman, "Justice and the 'Good Word,'" p. 25.

41. See *Miscellaneous Prose*, p. 39.

42. Ibid., p. 36.

43. Ibid., pp. 42–43. Duncan-Jones uses this passage to highlight the "manuscript tradition" (42).

44. Ibid., p. 43.

45. Ibid. Duncan-Jones quotes *OED*.

46. Ibid., p. 36. For a contrary position, see King, "Queen Elizabeth I," p. 50.

47. Feuillerat, vol. 3, p. 129.

48. Ibid., p. 125. A letter of 22 May 1746, quoted, in part, by Duncan-Jones.

49. Ibid.

50. Katherine Duncan-Jones has authorized my changing the word from "evil" in *Miscellaneous Prose*.

51. Copied in *Reasons for a War Against Spain* etc., 2nd edition (London: J. Wilford, 1738), pp. 38–40.

52. Languet attempted to divert Sidney from Italy on several occasions, on the grounds of personal safety, it seems, for a Protestant.

53. *Nicomachean Ethics* V, vii, 2. Loeb edition. Trans. H. Rackham (London: Heinemann, 1934), p. 294.

Chapter 4. Astrophil's "Tragicomedy of Love . . . Performed by Starlight"

1. Notably McCoy, *Rebellion in Arcadia*, pp. 69–109.
But see also Roswitha Mayr, *The Concept of Love in Sidney and Spenser* (Salzburg: Universitat Salzburg, 1978), for an extreme case of such "equation."

2. I quote from *The Poems of Sir Philip Sidney* by line number in the text.

3. Clark Hulse, "Stella's Wit: Penelope Rich as Reader of Sidney's Sonnets," in Margaret Ferguson, Maureen Quilligan and Nancy Vickers, eds. *Rewriting the Renaissance: The Discourses of Sexual Difference in Early Modern Europe* (Chicago: Univ. of Chicago Press, 1986), pp. 272–86.

4. James M. Osborn quotes the letter in *Young Philip Sidney: 1572–1577* (New Haven: Yale Univ. Press, 1972), p. 444.

Notes

5. Ringler, p. 447.
6. The two names are current, but Ringler has settled most readers on the former, because it means "love" and contains a nickname for "Philip," "Phil." Ringler, p. 458. I argue that "Phel" is simply a mistake for "Phil."
7. Ronald B. McKerrow, *The Works of Thomas Nashe*, 5 vols. (Oxford: Basil Blackwell, 1958), vol. 3, p. 329.
8. Ibid., vol. 4, p. 459 fn. 2 for a discussion of the reference.
9. Ibid., vol. 3, p. 329.
10. Ibid., p. 330.
11. Ibid., p. 329.
12. See the discussion of tragicomedy's catharsis in *Il Verrato, Ovvero Difesa di Quanto Ha Scritto M. Giason etc.* in *Opere di Battista Guarini*, ed. Marziano Guglielminetti, 2nd edition (Torino: Classici UTET, 1971), pp. 728–821, esp. 765, 775, where melancholy is discussed.
13. *The Works of Thomas Nashe*, vol. 3, p. 329.
14. Ibid., p. 231.
15. *John Donne, Coterie Poet* (Madison: Univ. of Wisconsin Press, 1986), p. 3. See also pp. 10, 11. In part, Marotti reflects comments he made in "'Love is not love': Elizabethan Sonnet Sequences and the Social Order," *ELH*, 49 (1982): 396–428, esp. pp. 399–406. Richard Helgerson develops ideas of immediate egoistic context in *Self-Crowned Laureates: Spenser, Jonson, Milton and the Literary System* (Berkeley: Univ. of California Press, 1983).
16. Ringler, p. 495, points out "What the poet will see when he looks in his heart is the image of Stella," certainly true, but the emotional response to her actual absence is also a cry of pain.
17. Ringler, p. xlvi.
18. See, for example, Dorothy Jones, "Sidney's Erotic Pen: An Interpretation of One of the *Arcadia* Poems," *Journal of English and Germanic Philology*, 73 (1974): 32–47.
19. Ringler, p. 487.
20. "The Last Act of Astrophil and Stella," *Mid-Hudson Language Studies* (1979): 62–76, p. 64.
21. *The Elizabethan Malady: A Study of Melancholia in English Literature from 1580 to 1642.* (East Lansing: Michigan State College Press), esp. pp. 36, 44, 70–71, 112, 126, 136–37.
22. *OED*, 1, for "harbinger."
23. "On the Pathetic Fallacy" in *Modern Painters. The Works of John Ruskin*, ed. E. T. Cook and Alexander Wedderburn, 39 vols. (London: George Allen, 1912), vol. 5, pp. 201ff.

Chapter 5. "Darknesse Cleare": Seven Levels of Starlover's Ambiguity

1. See Hulse, "Stella's Wit," and Duncan-Jones, "Sidney, Stella and Lady Rich."
2. Sidney's works, notably *Arcadia*, have become the source of a number of lists of "flowers." See chapter 2, fn. 1.
3. William Empson, *Seven Types of Ambiguity* (New York: New Directions, 1966, orig. London: Chatto and Windus, 1930).
4. *Sir Philip Sidney: Selected Prose and Poetry*, ed. Robert Kimbrough (New York: Holt Rinehart & Winston, 1969), p. 343, has "rare zeal."

5. For development of "Phil," see J. de Oliviera e Silva, "Naming and the Literary Context: Backgrounds to Sir Philip Sidney's *Philisides*," *Literary Onomastics Studies*, 7 (1980): 139–48.

6. Sidney is in a tradition that goes back to Catullus through Skelton's "Philip Sparrow."

7. Philip Sparrow's nickname as well.

8. Rosalie Colie, *Paradoxia Epidemica: The Renaissance Tradition of Paradox* (Princeton: Princeton Univ. Press, 1966), p. 92.

9. A kind of "mimetic rivalry" is suggested. For the concept, see René Girard, *Violence and the Sacred*, trans. Patrick Gregory (Baltimore: Johns Hopkins Univ. Pres, 1977), on reciprocal violence in Greek tragedy. See also Girard's upcoming book on Shakespeare. Also *Shakespeare's Political and Animal: Schema* and *Schemata in the Canon* (Newark: Univ. of Delaware Press, 1990).

10. Sonnets 24, 35, and 37 were omitted from the early editions.

11. Geoffrey Shepherd, in *Sir Philip Sidney: An Apology for Poetry or the Defence of Poesy* (London: Nelson, 1965), notes the wordplay, but he sees it as merely "brisk, rather empty," fn. to 115, 10ff, p. 184.

12. Richard Lanham, "*Astrophil and Stella*: Pure and Impure Persuasion," *English Literary Renaissance* 2 (1972): 100–15.

13. George Puttenham, *The Arte of English Poesie*, ed. Gladys Doidge Willcock and Alice Walker (Cambridge: Cambridge Univ. Press, 1936), p. 203.

14. *Directions for Speech and Style*, p. 36.

15. Ibid.

16. Ibid., p. 37; *The New Arcadia*, p. 368.

17. Colie, p. 91.

18. Note, for example, that Golding is largely uncensored. Only Sandys begins active bowdlerizing and deleting in his version, for example, of the tale of Orpheus "inventing" homosexuality in book 10 of the *Metamorphoses*,

19. Colie, p. 91ff.

20. Puttenham, p. 239.

21. *The Poetry of the Faerie Queene*, p. 36.

22. Ibid., p. 69.

23. McCoy, p. 100.

Chapter 6. The Sonneteer's Mock Encomium of Self

1. A. C. Hamilton, "Sidney and Agrippa," *Review of English Studies*, 7(1965): 151.

2. Ibid.

3. See especially, as Hamilton points out in the above, Gregory Smith in *Elizabethan Critical Essays* (Oxford, 1904), p. 393. Cf. J. W. H. Atkins, *English Literary Criticism: The Renascence* (London, 1947), p. 123; also the many references to Agrippa and Erasmus in Geoffrey Shepherd, ed., *An Apology for Poetry or the Defence of Poesy by Sir Philip Sidney* and Margaret Ferguson, *Trials of Desire*, pp. 157–58. Also see A. C. Hamilton, *Sir Philip Sidney: A Study of His Life and Works* (Cambridge: Cambridge Univ. Press, 1977), especially the chapter entitled "Sidney's Poetics," pp. 107–22.

4. *Plato's Symposium*, Loeb ed., pp. 215–16; and Desiderius Erasmus, *The Praise of Folly*, ed. and trans. Hoyt Hopewell Hudson (Princeton, N.J.: Princeton Univ.

Press, 1941), p. 36. See also Rabelais' odd amplification of this discussion in his preface to his third book, and Barbara Bowen's discussion in *The Age of Bluff*.

5. *English Literature in the Sixteenth Century*, pp. 343–47; and Morriss Partee, "Anti-Platonism in Sidney's 'Defence,' " *English Miscellany*, 22 (1971): 7–29.

6. *English Literature in the Sixteenth Century*, p. 344.

7. Rudenstine, pp. 51–52.

8. Lanham, *The Old Arcadia*, p. 338.

9. *Trials of Desire*, 137–62.

10. *Rebellion in Arcadia*, pp. 10, 20, 24–25, 75, 82, 94–97, 127, 128, 176. *The Elizabethan Prodigals*.

11. See, for example, Catherine Barnes, "The Hidden Persuader: The Complex Speaking Voice of Sidney's *Defence of Poetry*," *PMLA*, 86 (1971): 422–27.

12. *Praise of Folly*, p. 9.

13. Henrie Cornelius Agrippa, *Of the Vanitie and Uncertaintie of Artes and Sciences*, trans. James Sanford (London: Henry Wykes, 1569), folio pp. 183b–86a.

14. Edward Surtz, S. J. and J. H. Hexter, eds. Vol. 4 of *The Complete Works of St. Thomas More* (New Haven: Yale Univ. Press, 1965) p. 99.

15. Ibid.

16. *The Praise of Folly*, p. 10.

17. *Utopia*, p. 64. *Morosophis*. Surtz gives "wiseacres."

18. *Praise of Folly*, p. 10.

19. Ibid., p. 34.

20. Ibid., p. 32.

21. Ibid., p. 73

22. Ibid., p. 73

23. Shepherd writes, for example, that Sidney's introduction "employs a recognized method of indirect approach to the case and seeks to capture the goodwill of the audience by humourous anecdote, mock expostulation, and modesty formulas," p. 13.

24. See Barnes, "The Complex Speaking Voice," pp. 425–26. Also Levao, *Renaissance Minds and Their Fictions*, pp. 134–56.

25. See René Girard, *La Violence et la Sacré* (Paris: Grasset, 1972), pp. 63–101.

26. Feuillerat, 3:127.

Chapter 7. The Anti-Platonic Platonic Monologue

1. These figures were early gathered by Irene Samuels, for her article, "The Influence of Plato on Sir Philip Sidney's *Defense of Poesy*," *Modern Language Quarterly*, 1 (1940): 383–84. I suggest an expanded list to include *Philebus*, where delight and laughter are treated in similar ways to Sidney in *Miscellaneous Prose*, p. 115.

2. Henry S. Macran, ed., *The Harmonics of Aristoxenus* (Oxford: Clarendon Press, 1902), sections 30–31.

3. *Praise of Folly*, pp. 14, 15, 22, 26, 39, 47, 51, 79.

4. Of course, Plato noticeably ignores Pindar and reserves his praise for Tyrtaeus, but Tyrtaeus' mode of praise of governors etc. was apparently similar to our understanding of the "Pindaric mode."

5. Hazard Adams, ed., *Critical Theory Since Plato* (New York: Harcourt Brace Jovanovich, 1971), p. 154.

6. The original is found in Stephen Gosson, *The Schoole of Abuse*, ed. E. Arber (London: Alex. Murray, 1868), p. 65.
7. See also *Praise of Folly*, p. 8, and *Metamorphoses*, XI, pp. 146ff.

Chapter 8. Retroactive Reading

1. Forrest G. Robinson, for example, suggests that by his use of the term "speaking *Picture*," "Sidney means the poetic fusion of moral abstractions with actual character," *The Shape of Things Known: Sidney's Apology in Its Philosophical Tradition* (Cambridge, Mass.: Harvard Univ. Press, 1972), p. 100.
2. Alpers, p. 11.
3. Found in Lucretius, *De Rerum Natura*, I, 936–41 and IV, 11–16.
4. *Praise of Folly*, pp. 70–85; *Vanitie of the Artes, in toto*.
5. T. J. B. Spencer, ed., *Shakespeare's Plutarch*, trans. Thomas North (Baltimore: Penguin Books 1964), p. 303.
6. *Cranmer Bible*, 1539–1569. *II Samuel* 12: "And Nathan said to David: thou are the man."
7. See an elaborate discussion of this ruse in Margaret Ferguson, *Trials of Desire*, p. 144.
8. See *The New Arcadia*, p. 282. The relation of this passage and its original in *Old Arcadia* was the subject of a paper by Annabel Patterson at MLA 84, but I have yet to see it in print.
9. We are meant to ask, "What time is it?" I think the answer is both spring equinox (when "time" arbitrates indifferently "between the night and day") and pre-dawn twilight. Piers Ingersoll Lewis in "Literary and Political Attitudes in Sidney's *Arcadia*" (Cambridge, Mass.: Harvard Univ. Ph.D. diss., 1964), p. 54, and Jon Lawry in *Sidney's Two Arcadias: Pattern and Proceeding* (Ithaca: Cornell Univ. Press, 1972), p. 167, take it to be springtime, as does Skretkowicz (*The New Arcadia*, p. xxvi ff.) paralleling "It was in the . . ." of p. 179, in part, announcing winter. But it could also be pre-dawn, as it is in the opening of Heliodorus's *An Ethiopian Tale*. ("Day had begun to smile and the sun was shining upon the hilltop when . . ." in Heliodorus, *An Ethiopian Romance*, trans. Moses Hadas [Ann Arbor: Univ. of Michigan Press, 1957], p. 1), a temporal location that is specific and parallels the same afternoon described later in terms of the ultimate supervision of the sun who "then near his western home did shoot some of his beams" (8), and the pre-dawn three days later "in the time that the morning did strow roses and violets in the heavenly floor against the coming of the sun" (10).

As twilight, the expected encounter is between Uranus—sky—and Gaia—earth—a relationship found in Hesiod's *Theogony*—one ur-source of mythographic lore. As we will find later, in his evaluation of the motivation of his characters, our narrative voice leaves us with more than one possibility that is plausible. Twilight places us between day and night, and the equal length of day and night marks the springtime arrival of vegetation and equinoctial plenitude. In these opening words, we must work through apparent equivocation to a "double" conclusion that warns us of future complications in the narrative.

10. Of course, Hazlitt is a case in point. See Brian Vickers' review of the Oxford edition of *The New Arcadia* in *TLS* (November 18–24, 1988): 1285, captioned "A Wrong-headed Rewrite." But readers as diverse, and brilliant, as the late Bertrand Bronson and Michael Murrin have expressed to me blanket condemnation of what they see as a "generic" contamination of prose-style.

11. See Frances Yates, *The Art of Memory* (Chicago: Univ. of Chicago Press, 1966), pp. 263–64, 282–84, 312–19.

12. Peter Lindenbaum in *Changing Landscapes: Anti-Pastoral Sentiment in the English Renaissance* (Athens: Univ. of Georgia Press, 1986), p. 58, suggests in his searching analysis of the new beginning that the "abruptness" of this intrusion implies "that idealized Arcadian love and figures from the heroic world do not go very well together." I suggest that the abrupt confrontation is more paradoxical, contrasting Platonic love and suicide with common sense and compassion.

13. *Works,* ed. Herford and Simpson, vol. 1, p. 132.

14. A "place" to aid a rhetorician's memory should be permanent, perhaps elements of a building. In order to explain the concept of places as aids to memory, Sidney's rhetor, in his *Defence of Poetry,* suggests architectural features, such "as a certain room divided into many places well and thoroughly known" (101), mainly because those locations are solidly established and continuously available to view.

Chapter 9. The "Unflattering Glass": Sir Fulke Greville's Theory of Reader Identification and Sidney's *Arcadia*

1. John Gouws, ed., *The Prose Works of Fulke Greville, Lord Brooke* (Oxford: Clarendon Press, 1986), by page number in the text. As for the date of composition, see Gouws, pp. xxi–xxiv, and Ronald A. Rebholz, *The Life of Fulke Greville, First Lord Brooke* (Oxford: Clarendon Press, 1971), p. 23.

2. See Christopher Martin, "Misdoubting His Estate: Dynastic Anxiety in Sidney's *Acadia* [sic]," *ELR,* 18 (1988): 369–388, esp. pp. 374ff.

3. See Robert Stillman, "The Politics of Sidney's Pastoral: Mystification and Mythology in *The Old Arcadia,*" *ELH,* 52 (1985): 795–814, esp. p. 799.

4. Gouws's modernization, sound in itself, may obscure a secondary sense of "travail" that Greville would, I feel, encourage.

5. Gouws's editor's choice: I suggest, "Under a 'mask' " or *persona.*

6. Myrick, *Literary Craftsman,* p. 189.

7. Hazlitt, p. 324.

8. Ibid., p. 434.

9. Lindheim, p. 45.

10. Piers Lewis, "Literary and Political Attitudes," p. 128.

11. See McCoy, *Rebellion in Arcadia,* pp. 1–35; Montrose, "Celebration and Insinuation," pp. 3–35, Quilligan, "Sidney and His Queen," p. 171–96; and Alan Sinfield, "Power and Ideology: An Outline Theory and Sidney's *Arcadia,*" *ELH,* 52 (1985): 259–277.

12. See Patterson, *Censorship and Interpretation,* pp. 24–43, esp. pp. 28ff.

13. "Sidney's *Arcadia* and the Mixed Mode," *Studies in Philology,* 70 (1973): 269–78, p. 272.

14. On the notion of the female coterie, see Katherine Duncan-Jones, "Sidney, Stella, Lady Rich," pp. 170–92.

15. Perhaps some symptom of this "iconic" mind-set appears in Chapman's choice to publish first the "Shield of Achilles" before any narrative passage of his *Iliad.*

16. Separating "in" and "deed" also makes sense.

17. For an anticipation of my argument see Josephine Roberts's discussion in *Architectonic Knowledge in the New Arcadia (1590): Sidney's Use of the Heroic Journey.* Salzburg Studies in Literature (Salzburg: Universität Salzburg, 1978), pp. 174–75.

Chapter 10. The Irony of the *Eiron* and *Alazon*

1. Hoskins, p. 35.
2. "Sidney's *Arcadia* and the Mixed Mode," p. 272. Greenblatt quotes Guarini from Allan Gilbert, ed., *Literary Criticism: Plato to Dryden* (Detroit: Wayne State Univ. Press, 1962), p. 522.
3. Greenfield, pp. 57–68.
4. I suggest that the *1590 Arcadia* is incomplete, like so many English masterworks of the era, like *The Faerie Queene*, in part, because the political reconciliation in the form of the queen's marriage never takes place. Pamela and Philoclea, if they are partly modelled on Frances Walsingham and Penelope Devereux Rich, are also versions of Elizabeth. They never get to marry either, in the official, the revised, version. But with Sidney's departure into the Low Countries in 1584, the "arbor" of Wilton must have seemed remote, as well.
5. Hoskins, p. 41.
6. The *eiron*, (J. M. Edmunds, ed. *The Characters of Theophrastus*, Loeb edition [Cambridge: Harvard Univ. Press, 1953], pp. 40–41) dissembles with an ulterior motive. He represents the range of human speech acts that intentionally do not mean exactly what they seem at first to imply, like the moves of Sidney's narrator, and some of his internal narrators.

That the *eiron* is always in control, always masquerading, constitutes his generic difference from the other twenty-one characters of the early editions. (For instance, Casaubon's edition of 1952 mentioned in Hoskins, p. 95.) In fact, as a jester, the *eiron* can include all the other characters and their characteristics in himself. If he so chooses, in other words, he can play any of the others. He is exceptional and deserves to lead all the others, so to speak, because he is a fully self-conscious dissembler, a master, not a victim, of masking. Personal foible does not produce his affectation and any role may suit his purposes. Theophrastus's *eiron* has, of course, a designing character: "Now dissembling would seem, to define it generally, to be an affectation of the worse [and the less?] in word and deed" (40–41).

While this concept of irony as self-depreciation follows that of Plato's Socrates and Aristotle's definition in the *Ethics*, Theophrastus's elliptical examples of irony should be read with Quintilian's broader discussion of the fictive power of irony that led to the Renaissance reconciliation of Aristotelian and Neoplatonic notions of irony as figure and attitude of Apollo. Quintilian, as if directly emending Theophrastus, says that the simple name "*dissimulation*" does not "cover the whole range of this figure," (*The Institutio Oratoria of Quintilian*, ed. H. E. Butler, 4 vols. [London: W. Heinemann, 1922], IX.ii.44.) and shows many of its constructive versions. The *eiron* creates an "illusion" (VIII.vi.54) intentionally, which requires our interpretation, like some of Sidney's personae.

Partly through the influence of Theophrastus's theory and the example of Chaucer's peculiar self-deprecating narrative voice, Sidney's narrator, by means of exposition and indirect discourse exposes the probable truth of situations in the *Arcadia* by pretending to be "lower" or "lesser" in knowledge and position than he really is. Sidney in fact, singles out Chaucer's *Troilus and Criseyde*, for praise in his *Defence of Poetry*, saying "I know not whether to marvel more, either that he in that misty time could see so clearly, or that we in this clear age go so stumblingly after him" (112). "Go after" Chaucer's narrative voice, Sidney did, even, as here, with a hint of parody of Chaucer's narrator's and Pandarus's several disclaimers as followers of Love.

In his opening definition, Theophrastus's word "worse" ($\chi\hat{\epsilon}\rho o\nu$) could suggest so obviously pretending to be lesser that it is apparent to the other parties. Thus Theophrastus' *eiron* says "You amaze me" or "if so, he must have changed" (452–43), in order to "bluff" his listener. Here tongue in cheek becomes a narrator's mode of irony.

7. *Characters*, pp. 98–99. The concept of the *eiron* and the *alazon*, as critical source and target, form a key to understanding Sidney's own work. The *alazon* too is a dissembler, but he is not consciously pretending. He is the Muenchausen or braggart persona who, through foible or pride or misconception, says more than the truth, or something other than the truth, that the audience must ultimately recognize as false. In Theophrastus, "though he live in a hired house, he tells any that knows no better that he had this of his father, and is about to put it up for sale because it is too small for the entertaining of his friends" (102–3). Dreaming of a better life perhaps, the *alazon* fools himself into wandering from the truth in self-praise. As the *eiron* pretends to be less than he is, the *alazon* pretends to be more than he is, but the irony lies outside of his intention. He shows up in Menander, and, as *Miles Gloriosus*, he reappears in Latin Comedy as the boasting soldier. He is the unintentional producer of dramatic irony that figures in the scene we have discussed.

8. Hoskins, p. 41.

9. Notably C. S. Lewis, *English Literature in the Sixteenth Century,* pp. 335–36, but there is a consensus here among New and Old Historians.

Chapter 11. Sidney's Self-Effacement

1. Robertson, p. 3.

2. The first part of the "romance" of Parthenia and Argalus is an element of the Steward's tale to Musidorus. The conclusion and marriage is authorial narration in book 1. I have touched on their death in book 3 in chapter 9.

3. Ringler, p. 98.

4. Skretkowicz, pp. 92–105. The *painted muster* etc. is Greville's term, ibid., p. 94.

5. Robertson, p. 30.

6. Vickers' justly celebrated articles are "Diana Described: Scattered Women and Scattered Rhyme," *Critical Inquiry* 8 (1981): 265–79, and " 'The Blazon of Sweet Beauty's Best': Shakespeare's *Lucrece,*" in chapter 6 of Patricia Parker and Geoffrey Hartman, eds., *Shakespeare and the Question of Theory* (New York: Methuen, 1985), pp. 95–115. See also Eugene Vance's groundbreaking article, "Chaucer's *House of Fame* and the Poetics of Inflation," *Boundary* 7:2 (1979): 17–37. Hulse in "Stella's Wit," p. 276, remarks on "the *blazon,* in which her body is dismembered and consumed as a critic consumes a text."

7. *The New Arcadia,* p. 18.

8. *Amoretti,* 15.13–14.

9. (London: 1581), discussed in Roger Howell, *Sir Philip Sidney, The Shepherd Knight* (London: Hutchinson, 1968), pp. 85–89.

10. Ibid., p. 87, quoting Goldwell and Ringler, p. 345.

11. Ibid., p. 88.

12. Such sardonic maneuvers on the part of Sidney's narrator occur throughout the romance, perhaps culminating in the comparison of Amphialus's spaniel shaking himself dry to newly famous men spurning the men who helped them to greatness.

The narrator comments that the spaniel shakes "off the water as great men do their friends . . ." (189). The primary, naturalistic image of the dog and the shaken water remain, as does the pretty boy here. Sidney's ability to balance the ideal and ordinary or political fact has informed his implosive tactics throughout. His simile generally leads us into what we know only too well.

Bibliography

Adams, Hazard, ed. *Critical Theory Since Plato.* New York: Harcourt Brace Jovanovich, 1971.
Agrippa, Henrie Cornelius. *Of the Vanitie and Uncertaintie of the Artes.* Translated by James Sanford. London: Henry Wykes, 1569.
Alpers, Paul. *The Poetry of the Faerie Queene.* Princeton, N.J.: Princeton University Press, 1967.
Aristotle. *The Art of Rhetoric.* Loeb Edition. Translated by John Henry Freese. London: William Heinemann, 1926.
———. *Nichomachean Ethics.* Loeb Edition. Translated by H. Rackham. London: Heinemann, 1934.
Aristoxenus. *The Harmonics.* Edited by S. Macran. Oxford: Clarendon, 1902.
Ascham, Roger. *The Schoolmaster.* 2nd Edition. London: John Daye, 1571.
Atkins, John William Hey, ed. *English Literary Criticism: The Renascence.* London: Methuen, 1947.
Babb, Lawrence. *The Elizabethan Malady: A Study of Melancholia in English Literature from 1580 to 1642.* East Lansing: Michigan State College Press, 1951.
Bacon, Francis. *The Works.* Edited by James Spedding. 12 vols. London: Longmans, 1878.
Barnes, Catherine. "The Hidden Persuader: The Complex Speaking Voice of Sidney's *Defence of Poesie.*" *PMLA* 86 (1971): 422–27.
Booth, Stephen. *Shakespeare's Sonnets.* New Haven, Conn.: Yale University Press, 1977.
Bourdieu, Pierre. *Outline of a Theory of Practice.* Translated by Richard Nice. Cambridge: Cambridge University Press, 1977.
Bowen, Barbara. *The Age of Bluff: Paradox and Ambiguity in Rabelais and Montaigne.* Illinois Studies in Language and Literature, 62. Urbana: University of Illinois Press, 1972.
Buxton, John. *Sir Philip Sidney and the English Renaissance.* London: Macmillan, 1954.
Camden, William, *Remaines Concerning Britaine, Fifth Impression.* London: T. Harper for J. Waterson, 1636.
Colie, Rosalie. *Paradoxia Epidemica: The Renaissance Tradition of Paradox.* Princeton, N.J.: Princeton University Press, 1966.
Cotter, James Finn. "The Last Act of Astrophil and Stella." *Mid-Hudson Language Studies* (1979): 62–76.
Coulman, D. "Spotted to Be Known." *Journal of the Warburg and Courtauld Institutes* 20 (1957): 179–80.
Council, Norman. "'O Dea Certe'": The Allegory of *The Fortress of Perfect Beauty.*" *The Huntington Library Quarterly* 39 (1976): 329–42.

Craft, William. "Remaking the Heroic Self in the *New Arcadia.*" *SEL* 25 (1985): 45–67.

———. "The Shaping Picture of Love in Sidney's *New Arcadia.*" *Studies in Philology* 8 (1984): 395–418.

Cranmer Bible, 1539–69.

Danby, John. *Poets on Fortune's Hill.* London: Faber and Faber, 1952.

Davis, Walter. "Thematic Unity in the *New Arcadia.*" *Studies in Philology* 57 (1960): 123–43.

———. *A Map of Arcadia* in *Sidney's Arcadia.* New Haven: Yale University Press, 1965.

Dick, Oliver Lawson, ed. *Aubrey's Brief Lives.* Ann Arbor: University of Michigan Press, 1962.

Dobell, Bertram. "New Light upon Sir Philip Sidney's 'Arcadia.'" *Quarterly Review* 211 (1909): 74–100.

Dorsten, Jan Van. "Literary Patronage in Elizabethan England: The Early Phase." Chapter 7 of Guy Fitch Lytle and Stephen Orgel, ed. *Patronage in the Renaissance.* Princeton, N.J.: Princeton University Press, 1981, 191–206.

———. *Poets, Patrons, and Professors: Sir Phillip Sidney and the Leiden Humanists.* Leiden: Sir Thomas Brown Institute, 1962.

Duncan-Jones, Katherine. "Sidney, Stella and Lady Rich." In *Sir Philip Sidney: 1586 and the Creation of a Legend.* Edited by Jan Van Dorsten, Dominic Baker-Smith, and Arthur Kinney. Leiden: Leiden University Press, 1986, 170–92.

Empson, William. *Seven Types of Ambiguity.* London: Chatto and Windus, 1930.

———. *Some Versions of Pastoral.* London: Chatto and Windus, 1935.

Erasmus, Desiderius. *The Praise of Folly.* Edited and translated by Hoyt Hopewell Hudson. Princeton, N.J.: Princeton University Press, 1941.

Ferguson, Margaret. *Trials of Desire: Renaissance Defences of Poetry.* New Haven, Conn.: Yale University Press, 1983.

Feuillerat, Albert, editor. *The Prose Works of Sir Philip Sidney.* 4 vols. Cambridge: Cambridge University Press, 1912.

Fish, Stanley E. *Surprised by Sin: The Reader in Paradise Lost.* New York: St. Martin's Press, 1967.

Fraunce, Abraham. *The Arcadian Rhetorike.* Edited by Ethel Seaton. Oxford: Luttrell Society, 1950.

Gascoigne, George. *The Princely Pleasures. Kenilworth Illustrated.* Chiswick, 1821.

Girard, René. *Violence and the Sacred.* Translated by Patrick Gregory. Baltimore: Johns Hopkins University Press, 1977.

———. *La Violence et le Sacré.* Paris: Bernard Grasset, 1972.

Gosson, Stephen. *The Schoole of Abuse.* Edited by E. Arber. London: Alex. Murray, 1868.

Greenblatt, Stephen Jay. *Renaissance Self-Fashioning: From More to Shakespeare.* Chicago: University of Chicago Press, 1980.

———. "Sidney's *Arcadia* and the Mixed Mode." *Studies in Philology* 70 (1973): 269–78.

———. *Sir Walter Ralegh: The Renaissance Man and His Roles.* New Haven, Conn.: Yale University Press, 1973.

Greenfield, Thelma. *The Eye of Judgment: A Reading of the New Arcadia.* Lewisburg, Penn.: Bucknell University Press, 1982.

Greenlaw, Edwin A. "Sidney's Arcadia as an Example of Elizabethan Allegory." In *Kittredge Anniversary Papers.* Boston: Ginn, 1913, 327–37.

Greville, Fulke, First Lord Brooke. *The Prose Works.* Edited by John Gouwys. Oxford: Clarendon Press, 1971.

Guarini, Battista. *Opere.* Edited by Marziano Guglielminetti. 2nd. edition. Torino: Classici UTET, 1971.

Hager, Alan. "British Virgil: Four Renaissance Disguises of the Laocoön Passage of Book 2 of the *Aeneid.*" *SEL* 22 (1982): 21–38.

———. "The Exemplary Mirage: Fabrication of Sir Philip Sidney's Biographical Image and the Sidney Reader." *ELH* 48 (1981): 1–16.

———. *Shakespeare's Political Animal: Schema and Schemata in the Canon.* Newark: University of Delaware Press, 1990.

Hamilton, A. C. "Sidney and Agrippa." *Review of English Studies* 7 (1965): 151–57.

———. *Sir Philip Sidney: A Study of His Life and Works.* Cambridge: Cambridge University Press, 1977.

Hazlitt, William. *The Collected Works.* Edited by A. R. Waller and Arnold Glover. 12 vols. London: J. M. Dent, 1902.

Helgerson, Richard. *The Elizabethan Prodigals.* Berkeley: University of California Press, 1976.

———. *Self-Crowned Laureates: Spenser, Jonson, Milton and the Literary System.* Berkeley: University of California Press, 1983.

Heliodorus. *An Ethiopian Romance.* Translated by Moses Hadas. Ann Arbor: University of Michigan Press, 1957.

Herrick, Marvin T. *Italian Comedy in the Renaissance.* Urbana: University of Illinois Press, 1960.

Hoskins, John. *Directions for Speech and Style by John Hoskins.* Edited by Hoyt H. Hudson. Princeton: Princeton University Press, 1935.

Hulse, Clarke. "Stella's Wit: Penelope Rich as Reader of Sidney's Sonnets." In *Rewriting the Renaissance: The Discourses of Sexual Difference in Early Modern Europe.* Edited by Margaret Ferguson, Maureen Quilligan, and Nancy Vickers. Chicago: Chicago University Press, 1986, 272–86.

Jones, Dorothy. "Sidney's Erotic Pen: An Interpretation of One of the *Arcadia* Poems." *Journal of English and Germanic Philology* 73 (1974): 32–47.

Judson, Alexander C. *Sidney's Appearance: A Study in Elizabethan Portraiture.* Indiana University Publications in the Humanities Series, 51. Bloomington: Indiana University Press, 1958.

Jusserand, J. J. *The English Novel in the Time of Shakespeare.* London: Unwin, 1890, reprinted in New York: AMS, 1965.

Kalstone, David. *Sidney's Poetry: Contexts and Interpretations.* New York: Norton, 1965.

Kimbrough, Robert, editor. *Sir Philip Sidney: Selected Prose and Poetry.* New York: Holt, Rhinehart, and Winston, 1969.

———. *Sir Philip Sidney.* New York: Twayne, 1971.

Kimbrough, Robert, and Philip Murphy. "The Helmingham Hall Manuscript of

Sidney's *The Lady of May:* A Commentary and Transcription." *Renaissance Drama.* New Series 1 (1968): 103–19.

King, John H. "Queen Elizabeth I: Representations of the Virgin Queen." *Renaissance Quarterly* 43 (1990): 30–74.

Kinney, Arthur, ed. *Essential Articles for the Study of Sir Philip Sidney.* Hamden, Conn.: Archon, 1986.

Lamb, Charles. "Some Sonnets of Sir Philip Sydney," in *The Works of Charles and Mary Lamb.* Edited by E. V. Lucas. 7 vols. London: Methuen, 1904, vol. 2, 213–20.

Lanham, Richard. "*Astrophil and Stella:* Pure and Impure Persuasion." *ELR* 2 (1972): 100–115.

———. *The Old Arcadia* in *Sidney's Arcadia.* New Haven: Yale University Press, 1965.

———. "Sidney: The Ornament of His Age." *Southern Review: Australian Review of Literary Studies* 2 (1967): 319–40.

Lawry, Jon. *Sidney's Two Arcadias: Pattern and Proceeding.* Ithaca: Cornell University Press, 1972.

Levao, Ronald. *Renaissance Minds and Their Fictions: Cusanus, Sidney, Shakespeare.* Berkeley: University of California Press, 1985.

Levine, Joseph, ed. *Great Lives Observed: Elizabeth I.* Englewood Cliffs, N.J.: Prentice-Hall, 1969.

Lewis, C. S. *English Literature in the Sixteenth Century, Excluding Drama.* Oxford: Clarendon, 1964.

Lewis, Piers Ingersoll. "Literary and Political Attitudes in Sidney's *Arcadia.*" Unpublished Dissertation, Harvard University, 1964.

Lindenbaum, Peter. *Changing Landscapes: Anti-Pastoral Sentiment in the English Renaissance.* Athens: University of Georgia Press, 1986.

Lindheim, Nancy. *The Structures of Sidney's Arcadia.* Toronto: University of Toronto Press, 1982.

Litvak, Joseph. "Back to the Future: A Review Article on the New Historicism, Deconstruction, and Nineteenth-Century Fiction." *TSLL* 30 (1988): 120–49.

Lucretius. *De Rerum Natura.* Loeb edition. Translated by W. H. D. Rouse. London: W. Heinemann, 1924.

Marotti, Arthur. *John Donne: Coterie Poet.* Madison: University of Wisconsin Press, 1986.

———. "'Love is not love': Elizabethan Sonnet Sequences and the Social Order." *ELH* 49 (1982): 396–428.

Martin, Christopher. "Impeding the Progress: Sidney's *The Lady of May.*" *Iowa State Journal of Research* 60 (1986): 395–405.

———. "Misdoubting His Estate: Dynastic Anxiety in Sidney's *Arcadia,*" *ELR* 18 (1988): 369–88.

Mayr, Roswitha. *The Concept of Love in Sidney and Spenser.* Salzburg: Universität Salzburg, 1978.

McCoy, Richard. *Sir Philip Sidney: Rebellion in Arcadia.* New Brunswick, N.J.: Rutgers University Press, 1979.

Miller, Clarence H., editor. *Moriae Encomium id est Stultitiae Laus (1979).* In *Opera*

Omnia (Erasmus), 16 vols. Amsterdam: North Holland Publishing Company, 1969–83.

Moffet, Thomas. *Nobilis, or a View of the Life and Death of a Sidney and Lessus Lugubris*. Edited by Virgil B. Heltzel and Hoyt H. Hudson. San Marino: Huntington Library, 1940.

Montrose, Louis. "Celebration and Insinuation: Sir Philip Sidney and the Motive of Elizabethan Courtship." *Renaissance Drama* 18 (1977): 3–35.

———. "The Elizabethan Subject and the Spenserian Text." In *Literary Theory/Renaissance Texts*. Edited by Patricia Parker and David Quint. Baltimore: Johns Hopkins University Press, 1986, 303–40.

———. "'Eliza, Queene of Shepheardes,' and the Pastoral of Power." *ELR* 10 (1980): 153–82.

———. "Of Gentlemen and Shepherds: The Politics of Elizabethan Pastoral Form." *ELH* 50 (1983): 415–59.

———. "Renaissance Literary Studies and the Subject of History." *ELR* 16 (1986): 5–12.

More, Thomas. *Utopia*. Edited and translated by Edward Surtz, S. J. and J. H. Hexter. *Volume 4 of the Complete Works of St. Thomas More*. New Haven, Conn.: Yale University Press, 1965.

Myrick, Kenneth. *Sir Philip Sidney as a Literary Craftsman*. 2nd edition, orig. 1935. Lincoln: University of Nebraska Press, 1965.

Nashe, Thomas. *The Works*. Edited by Ronald B. McKerrow. 5 vols. Oxford: Basil Blackwell, 1958.

Naunton, Sir Robert. *Fragmenta Regalia, 1641*. In *The Harleian Manuscript*. London: John White, 1809.

Norbrook, David. *Poetry and Politics in the English Renaissance*. London: Routledge and Kegan Paul, 1984.

Oliviera e Silva, J. de. "Naming and the Literary Context: Backgrounds to Sir Philip Sidney's *Philisides*." *Literary Omastics Studies* 7 (1980): 139–48.

Orgel, Stephen. *The Jonsonian Masque*. Cambridge, Mass.: Harvard University Press, 1965.

———. "Sidney's Experiment in Pastoral: *The Lady of May*." *Journal of the Warburg and Courtauld Institutes* 26 (1963): 198–203.

Osborn, James M. *Young Philip Sidney: 1572–1577*. New Haven, Conn.: Yale University Press, 1972.

Partee Morriss. "Anti-Platonism in Sidney's 'Defence.'" *English Miscellany* 22 (1971): 7–29.

Patterson, Annabel. *Censorship and Interpretation: The Conditions of Writing and Reading in Early Modern Europe*. Madison: University of Wisconsin Press, 1984.

Peck, D. C., ed. *Leicester's Commonwealth: The Copy of a Letter Written by a Master of Art of Cambridge (1584) and Related Documents*. Athens: Ohio University Press, 1985.

Peele. George. *Polyhymnia*. London: Richard Ihoner, 1590.

Philip (Phillips), John. *Life and Death of Sir Philip Sidney*. London: Robert Waldegrave, 1587.

Pickett, Penny, "Sidney's Use of *Phaedrus* in *The Lady of May*," *SEL* 16 (1976): 33–50.

Plato. *Symposium*. Edited by R. G. Bury. Cambridge: W. Heffer, 1909.

Plutarch. *Shakespeare's Plutarch*. Edited by T. J. B. Spencer. Translated by Thomas North. Baltimore: Penguin Books, 1964.

Poirier, Michel. *Sir Philip Sidney: Le Chevalier Poete Elizabéthain*. Lille: Université de Lille, 1948.

Powell, Anthony, editor. *Brief Lives and Other Selected Writings by John Aubrey*. New York: Charles Scribner's Sons, 1949.

Praz, Mario, "Sidney's Original *Arcadia*." *London Mercury* 15 (1926–27): 507–14.

Progresses and Public Processions of Queen Elizabeth. 3 vols. London: T. Nichols and Son, 1823.

Puttenham, George. *The Arte of English Poesie*. Edited by Gladys Doidge Willcock and Alice Walker. Cambridge: Cambridge University Press, 1936.

Quilligan, Maureen. "Sidney and His Queen." In *The Historical Renaissance: New Essays on Tudor and Stuart Literature and Culture*. Edited by Heather Dubrow and Richard Strier. Chicago: University of Chicago Press, 1988, 171–96.

Ramus, Peter. *Arguments in Rhetoric against Quintilian: Translation and Text of Peter Ramus's Rhetorical Distinctions in Quintilianum (1549)*. Translated by Carole Newlands. Introduction by James J. Murphy. DeKalb: Northern Illinois University Press, 1986.

Reasons for a War against Spain etc., 2nd edition. London: J. Wilford, 1738.

Roberts, Josephine. *Architectonic Knowledge in the New Arcadia (1590): Sidney's Use of the Heroic Journey*. Salzburg: Studies in English Literature. Salzburg: Universität Salzburg, 1978.

Robinson, Forrest G. *The Shape of Things Known: Sidney's Apology in Its Philosophical Tradition*. Cambridge, Mass.: Harvard University Press, 1972.

Rogers, Thomas. *Leicester's Ghost*. Edited by Franklin B. Williams, Jr., Chicago: University of Chicago Press, 1972.

Rudenstine, Neil. *Sidney's Poetic Development*. Cambridge, Mass.: Harvard University Press, 1967.

Ruskin, John. *The Works*. Edited by E. T. Cook and Alexander Wedderburn. 39 vols. London: George Allen, 1912.

Samuel, Irene. "The Influence of Plato on Sir Philip Sidney's 'Defense of Poesy.'" *Modern Language Quarterly* 1 (1940): 383–84.

Shepherd, Geoffrey, ed. *Sir Philip Sidney: An Apology for Poetry or the Defence of Poesy*. London: Nelson, 1965.

Sidney, Sir Philip. *The Countess of Pembroke's Arcadia (The New Arcadia)*, Edited by Victor Skretkowicz. Oxford: Clarendon press, 1987.

———. *The Countess of Pembroke's Arcadia (The Old Arcadia)*. Edited by Jean Robertson. Oxford: Clarendon, 1973.

———. *The Miscellaneous Prose*. Edited by Katherine Duncan-Jones and Jan Van Dorsten. Oxford: Clarendon, 1973.

———. *The Poems*. Edited by William Ringler, Jr. Oxford: Clarendon, 1962.

Siebeck, Berta. *Das Bild Sir Philip Sidneys In Der Englischen Renaissance*. Weimar: Hermann Bohlaus, 1939.

Sinfield, Alan. "Power and Ideology: An Outline Theory and Sidney's *Arcadia*." *ELH* 52 (1985): 259–77.

Smith, George Gregory, ed. *Elizabethan Critical Essays.* 2 vols. Oxford: Clarendon Press, 1904.
Spenser, Edmund. *The Works: A Variorum Edition,* ed. Edwin Greenlaw et al. 10 vols. Baltimore: Johns Hopkins Univ. Press, 1932–1957.
Stillman, Robert. "Justice and the 'Good Word' in Sidney's *The Lady of May.*" *SEL* 24 (1984): 23–38.
———. "The Politics of Sidney's Pastoral: Mystification and Mythology in *The Old Arcadia,*" *ELH* 52 (1985): 795–814.
———. *Sidney's Poetic Justice: The Old Arcadia, Its Eclogues, and Renaissance Pastoral Traditions.* Lewisburg: Bucknell Univ. Press, 1986.
Stone, Lawrence. *Crisis of the Aristocracy: 1558–1641.* Oxford: Clarendon Press, 1965.
Strickland, Ronald. "Pageantry and Poetry as Discourse: The Production of Subjectivity in Sir Philip Sidney's Funeral." *ELH* 57 (1990): 19–36.
Tillyard, E. M. W. *The Elizabethan World Picture.* New York: Vintage, 1966.
———. *The English Epic and Its Background.* New York: Oxford Univ. Press, 1954.
Trevor-Roper, H. R. *Archbishop Laud: 1573–1645.* London: Macmillan, 1940.
Vance, Eugene. "Chaucer's *House of Fame* and the Poetics of Inflation." *Boundary,* 7, ii (1979): 17–37.
Vickers, Brian. "A Wrong-Headed Rewrite" (review of the Oxford edition of *The New Arcadia*) *TLS* (November 18–24, 1988).
Vickers, Nancy. "'The blazon of sweet beauty's best': Shakespeare's *Lucrece.*" *Shakespeare and the Question of Theory.* Edited by Patricia Parker and Geoffrey Hartman. New York: Methuen, 1985, 95–115.
———. "Diana Described: Scattered Women and Scattered Rhyme." *Critical Inquiry* 8 (1981): 265–79.
Virgil. *Complete Works.* Translated by H. Rushton Fairclough. Loeb edition. 2 volumes. London: Heinemann, 1932.
Wallace, Malcomb. *The Life of Sir Philip Sidney.* Cambridge: Cambridge University Press, 1915.
Walzer, Michael. *Obligations: Essays on Disobedience, War and Citizenship.* Cambridge, Mass.: Harvard University Press, 1970.
———. *The Revolution of the Saints: A Study of the Origins of Radical Politics.* Cambridge, Mass.: Harvard University Press, 1965.
Weiner, Andrew. *Sir Philip Sidney and the Poetics of Protestantism.* Minneapolis: University of Minnesota Press, 1978.
Whetstone, George, *Sir Philip Sidney, His Honorable Life etc.* London: T. Cadman, 1587.
Willett, C. and Phillis Cunnington. *Handbook of English Costume in the Sixteenth Century.* London: Faber & Faber, Ltd., 1954.
Williams, Neville. *Elizabeth, Queen of England.* London: Weidenfeld & Nicholson, 1967.
Wilson, Thomas. *The Arte of Rhetorique.* Facsimile Edition. Edited by Robert Hood Bowers. Gainesville: Scholars' Facsimiles and Reprints, 1962.
Wolff, Samuel Lee. *The Greek Romances in Elizabethan Prose Fiction.* New York: Columbia University Press, 1912.

Yates, Frances. *The Art of Memory.* Chicago: Chicago University Press, 1966.

———. *Astraea: The Imperial Theme in the Sixteenth Century.* London: Routledge & K. Paul, 1975.

———. "Elizabethan Chivalry: The Romance of the Accession Day Tilts." *Journal of the Warburg and Courtauld Institutes,* 20 (1957): 4–25.

———. *Giordano Bruno and the Hermetic Tradition.* Chicago: Chicago University Press, 1964.

———. "Queen Elizabeth as Astraea." *Journal of the Warburg and Courtauld Institutes* 10 (1947): 27–82.

Index

Abradatas, 135
Accession Day Tilt (1590), 24
Achilles (Homer), 168
Acts and Monuments (John Foxe), 21
Ad hominem argument, 115–17, 119
Adams, Hazard, 126–27, 201 n.5
Adolescens, 15, 65, 80
Aeneas (Virgil), 100, 131–32, 149
Aeneid (Virgil), 48–49, 100, 131–32, 149, 182
Agrippa, Henry Cornelius, 103, 105–8, 113, 132, 200 n.3, 201 n.3, 202 n.4
Agrippa, Menenius, 9, 87, 108–9, 116, 133
Ajax (Homer), 52
Alazoneia, 14–15, 167, 173–75, 187, 205 n.7
Alcibiades, 103, 116–17, 126
Alencon, Duc d', 51–54, 59, 184, 196 n.7
Alexander the Great, 52
Allegory, 37, 39–40, 42
Alpers, Paul, 14, 100–1, 131, 189 n.23, 200 n.21, 202 n.2
Amoretti (Edmund Spenser), 179, 182, 205 n.8
Amorous fallacy, 142, 152, 172–73
Andromache (Homer), 169
Anti-Idealism, 19–20, 44–45, 69–81, 115–29, 136–44, 173–75
Apollo, 76
Apollodorus (Plato), 106
Apology (Plato), 106
Apuleius, 165
Araygnement of Paris, The (George Peele), 196 n.26
Argus, 73
Ariadne, 147
Aristophanes, 82, 117
Aristotle, 9, 14, 62, 115, 125, 128, 130, 174, 189 n.9, 204 n.6

Aristoxenus, 116, 201 n.2
Armstrong, Archibald, 188 n.5
Art of memory, the, 140–41, 177
Arte of Rhetorique, The (Thomas Wilson), 196 n.25
Arte of English Poesie, The (George Puttenham), 200 n.13
Arthurian ideal, 33
Arundel, Earl of (Philip Howard), 184
Ascham, Roger, 197 n.29
Astraea, 22, 51, 190 n.12
Astronomy: Babylonian, 32; Copernican, 32; Ptolemaic, 32
Astrophel (Edmund Spenser), 21, 65, 199 n.6
Astrophil and Stella, 13, 21, 34, 36, 63–102, 110, 183, 193 n.11
Athena, 10, 47, 116, 118, 176
Atkins, J. W. H., 200 n.3
Atlas, 96
Aubrey, John, 31, 192 n.52
Augustus Caesar, 55–56, 60
Aurora, 76

Babb, Lawrence, 74, 199 n.21
Bacon, Francis, 20, 22, 25, 27, 51, 191 nn. 16, 20, 25, and 26, 198 n.38 198 n.38
Baker-Smith, Dominic, 192 n.44
Barnes, Catherine, 201 nn. 11 and 24
Basilisk, image of, 10, 50, 197 n.35
Bathsheba, 133–34
Beaumont, Francis, 193 n.9
Belphoebe (Spenser), 28
Bembo, Pietro, 128
Bestiary, 164
Blake, William, 12
Blatant Beast, the (Spenser), 56–61
Blazon, 90, 99, 169, 177–84
Blount, Charles, 26
Booth, Stephen, 14, 190 n.23

215

Bourdieu, Pierre, 191 n.19
Bowen, Barbara, 9, 189 n.9, 201 n.4, 205 n.7
Bowers, Robert, 196 n.25
Bradley, A. C., 80
Brief Lives (John Aubrey), 31, 192 n.52
Briefe Declaration of the Shews (1581) (Henry Goldwell), 184
Bronson, Bertrand, 202 n.10
Bruno, Giordano, 38, 190 n.4
Burleigh, Earl of (William Cecil), 23
Butler, H. E., 204 n.6
Buxton, John, 21, 190 n.4
Byrd, William, 70

Calidore (Spenser), 14, 25, 57
Calliope, 68
Calvin, John, 19, 42, 125
Camden, William, 191 n.36
Campion, Edmund, 22, 190 n.11
Canterbury Tales (Geoffrey Chaucer), 164
Career melancholy, 14, 73, 80, 82–83
Casaubon, Isaac, 204 n.6
Cassandra, 48, 108
Castalian streams, 68
Catherine of Medici, 56
Cato, Marcus Porcius, the elder, 172
Catullus, 95, 200 n.6
Cecil, Thomas, 53, 56
Chapman, George, 82, 203 n.15
Characters (Imagines) (Theophrastus), 171–74, 204 n.6, 205 n.7
Charles I (England), 150, 188 n.5
Chaucer, Geoffrey, 14, 135, 138, 164, 167, 175, 185, 204 n.6
Chronographia, 98, 136
Cicero, 21, 59
Clarindon, 56
Clauserus, 128
Colie, Rosalie, 86, 93, 95, 200 nn. 8, 17, and 19
Collective ideal, 7, 44, 45, 49, 80, 156
Collective violence, 8, 48, 149
Collins, Arthur, 10, 189 n.11
Commedia dell'Arte, 15, 46
Comus (John Milton), 34–35
Concordia discors (and *discordia concors*), 37, 83, 91, 93, 106, 146
Connell, Dorothy, 41, 48, 194 n.21, 195 nn. 1 and 2, 197 n.31, 198 n.37

Cook, E. T., 199 n.23
Coriolanus (William Shakespeare), 133, 189 n.15
Cosmic melancholy, 14
Cotter, James Finn, 72, 199 n.20
Coulman, D., 29, 192 n.43
Council, Norman, 190 n.15
Court jester, 7, 10, 15, 105–11
Courtly heroism, 33, 34
Craft, William, 37, 195 n.25
Cranmer Bible, 134, 202 n.6
Cromwell, Oliver, 34
Cunnington, Phyllis, 188 n.4
Cupid (Eros) (Love), 47, 50, 64, 77, 96, 99, 106, 115, 137, 159–66, 181–82
Cusanus (Nicholas of Cusa), 37
Cynthia, 22, 28
Cyrus, 126, 131, 135
Cythera, 140–41

Danby, John, 167, 194 n.11
Daniel, Samuel, 65, 156
Dante, 119, 148
Darius, 134
David, 109, 133–34
Davis, Walter, 194 n.11
De la Pole, Duke of Suffolk, 60
de Oliviera e Silva, J., 200 n.5
De Vere, Robert, Duke of Ireland, 60
Deconstruction, 12, 32
Defence of Leicester, The, 13, 41, 56–62
Defence of Poetry, 11, 13, 19, 20, 21, 28, 33–34, 36–39, 44, 46, 51, 63–65, 79, 82, 87, 96, 100–1, 103–37, 144, 147, 156, 181, 202 n.14, 204 n.6
Dennis, John, 74
De Rerum Naturae (Of the nature of things) (Lucretius), 202 n.3
Diana, 10, 22
Dick, Oliver Lawson, 192 n.52
Dido (Virgil), 132
Dionysius (tyrant of Syracuse), 116
Dionysus, 176
Directions for Speech and Style, 90–91, 167, 171–75, 205 n.8
Discorsi (Niccolò Machiavelli), 174
Discourse on Irish Affairs, 41
Dissimulation, 7–9
Dobell, Bertram, 30, 192 n.51
Donne, John, 199 n.15

Dorsten, Jan Van, 21, 188 n.8, 190 n.4, 192 n.44
Douland, Robert, 70
Drake, Francis, 23
Dubrow, Heather, 189 n.13
Duchess of Malfi, The (John Webster), 74
Ducan-Jones, Katherine, 29–30, 45, 56–57, 188 n.8, 191 n.36, 192 n.42, 195 nn. 2 and 3, 198 n.43, 198 n.50, 199 n.1, 203 n.14
Dyer, Edward, 20

Eden, 45, 51, 123
Edmunds, J. M., 204 n.6
Edward II, 61
Edward IV, 49
Edward VI, 49
Egyptology, 129
Eironeia, 14–15, 167, 171–73, 185–87, 204 n.6, 205 n.7
Eliza, 10, 22, 41, 56, 148, 186, 190 n.15
Elizabeth I, 7, 10, 12–15, 19–20, 22–25, 27–28, 30, 33–34, 41–42, 47–49, 51–56, 59–62, 80, 96, 128, 140, 145–50, 156, 177, 179, 184, 186, 190 n.15, 192 n.40, 195 n.2, 196 n.7, 197 n.33, 198 n.37, 204 n.4
Elizabeth of York, 25
Empson, William, 83, 188 n.2, 199 n.3
Erasmus, Desiderius, 11, 13, 103, 105–12, 130–32, 200 nn. 3 and 4, 201 n.12, 202 nn. 7 (chap. 7) and 4
Eryximachus (Plato), 106, 117
Esoteric goals, 20, 30
Essex, 42
Essex, Earl of (Robert Devereux), 23–25, 29, 51, 64
Essex, first Earl of (Walter Devereux), 63–64, 195 n.2, 198 n.37
Ethiopian Tale, An (Ethiopica) (Heliodorus), 202 n.9
Euphues, or The Anatomy of Wit (John Lyly), 65
Evil Eye, 50
Exoteric goals, 20, 35, 54–55, 67, 117–18, 129

Faerie Queene, The (Edmund Spenser), 14–15, 57, 80, 100–1, 149, 156, 204 n.4
Fairclough, H. Rushton, 197 n.30

Falstaff (William Shakespeare), 169
Fantastic imitation, 125–27
Ferdinand (John Webster), 74
Ferguson, Margaret, 12–13, 37, 103, 104–5, 189 nn. 12 and 21, 195 n.24, 198 n.3, 200 n.3, 201 n.9, 202 n.7
Feuillerat, Albert, 198 n.47, 201 n.26
Fish, Stanley, 14, 189 n.23, 195 n.26
Fletcher, John, 82, 193 n.9
Folly *(Stultitia)* (Erasmus), 11, 105–12, 119, 127
Ford, John, 82
Four Foster Children of Desire, 41, 184–87
Foxe, John, 21
Fraunce, Abraham, 20, 29, 192 n.1
Freese, John Henry, 189 n.10
Freudian analysis, 12

Gaia, 202 n.9
Ganymede, 96
Gargantua (Rabelais), 201 n.4
Gascoigne, George, 42, 181, 197 n.29
Gaveston, Earl of Cornwall, 60
Gifford, George, 192 n.44
Gilbert, Allan, 204 n.2
Girard, René, 87, 200 n.9, 201 n.25
Glover, Arnold, 192 nn. 55 (chap 1) and 1
Golden Ass, The (Apuleius), 165
Golding, Arthur, 200 n.18
Goldwell, Henry, 184, 205 n.10
Gosson, Stephen, 115–17, 121, 202 n.6
Gothic imagery, 66, 73–77, 79
Gouws, John, 191 n.19, 203 nn. 1, 4, and 5
Gray, William, 19
Green world, 7, 45, 48
Greenblatt, Stephen, 11–12, 14, 27–28, 157–59, 166–68, 189 n.12, 190 n.24, 191 n.31, 203 n.13, 204 n.2
Greenfield, Thelma, 196 n.7, 204 n.3
Greenlaw, Edwin, 37, 190 n.24, 193 n.1
Gregory, Patrick, 200 n.9
Greville, Fulke, 9, 15, 20–22, 27–28, 30, 32, 145–50, 184, 181 n.19, 191 nn. 30 and 37, 193 n.1, 203 n.1, 205 n.4
Grey, Lady Elizabeth, 65
Grey, Lady Jane, 60
Guarini, Giovanni Battista, 65, 199 n.12, 204 n.2
Guglielminetti, Marziano, 199 n.12

Hadas, Moses, 202 n.9
Hamilton, A. C., 103, 167, 194 n.11, 198 n.37, 200 nn. 1 and 3
Hamlet (William Shakespeare), 74, 82
Hamlet (William Shakespeare), 74, 80, 82
Harmonics, The (Aristoxenus), 116, 201 n.2
Harrington, John, 72
Hartman, Geoffrey, 205 n.6
Hazlitt, William, 31, 34–36, 38, 82, 143, 152–53, 192 nn. 55 (chap. 1) and 1, 193 n.5, 202 n. 10
Hector (Homer), 168–69
Hegel, Georg Wilhelm Friedrich, 80
Helgerson, Richard, 12, 21, 37, 43, 105, 189 n.12, 190 n.4, 194 n.12, 196 n.12, 199 n.15, 201 n.10
Heliodorus, 202 n.9
Helmingham Hall Manuscript, 42, 44, 46, 195 n.3
Heltzel, Virgil, 190 n.7, 191 n.35
Henry VI, 61
Henry VII, 25
Henry VIII, 12, 105, 108
1 Henry IV (William Shakespeare), 169
Heraclitus, 48
Herbert, William, 21
Hercules, 95, 176
Herrick, Marvin T., 196 n.24
Hesiod, 128, 202 n.9
Hexter, J. H., 201 n.14
History of Henry VII, The (Francis Bacon), 191 n.26
Holbein the Younger, 111
Holofernes (Shakespeare), 46
Homer, 52, 128, 169
Horace, 43, 95
Hoskins, John, 9, 15, 20, 32, 90–91, 167, 171–75, 192 n.1, 200 n.14, 204 nn. 1 and 5, 205 n.8
Hotspur (William Shakespeare), 169
Howe, P. P., 192 n.1
Howell, Roger, 42, 205 n.9
Hudson, Hoyt, 190 n.7, 191 n.35, 192 n.1, 200 n.4
Hulse, Clark, 198 n.3, 199 n.1, 205 n.6
Hythlodaeus (Thomas More), 105, 107–8

Iago (William Shakespeare), 82
Icarus, 122

Icastic imitation, 125–27, 183
Iliad (Homer), 52, 168–69, 203 n.15
In Felicem Memoriam Elizabethae Regina Angliae (Francis Bacon), 191 n.20, 198 n.38
Infanticide, image of, 94–95, 176
Ion (Plato), 124
Iris, 181–82

James I, 188 n.5
Jezebel, 56
Jones, Dorothy, 199 n.18
Jonson, Ben, 30, 32, 139, 199 n.15, 203 n.13
Judson, Alexander, 190 n.3
Juno, 47, 181–82
Jupiter (Zeus), 10, 95, 176
Jusserand, J. J., 192 n.1

Kalstone, David, 102, 193 n.11
Kant, Immanuel, 126
Kimbrough, Robert, 43, 167, 194 n.11, 195 n.5, 196 n.9, 199 n.3
King, John H., 190 n.15, 198 n.46
Kinney, Arthur, 9, 188 n.7, 192 n.44
Knowles, Lettice, 195 n.2

Lady of May, 13, 21, 23, 34, 39, 41–52, 132, 191 n.17, 193 n.11
Lamb, Charles, 34–36, 38, 193 n.1
Lamb, Mary, 193 n.1
Lancaster, house of, 197 n.33
Landino, Cristofero, 129
Languet, Hubert, 198 n.52
Lanham, Richard, 12, 13, 15, 21, 63, 88, 104, 190 nn. 4, 6, and 9, 193 n.11, 194 n.11, 200 n.12, 201 n.8
Laud, Archbishop William, 188 n.5
Laura (Petrarch), 54
Lawry, Jon, 202 n.9
Lee, Henry, 25, 33, 51
Leicester, Earl of (Robert Dudley), 12–13, 15, 22–25, 27–28, 41, 43, 46, 51–52, 56, 60–62, 64, 86, 188 n.1, 195 n.2, 196 n.19, 198 n.37
Letter to the Queen, Concerning Monsieur, 13, 52–56
Levao, Ronald, 194 n.21, 201 n.24
Levine, Joseph, 23, 191 n.21
Lewis, C. S., 30, 31, 36, 44, 104, 192 nn. 47, 54, and 56, 196 n.20, 201 n.5, 205 n.9

Index

Lewis, Piers, 155, 202n.9, 203n.10
Lindenbaum, Peter, 203n.12
Lindheim, Nancy, 37–38, 154, 167, 189n.22, 194n.18, 195n.27, 203n.9
Litvak, Joseph, 12, 189n.18
Livy, 133
Locus amoenus, 154
Love Melancholy, 14–15, 47, 65–66, 73–74, 80, 82–83
Love's Labor's Lost (William Shakespeare), 46
Lucas, E. V., 193n.1
Lucian, 105
Lucrece (William Shakespeare), 205n.6
Lucretius, 132, 202n.3
Luna, 28
Lycanthropy, 74, 75–77, 98
Lyly, John, 65
Lytle, Guy, 190n.4

McCoy, Richard, 12–13, 21, 37, 43, 63, 102, 105, 189nn. 12, 19, and 20, 190n.4, 191n.19, 192n.48, 194n.13, 196n.10, 198n.1, 200n.23, 201n.10, 203n.11
Machiavelli, Niccolò, 11, 25, 27, 56, 174
McKerrow, Ronald B., 199n.7
Macran, Henry S., 201n.2
Male pregnancy and birthing, image of, 69, 94–95, 176–77
Mark Antony, 59
Marlowe, Christopher, 45, 136
Marotti, Arthur, 66, 199n.15
Martin, Christopher, 43, 196n.11, 203n.2
Marxian analysis, 12
Mary, Queen of Scots, 26–28, 53, 55
Maximilian II (Holy Roman Emperor), 20
Mayr, Roswitha, 198n.1
Melibee (Spenser), 14, 45
Menander, 205n.7
Merchant of Venice (William Shakespeare), 175
Metamorphoses (Ovid), 95–96, 163–66, 200n.18, 202n.7
Metaphysics (Aristotle), 128
Midas (Ovid), 129
Midas (John Lyly), 65
Middleton, Thomas, 82
Midsummer Night's Dream (William Shakespeare), 81

Miles Gloriosus (Terence), 13, 56, 60, 205n.7
Miller, Clarence, 189n.16
Milton, John, 14, 34, 91, 149, 199n.15
Moffet, Thomas, 21, 27, 29–30, 190n.7, 191n.35, 192n.49
Molyneux, Edmund, 57
Momus, 129, 181–82
Montague, George, 56
Montaigne, Michel de, 9, 12–13, 87, 103
Montrose, Louis, 12, 43, 189n.12, 196nn. 10 and 26, 203n.11
Morality play, 39
More, Thomas, 12–13, 105, 107–8, 201n.14
Mueller, Janel, 197n.29
Murphy, James J., 197n.30
Murphy, Philip, 43, 195n.5, 196n.9
Murrin, Michael, 202n.10
Myrick, Kenneth, 151, 191n.34, 203n.6

Nashe, Thomas, 9, 20, 32, 65–66, 199n.7
Nathan (prophet), 9, 133–34
Nature, Lady, 67–68, 83, 186
Naunton, Robert, 191n.40
Nelson, Viscount Horatio, 27
Neologism, 83–87
New Arcadia, 9, 13, 15, 20–21, 26, 28–29, 34–37, 39, 82, 84–85, 91, 129–30, 135–73, 176–87, 188n.6, 190n.2, 202n.9, 204n.4
New historicism, 8–9, 12, 40
New comedy, 46
Newlands, Carole, 197n.30
Nice, Richard, 191n.19
Nichols, John, 10, 195n.2, 197n.33
Nicomachean Ethics (Aristotle), 62, 174, 198n.53, 204n.6
Norbrook, David, 37, 195n.22
Norfolk, 48
North, Thomas, 133
Northumberland, Earl of (John Dudley), 60
Norwich, 197n.33

Oblique indirect discourse, 151–53
Ocean to Cynthia (Walter Ralegh), 52
Old Arcadia, 7–9, 13, 21, 26, 28–29, 34, 37–38, 82, 84–85, 93, 129–30, 135–36, 138, 173–84
Ophelia (William Shakespeare), 82

Orgel, Stephen, 23, 43–44, 190 n.4, 191 n.17, 196 n.16
Orsino (William Shakespeare), 143
Osborne, James M., 198 n.4
Othello (William Shakespeare), 82
Ovid, 95–96, 129, 200 n.18, 202 n.7
Ovidian mode, 96, 159, 163–66
Oxford, Earl of (Edward De Vere), 23, 57, 137
Oxymoron, 75, 90–93

Pan, 23, 181–82
Pantagruel (Rabelais), 127
Panurge (Rabelais), 87
Paradise Lost (John Milton), 34–35, 91, 149, 193 n.3
Paradox, 38, 41, 68–69, 72, 83, 86–87, 91–92, 104, 106, 118, 120, 124, 183, 184, 186–87
Paris (Son of Priam), 47
Parker, Patricia, 189 n.12, 205 n.6
Parliament, 7, 156
Parmenides, 117
Parnassus, 68
Parsons, Robert, 57
Partee Morris, 104, 201 n.5
Pastoral mode, 7–8, 45, 48–51, 80
Patterson, Annabel, 37, 44, 195 n.23, 196 n.18, 202 n.8, 203 n.11
Paul, 115
Peck, D. C., 198 n.37
Peele, George, 24, 196 n.26
Pembroke, Countess of (Mary Sidney), 20, 65, 82, 110, 157–58, 176–77
Pembroke, Earl of (William Herbert), 157
Penshurst, 29, 166
Persona, theory of, 7, 34, 54, 60, 64–65, 74, 79, 82–84, 102, 105–8, 111, 115, 117, 119, 121, 123, 126, 129, 133, 139, 143, 156, 164, 167–77, 180, 183
Petrarca, Francesco, 21, 54, 66, 79
Petrarchan mode, 44, 49–50, 64, 68, 70, 80, 92, 159–66, 179–81, 193 n.11
Phaedrus (Plato), 43, 116
Phalaris of Agrigento, 96–97, 162
Pharmakos, 80, 150
Philebus (Plato), 201 n.1
Philip II (Spain), 61, 192 n.40
Philip, John, 22, 190 n.10
Phoenix, image of, 66, 78–81

Pickett, Penny, 43, 196 n.13, 197 n.30
Pindar, 201 n.4
Pindaric mode, 119, 201 n.4
Plato, 82–83, 88, 103, 105–6, 109–10, 115–29, 140, 163, 174, 180, 200 n.4
Platonism, 42–45, 65, 94, 115, 121, 127, 129, 131, 136–44, 173–75, 182, 202 nn. 9 and 12
Plautus, 46, 80
Plebeians, 50, 87, 108–9
Plutarch, 126, 133, 202 n.5
Poetics (Aristotle), 130
Poirier, Michel, 27, 191 n.29
Pollard, Alfred, 80
Polyhymnia (George Peele), 191 n.23
Ponsonby, William, 195 n.28
Powell, Anthony, 192 n.53
Prague, 112
Praise of Folly (Erasmus), 11, 103, 105–12, 119, 127, 200 n.4, 201 nn. 12 (chap. 6) and 3, 202 nn. 4 and 7
Praz, Mario, 193 n.1
Pre-Socratic philosophy, 135
Princely Pleasures, The (George Gascoigne), 42, 197 n.29
Prometheus, 96
Protestant League, 22, 43, 51, 53, 196 n.7
Ptolemaic astronomy, 32
Pugliano, John Pietro, 20, 111–14, 117
Puttenham, George, 89, 98, 136, 200 n.13
Python, Monty (B.B.C. television show), 19, 190 n.1

Quilligan, Maureen, 189 n.13, 191 n.19, 198 n.3, 203 n.11
Quint, David, 189 n.12
Quintilian, 204 n.6

Rabelais, 9, 12, 13, 87, 103, 201 n.4
Ralegh, Walter, 11, 20, 21, 23, 28, 30, 52
Ramus (Pierre de la Rame), 38, 197 n.30
Rawlinson Manuscript, 72
Reader response, theory of, 9–14, 130–66
Rebholz, Ronald, 203 n.1
Recusancy, 44–45, 48–49, 51, 197 n.31
Republic (Plato), 83, 109–10, 119–23
Rhetoric (Aristotle), 9, 14, 189 n.10

Index

Rhetoric (Institutio Oratoria) (Quintilian), 204 n.6
Rich, Lord, 41, 63–64, 86–87, 90
Rich, Penelope Devereux, 20, 29–30, 63–64, 82, 84, 86–87, 110, 157–58, 192 n.48, 204 n.4
Richard II, 61
Richard III, 25
Ringler, William, 43, 64, 70, 102, 188 n.3, 191 n.18, 192 n.48, 196 nn. 7 and 19, 199 nn. 6 and 16, 205 nn. 3 and 10
Roberts, Josephine, 203 n.17
Robertson, Jean, 43, 188 n.6, 205 n.1
Robinson, Forrest, 202 n.1
Robsart, Amy, 59, 198 n.37
Rogers, Thomas, 198 n.37
Romanticism, 34–36, 127
Romeo (Shakespeare), 82
Romeo and Juliet (William Shakespeare), 82
Rudenstine, Neil, 104, 193 n.11, 194 n.11, 195 n.29, 201 n.7
Ruskin, John, 78, 199 n.23

St. Bartholomew's Day Massacre (24 August 1572), 188 n.1, 197 n.30
St. Paul's Cathedral, 27
Sallust, 137
Samuels, Irene, 201 n.1
Sandys, George, 200 n.18
Sannazaro, Jacopo, 45, 193 n.11
Saturn, 29, 179, 181–82
Savagery, 7–8
Scaliger, Joseph Justus, 128
Schoole of Abuse, The (Stephen Gosson), 115–17, 121, 202 n.6
Schoolmaster, The (Roger Ascham), 197 n.29
Scipio Africanus, 21
Scott, Walter, 61
Seaton, Ethel, 192 n.1
Self-Fashioning, 11, 14–15, 190 n.24
Serio ludere, 11, 15, 41, 46, 106, 182, 187
Shakespeare, William, 14, 46, 74, 80–82, 87, 102, 133, 143
Shepheardes Calender (Edmund Spenser), 57
Shepherd, Geoffrey, 103, 200 n.11, 201 n.23
Shepherd knight, 25–26, 187

Sibyl (Virgil), 123
Sidney, Lady Mary Dudley, 177
Sidney, Robert (future Earl of Leicester), 112–13
Siebeck, Berta, 27, 191 n.28
Sinfield, Alan, 203 n.11
Sinon (Virgil), 155
Skelton, John, 200 n.6
Skretkowicz, Victor, 192 n.41, 197 n.35, 202 n.9, 205 n.4
Smith, Gregory, 103, 200 n.3
Smith Nowell, 191 n.19
Socrates, 13, 82–83, 88, 106, 115–26, 140, 163, 174, 204 n.6
Song of Solomon, 142
Sonnets (William Shakespeare), 14
Sophist, the (Plato), 125
Sparrow, Philip (John Skelton), 200 n.7
Sparta, 116
Spedding, James, 191 n.16, 198 n.38
Spencer, T. J. B., 202 n.5
Spenser, Edmund, 14, 21, 30, 32, 52, 57, 65, 80, 100–1, 149, 156, 179, 182, 190 n.24, 193 n.11, 199 n.15
Spenser, Elizabeth, 179
Sprezzatura, 28
Stillman, Robert, 43, 46–47, 195 n.26, 196 n.14, 197 n.30, 198 n.40, 203 n.3
Stoicism, 43, 118–19
Stone, Lawrence, 37
Strickland, Ronald, 191 n.27
Strier, Richard, 189 n.13
Stubbs, John, 53
Suffolk, 48
Sumptuary laws, 7
Surtz, Edward, 201 nn. 13 and 17
Symposium (Plato), 163, 175, 180

Tarlton, Richard, 196 n.19
Tasso, Torquato, 45
Terence, 46, 57, 80
Theocritus, 45
Theogony (Hesiod), 202 n.9
Theophrastus, 14, 171–74, 204 n.6, 205 n.7
Theseus (Shakespeare), 81
Thraso (Terence), 13, 56, 60
Tilbury, 61
Tillyard, E. M. W., 11, 36, 167, 190 n.5
Timon (Shakespeare), 82, 102
Tragicomedy, 63–81, 175

Transvestitism, 7, 149–50, 169–70
Trevor-Roper, H. R., 188 n.5
Troilus and Cressida (William Shakespeare), 82, 102, 192 n.55
Troilus and Criseyde (Geoffrey Chaucer), 204 n.6
Troy, 132
Twelfth Night, or What You Will (William Shakespeare), 143
Tyrtaeus, 201 n.4

Ulysses, 100, 155
Undifferentiation, 8, 13, 145–53
Uranos, 202 n.9
Uriah, 134
Utopia (Thomas More), 105, 107–8, 201 n.17

Vampirism, image of, 74–77
Vance, Eugene, 205 n.6
Vanishing distinctions, concept of, 37–39, 62
Vanitie and Uncertaintie of the Artes and Sciences, Of the (Henry Cornelius Agrippa), 103, 105–8, 113, 132, 201 n.13, 202 n.4
Vasari, Girgio, 131
Vates, 128
Venus, 47, 77, 179
Veronese, Paolo, 21, 131
Vestal Virgin, 22
Vickers, Brian, 202 n.10
Vickers, Nancy, 179, 198 n.3, 205 n.6
Virgil, 44, 48–49, 95, 100, 123, 131–32, 148–49, 154–55, 182, 197 n.30
Vulcan, 181–82

Walker, Alice, 200 n.13
Wallace, Malcolm, 10, 21, 22, 30, 189 nn. 11 and 14, 190 nn. 8 and 11, 191 n.19, 192 n.51
Waller, A. R., 192 nn. 55 (chap. 1) and 1
Walpole, Horace, 56
Walsingham, Frances (Sidney, then Devereux), 20, 24, 30, 31, 82, 110, 157–58, 204 n.4
Walsingham, Francis, 22, 24, 26, 27, 43, 188 n.1, 197 n.30
Walzer, Michael, 11, 189 n.15
Wanstead Garden, 41–42, 48, 51, 86
Ward, John, 70
Warwick, Earl of (Ambrose Dudley), 188 n.1
Webster, John, 74, 82
Wedderburn, Alexander, 199 n.23
Weiner, Andrew, 195 nn. 25 (chap. 2) and 2
Whetstone, George, 191 n.36
Willcock, Gladys, 200 n.13
Willett, C., 188 n.4
Williams, Franklin, 198 n.37
Williams, Neville, 191 n.27
Wilson, Thomas, 196 n.25
Wilton, 56, 65, 69, 137, 144, 157–58, 166, 204 n.4
Windsor, Lord Henry, 184
Wolff, S. L., 193 n.1
Woodstock (1573), 22
Wotton, Edward, 113

Xenophon, 82, 126, 134–35

Yates, Frances, 21–22, 41, 190 nn. 4, 12, 13, and 14, 198 n.39, 203 n.11
York, house of, 25, 197 n.33

Zephyr, 77
Zopyrus, 134